ECONOMIC GROWTH AND RESOURCES

Vol. 4

NATIONAL AND INTERNATIONAL POLICIES

ECONOMIC GROWTH AND RESOURCES —

Proceedings of the Fifth World Congress of the(International Economic Association)held in Tokyo, Japan, 1977

VOLUME 4

NATIONAL AND INTERNATIONAL POLICIES

EDITED BY

IRMA ADELMAN

St. Martin's Press　New York

330.9
I 6l e

© International Economic Association 1979

All rights reserved. For information write:
St. Martin's Press, Inc., 175 Fifth Avenue, New York, N.Y. 10010

Printed in Great Britain

First published in the United States of America in 1979

ISBN 0-312-23317-5

Library of Congress Cataloging in Publication Data

International Economic Association.
   Economic growth and resources.

   Includes bibliographies and indexes.
   CONTENTS: v. 1. The major issues, edited
by E. Malinvaud. — v. 2. Trends and factors,
edited by R. C. O. Matthews. — v. 3. Natural
Resources, edited by C. Bliss. [etc.]
   1. Economic development — Congresses.
2. Economic policy — Congresses. 3. Natural
resources — Congresses. 4. Japan — Economic
conditions — 1945–   — Congresses. I. Title.
HD82.I45   1979a   330.9   79-4430

ISBN 0-312-23314-0 Volume I.   The Major Issues
ISBN 0-312-23315-9 Volume II.   Trends and Factors
ISBN 0-312-23316-7 Volume III. Natural Resources
ISBN 0-312-23317-5 Volume IV. National and International Policies
ISBN 0-312-23318-3 Volume V.   Problems Related to Japan

Contents

Introduction

Irma Adelman

Berkeley, California

THE MAJOR THEMES OF THIS VOLUME

This volume combines two major themes: North–South relations, particularly the New International Economic Order, and the nature of economic growth in the mature economies of the industrial world. The papers in this volume were presented to the International Economic Association World Congress in two separate sections and are, therefore, only loosely related to each other.

Nevertheless, one can detect some underlying communalities. There is a common atmosphere permeating discussions in both sections. There is a feeling that the combination of exogenous shocks, changes in ideology and perceptions, and endogenous dynamics of growth and development have created very serious economic and sociopolitical strains. The nature of optimal adjustments to these strains is not at all clear, but what is evident is that most likely structural rather than marginal adjustments will be required to absorb these strains. Both in international relations and in the management of the growth of advanced economies, the structural adjustments are likely to extend beyond the purely economic and into political relations and sociocultural change. The papers in both sections examine various aspects of such potential structural adjustments.

National Economic Policies

The framework of the discussion in this section is given by the Stoleru paper. He categorises the major economic problems facing developed nations in the coming decades as falling under four headings: inflation, employment, social consensus, and international equilibrium. He then goes on to sketch the major outlines of the new sociopolitical and factual situation with which policy and theory in each of these areas must come to grips. The other papers in this section each address either one or several of the issues raised by him.

Several papers touch on issues relating to economic growth. Ostrowsky and Sadowski provide a model for choosing a growth rate in which the rate of growth is chosen so that the benefits from growth exactly balance the costs of growth.

Gelting discusses the relationship between employment and economic growth in the long run. The question he raises (with inconclusive results) is

what effect the lower levels of employment, which one may expect to be
characteristic of the sixties, will have on the rate of growth of factor
productivity.

Perkins suggests a way to combine anti-inflationary policy with employment
stimulation. He argues for the combination of an expansionary budgetary
policy with a tight monetary policy. He believes that such a combination can
be achieved by financing a rise in government spending by borrowing from the
public.

Scitovsky looks to changes in consumption patterns and life styles to save
on energy consumption while raising consumer satisfaction.

Finally, in a very thoughtful paper which provides a good transition to the
next section of the book, Streeten discusses the problems raised for
international co-existence by the failures of the development process in
developing countries and provides various hypotheses concerning the origins of
these failures.

The New International Economic Order

There is a sense of crisis and confrontation permeating political discussions
among developed and developing nations. This crisis manifests itself in a
renewed struggle for the redistribution of the world product and of world
power. This struggle has been sparked by two phenomena: the recognition of
the failures of the development pattern of the fifties and sixties and the 'oil
crisis'. The oil crisis indicated that bold, concerted action by a group of
developing countries *could* lead to a drastic redistribution of world income and
power, and the failures of development highlighted the need for such
redistribution.

The discussion in this second part of the volume relates to the moral and
philosophical bases for a New International Economic Order as well as to the
potential effectiveness of individual technical proposals for reform.

Along political lines, the New International Economic Order is a clamour
for reforms designed to effectuate a change in the purposes served by the
international economic order. As emphasised by Rickard Lang, in particular,
in the past the international economic order has primarily served the needs of
development strategies of developed countries. It has consisted of a system of
international economic relations resulting in the perpetuation of the
underdeveloped status of developing countries. The calls for reform argue that
the international economic order should now be restructured so as to serve to a
much larger extent the needs of development strategies of the *developing*
countries. As Pajestka emphasises, this implies a *process* rather than a once-
and-for-all change; as Lang, Pajestka and Kohlmey stress, the successful
implementation and operation of the New International Economic Order
requires a change in the system of international power relations.

However, two participants – Pajestka and Chakravarty – correctly stress
that, even with major changes in the international economic order, one cannot

expect economic development to eradicate poverty in the absence of
appropriate internal policies for structural reform and for the rationalisation of
internal incentive systems. What is required is internal redistribution of wealth
and power; appropriate growth promoting strategies supported by appropriate
resource allocation and incentive systems; and the creation of the institutional,
sociocultural, organisational, and factor-endowment preconditions for self-
reliant development. The direction of structural change and growth will then be
endogenous, and the New International Economic Order will be used to spark
and support the endogenously designed pattern of dynamic domestic change.

The rest of the papers in this section deal with more technical issues relating
to the purely economic aspects of the international economic order.

With respect to the commodity pattern of trade, Balassa presents some
statistical evidence in favour of the proposition that changes in the patterns of
manufactured exports of developing countries can be expected to go through a
set of typical dynamic sequences resulting from changes in their patterns of
comparative advantage. As economies develop, their patterns of comparative
advantage move from labour-intensive to either skill-intensive or capital-
intensive exports depending on their past accumulation policies. If they have
stressed accumulation of physical capital (as have Brazil and Mexico) their
future comparative advantage will be in capital-intensive exports. If they have
stressed the build-up of human capital (as have Korea, Taiwan, Singapore and
Hong Kong), their future comparative advantage will lie in skill-intensive
exports. He argues that, in view of the existence of this hierarchy of
specialisation, the demand constraints on the exports of developing countries
are considerably less severe than one would think *a priori*. With countries
progressing on the comparative advantage scale, their exports can supplant the
exports of countries that graduate to higher lever. To the extent that one
developing country replaces another in the imports of a particular commodity
by the developed countries, the problem of adjustment in the latter group of
countries does not arise. It is only where the products of newly graduating
developing countries compete with the products of developed countries that
demand constraints will be felt. Thus, Balassa sees much scope for export-
oriented policies in LDCs within the current international economic order.

Myint, looking at an earlier stage of economic development than Balassa,
stresses the beneficial impact on economic development of primary exports. He
argues that the expansion of peasant exports from the traditional sector of an
underdeveloped economy tends to promote development both directly and
indirectly. The direct effect is due to a fuller and more effective utilisation of
their underutilised resources in the subsistence sector. The indirect effect stems
from the induced extension and improvement of their domestic economic
organisation. More generally, he concludes that free-trade and export-
expansion policies tend to promote the economic development of LDC.

With respect to exchange rate regimes, Corden considers the implications
for growth, stability and the international division of labour of four exchange
rate systems: the present system and that preceding the Bretton Woods system

as well as two polar theoretical systems – completely fixed rates and free-floating rates. He concluded that their implications for growth are rather indirect. Exchange rates are monetary phenomena, and the exchange rate regime is important mainly for affecting domestic monetary policy and, more generally, domestic aggregate demand policies. The exchange rate regime influences the transmission of disturbances and monetary trends between countries and the degree to which countries can carry on independent monetary policies. The effects of exchange rates on such matters as economic growth depend on how the internal demand policies affect economic growth. But the central issue turns out to be *not* the exchange rate-growth relationship but rather the extent of integration or lack of integration into the world economy.

In a fixed rate system, economies are monetarily integrated and must inflate when the rest of the world inflates. Hence, in that system, the monetary policies of the major economies (United States, Germany and Japan) will govern the economies of all other nations participating in international trade. By contrast, a flexible exchange rate system gives countries monetary independence; a country can inflate ahead of the rest of the world, reconciling its excess inflation with continuous depreciation of the currency, or it can follow a less inflationary policy than the rest of the world, appreciating its currency appropriately. Thus, Corden concludes that the movement from Bretton Woods to the present has increased the monetary independence of many countries. Nevertheless, domestic monetary policies are still affected by the outside world through external influences on domestic prices.

The final paper in this section concerns the potential benefits to developing countries of indexing their prices so as to keep their international terms of trade fixed. Bénard uses a simple aggregative, static model to examine this issue. The model he employs consists of (i) aggregate supply and demand functions to primary exports, (ii) a cost function for a composite manufacturing good, and (iii) an equilibrium condition which specifies that demand equal supply for primary exports. Paradoxically, Bénard concludes that indexation, which aims at making developing countries escape from vulnerability to random shocks arising from fluctuations in world markets, will make them more rather than less vulnerable to such shocks by compelling their production to adapt to these fluctuations.

The overall import of the technical papers is that no panaceas can be expected from changes in specific features of the international economic order and that there is much scope for gains to developing countries from appropriate export-oriented development in the present international economic order.

The conclusion from the philosophical papers is that the international economic order can provide the dynamic impetus for growth only for a rather limited period. Unless this dynamic impetus is supported by appropriate domestic policies in developing countries, and unless it is used to generate the internal structural changes necessary for growth with equity, long-term equitable development will not materialise.

Part I
National Policies

1 Economic Management with Moderate Growth

Lionel Stoleru*

Paris, France

I. THE PRESENT AGE

The third quarter of our century, from 1950 to 1975, is universally recognised as an exceptional one. We have, since the war, had exceptional economic growth, an exceptional expansion of world trade, exceptional progress in technology and communications.

As economists we can add: our calling has gained exceptional prestige. Some of us are indebted to Keynes for the tools by which to adapt demand to the pace of production and to follow the rules of the system of fixed exchange rates. Others owe to Marx the basic concepts upon which to construct a planned economy and a price system resting upon the value of labour embodied in goods. To both, post-war research and the development of computers gave access to the technique of model building for predicting or planning the course of the economy. We have had a proliferation of short-term models, growth models, models of aid to developing countries, models of decentralisation of decisions and of price simulation in socialist economies. There was a hint, sometimes, of an ideological rapprochement around the idea of market prices, observed prices for one school and calculated ones for the other, but in any case leading up to the same rules of economic management. After Einstein, economists too had found unity in relativity.

This beautiful harmony soon came to an end. Conceptually, it was shattered by the Club of Rome, and factually by the demise of fixed parities in 1971, by the end of cheap energy in 1973 and by the new distribution of power among the developed and the developing countries. While structural imbalances are spreading throughout the world and uncertainties grow, economists have discovered that though they were supposed to be the doctors, they were incapable of curing the torpor that was gripping the world. For a time they belittled the sickness, waiting for growth to revive or trying to stimulate it by the usual treatments in the hope of re-creating their familiar universe. Now at last they are bowing to the facts and admit that the last quarter of our century is not, economically, going to be the continuation of the preceding twenty-five years, that it is going to be different especially by virtue of a

---

*Translation by Elizabeth Henderson.

profound change in the pace and type of growth. Economists will have to alter
their approach – but how? I propose here, in the light of the first lessons of
recent years, to formulate a very tentative outline of the new economics that we
must create, to wit, economic management with moderate growth.

II. TWO NEW ELEMENTS

At the level of diagnosis, two fundamental new elements have to be taken into
account: the appearance of natural limits to growth, and the end of adaptation
between growth factors and demand.

As regards the *natural limits to growth*, we have to go beyond the strict
concepts of the Club of Rome and recognise that the new constraints are not so
much of physical as of economic and political origin. The energy crisis of 1973
did not lead to rationing anywhere except in the Netherlands, where for one
weekend people abstained from driving their cars. It did lead, instead, to some
economic reappraisal with regard to prices, to the use of various forms of
energy, to investment choices especially in the nuclear field, and to policy
options in terms of national independence. President Carter's recent decisions
are a case in point. The energy crisis furthermore led to a new balance of
power, in which the industrial countries so far in possession of the three
attributes of economic power, namely money, markets and technology,
partially lost the first two and retain only the third. Hence these new triangular
forms of co-operation in which development proceeds with the help of the
technology of an industrial country, the money of an oil-producing country
and the market of a developing country.

Meanwhile thinking has switched from the world-wide approach of the first
(Meadows) report of the Club of Rome, to equilibrium by zones in the Pestel-
Mesarovic report and to the search for a new international order in the
Tinbergen report, in the North–South conference and in the Jamaica
agreements. Politicians and economists are desperately looking for new rules of
the game which, however pragmatic they may be, would at least be preferable
to the present uncertainty and would demonstrate that concerted action is
better than confrontation.

Whether it is petroleum we are talking of or coffee or some other raw
material, or the dollar or flexible exchange rates, we must recognise that the
new rules of the economic game as it will be played during the last quarter of
this century will not be known for many years. For politicians this will mean
that in the conduct of national economies planning will give way to strategy
with its multiple tactical elements, and for economists that models will be
replaced by scenarios.

The second new element in diagnosis is the end of the reign of *growth
factors*. We have lived through 25 years in which, to be sure, economic
crises – Korea, Vietnam and others – did occur, but in which they were no
more than accidents along an economic path defined by the factors of growth,
that is labour, capital and technology.

According to theory, as adjusted notably by Denison to observations made in the leading countries of the OECD, economies were progressing at a natural rate of growth, which was not the same as Harrod's and was the direct result of each country's disposable supply of these three factors. Natural growth, for example, was all the faster the larger was a country's disposable labour supply, on the pattern of Western Germany during the period of large-scale immigration from Eastern Germany. In France, where the labour force was no larger in 1970 than it had been in 1920, growth was due to technical progress, and in Japan the major influence was capital investment. In other words, each country got what it deserved, *itself*, by its own efforts in work, investment and productivity. Consequently, if there was unemployment it could only be by accident, as a result of bad economic management, since in the medium term any additional supply of labour found its way into additional growth. The role of the economist was that of an aircraft pilot steering by the automatic pilot and having to make sure only that the trip was not too bumpy when the aircraft ran into a thunderstorm.

Things have changed. No one today would dare organise a country's economic growth on the basis of its own growth factors. No one would dare rely on an increase in the labour force for accelerating growth; and indeed economists, reversing cause and effect, are trying to increase employment by stepping up the pace of growth – without, incidentally, much faith in the efficacy of this method alone. What has happened is that in the course of just a few years we have changed over from growth determined in the medium term by the supply of factors of production to growth determined in the medium term by the demand for goods, as in a short-term Keynesian model. There is this difference, though, that the Keynesian model is no longer a one-country model but a world model. No longer is it the traditional imbalance between national saving and national investment which prevents the economy from achieving full growth; it is the imbalance between the surplus of some countries and the deficit of others, whatever is done to recycle the corresponding petrodollars. In other words, economic policy now has to absorb the Keynesian disequilibrium not in time but in space. This is an altogether different task, for it transcends the limits of any national design.

III. THE IMPLICATIONS FOR POLICY

If this diagnosis is correct, we must in the first place accept its negative consequences. A whole batch of the traditional economic remedies must simply be written off.

Take *reflation*: applied in one country only, it is now totally incapable of relaunching the growth process, except by a return to a closed economy via protectionism. The disproportion between the recovery effort possible at national level and the magnitudes involved in world imbalance is so enormous that national reflation is powerless and indeed harmful, because it works only in money terms and at once turns into inflation.

But co-ordinated international reflation can displace the Keynesian world disequilibrium towards a point of higher activity, and this is why agreements such as that proclaimed at the May 1977 London Economic Summit between the United States, Japan and the Common Market are so important.

Then there was the trade-off between *inflation and unemployment*. The theoretical foundation of the Phillips curve was the gap between wage rates actually offered and wage claims in terms of expectations, so that any easing of labour supply could have stabilising effects on prices, at least in the short run. In the new model this mechanism has disappeared. The acceptance of an additional price and wage rise no longer creates additional jobs, but on the contrary, impairs competitiveness and so aggravates unemployment. Stagflation has taken the place of the Phillips curve.

Finally, there was the remedy of *devaluation*. Time was when economic policy makers, unable to achieve economic recovery by domestic means, could resort to devaluation and start again on a sound basis. This is no longer so, for two reasons. First, flexible exchange rates take care, day by day, of *de facto* devaluations of a country's currency and thereby dilute the structural effect of such a device. Secondly, and this is more important, devaluation does not put a country's economy on a sound basis, but undermines it – witness the recent examples of Great Britain and Italy. The cost of necessary imports grows, in the absence of world demand exports expand less than expected, and the balance of payments goes from bad to worse. The countries with the most overvalued currencies have the strongest balance of payments, at a time when the United States, in an ultimate paradox, is trying to undervalue its currency so as to preserve a payments deficit most useful for the re-establishment of world equilibrium. What a strange back-to-front contest!

Is the economist, then, reduced to total impotence, or can we find some new mechanism of positive action?

Let us see what the elements of such action are in respect of each of the four major problems of our epoch, that is, *inflation, employment, social consensus, and international equilibrium*.

IV. POLICY FOR INFLATION

As regards *inflation*, we must be clear in our minds that it is no longer what it used to be. Demand inflation, the hitherto usual form, has become a minor aspect of a process nowadays mainly determined by an international component and by the formation of incomes.

The international component consists in the first place of raw materials. But it is a deceptive one. In a world economy growing less fast, rising oil prices certainly push up production costs in the non-oil producing countries, but in so doing they generate a domestic price rise which, unmatched by real income growth, erodes purchasing power and in the longer run has a *deflationary* effect. This is indeed what the fourfold rise in the price of oil in 1973 did for the period 1973–77.

It is the formation of incomes, then, which is the key to the battle against inflation. On the one hand, the loss of economic substance due to slower growth is hard to accept for social groups used to a fast increase in purchasing power. On the other hand, the system of floating exchange rates weakens the mechanism of automatic adjustment via foreign trade; if prices and wages rise not by 3 and 5 per cent annually, but by 13 and 15 per cent, the process can be made to look painless by letting the parity slide by an extra 10 per cent.

The most promising weapon against inflation thus seems to be *incomes policy*. It is astonishing how quickly the ideological resistances of the early seventies have crumbled; the United States, Great Britain, Germany, France have all, in varying degrees, introduced policies to control prices, wages and profits in an effort to stem the inflationary wave of 1973–75. Most often the effort has been successful.

V. POLICY FOR EMPLOYMENT

For *employment*, we need an entirely new economic policy. Full employment without full growth cannot be secured by the traditional means, as was made only too clear at a meeting of experts called in March 1977 by the OECD in Paris, at France's request.

First of all the fruits of growth must be distributed in a different way, with more emphasis on increasing leisure rather than purchasing power. An organised return to shorter working time, alongside the adaptation of purchasing power, will improve the distribution of access to jobs, on the one condition that nothing irreversible is done. The door must be left open for a gradual return to more satisfactory rates of world economic growth, and from this point of view such measures as bringing retirement age forward must be handled with the utmost caution.

Then we have to find out more about how much different components of demand contribute to full employment. To do this we must examine the problems of industries based on unskilled labour as well as the effects of capital/labour substitution. It is not a question of holding back technical progress, but of achieving a better balance between the share of capital and the share of labour in the production of goods. By way of example, we may mention the problems of conserving and saving raw materials: in trying to solve the energy problem, more jobs are created by regulations on the heat insulation of premises than by the construction of a nuclear power station.

We also need a more precise definition of labour supply. In France, for instance, it is misleading to describe the employment situation by saying that 21 million persons are employed and 1 million unemployed. What we should say is that there are 31 million persons of working age, of whom 21 million are at work, 1 million are trying to find work, and 9 million are not looking for work. The crucial matter is the mechanism of distribution among these three categories; it depends on how many jobs are wanted by women, by the young and the elderly, and also on the problems of alternation between work and training.

Finally, we need to know more about the means by which to influence the adjustment between supply and demand on the labour market. Equilibrium is certainly not achieved solely by the wage level and we must learn to control other aspects, such as job location.

VI. SOCIAL CONSENSUS

This element of economic policy, which is only too often underestimated, becomes essential in the new conditions of growth, for at least two reasons.

The first has to do with social justice. To be sure, rapid growth does not in itself reduce inequalities, but at least it masks individual grievances in a general economic euphoria. At a time of slower general prosperity gains, social injustices are more keenly felt, and equitable distribution is demanded the more insistently the less there is to distribute. The protection of the weak then becomes a primary concern of economic policy, and it is a task the more difficult to discharge as individual economic security is incompatible with world-wide uncertainty. Nevertheless, the countries that have come through the crisis best are those which have met this challenge.

The second reason is connected with the fight against inflation and the related matter of incomes policy. Incomes policy presupposes a modicum of social consensus, because only a freely accepted discipline allows lasting management of prices and wages. The countries which have succeeded in stabilising their prices, and thus in raising purchasing power once more, are those where trade unions, employers and government have come to the most effective agreement on moderating nominal rises. A genuine incomes policy is not a policy of sacrifice, it is a policy of investment for the future, resulting in a national gain of purchasing power.

Hence, social cohesion, once a purely political objective, becomes in the present setting a major economic objective necessary for the re-establishment of basic balance.

VII. INTERNATIONAL EQUILIBRIUM

International equilibrium is the fourth and last of the major aspects of any country's new economic policy. Unless it yields to the siren call of protectionism, no country can nowadays maintain its own economic equilibrium without an active policy of international co-operation, the main elements of which were defined at the North–South Conference as follows:

(1) participation in a world organisation of markets for the principal raw materials within the Common Fund for commodity buffer stocks agreed in principle at the London Economic Summit in May 1977;

(2) acceptance of a system of foreign trade giving developing countries access to the market of developed countries in an organised manner, as under the generalised preferences or the Lomé agreement;

(3) participation in technology transfers which will help the Third World

on the way to industrialisation, especially in the first processing of raw materials;

(4) contributions to financial aid needed in order to narrow the gap between rich and poor countries.

This kind of international economic policy used to be seen as a policy of aid; it has now become a policy of survival. The 1971–73 crisis revealed the now glaring truth that we are all in the same boat, a fragile Noah's ark which has to be steered through perilous seas to a safe landing. No longer can any one country prosper at the expense of others; all of them need to pull together now in quest of the best possible world equilibrium.

VIII. CONCLUSION

If we, as economists, manage to understand what new economic policy is required in the new circumstances, and if we can induce our governments to act accordingly, then we can hope, not perhaps to regain the prestige we had during the quarter-century of rapid growth, but at least to make up for our loss of prestige by becoming more useful.

2 On the Level of Employment and the Rate of Economic Growth

Jørgen H. Gelting

Aarhus University, Denmark

I. THE NEED TO RECONSIDER EARLIER ASSUMPTIONS

More than forty years ago Keynes conjectured that typically over the business cycle real wages and money wages would move inversely, money wages rising and real wages falling during expansion and the other way round during contractions. In a paper published three years later Dunlop showed – as Pigou had done more than ten years earlier in his book *Industrial Fluctuations* – that preponderantly the changes in both money and real wages are positively related to changes in the level of economic activity.

Keynes' conjecture was evidently based on neo-classical short-run production theory, according to which the combination of an increased number of workers with a substantially unchanged stock of real capital must cause the marginal product of labour to fall. Since about 1960 a great many studies have appeared establishing that generally in the short run apparent output per man-hour varies directly with economic activity, implying a short-run output elasticity of employment appreciably below one. Further, while the employed labour force cannot be smaller than that technically required for the production of actual output, it may well be and mostly is larger. What is observed, then, is not a technological but an economic relationship between output and the demand by firms for workers and hours.

Much less attention has been paid in economic research and literature to the long-run relationships between output, employment, output per man-hour and the rate of economic growth. However, issues of considerable importance are involved among which two will be emphasised here: assuming that employment levels in the industrial countries for many years ahead will persist distinctly lower than in the 1960s, will this (apart from a period of adjustment, which may well take quite a few years) occasion a decline in the rate of economic growth, primarily through less rapidly advancing productivity? Further, irrespective of whether the Phillips curve is thought to represent a permanent or only a temporary trade-off, the character and strength of any long-run relation between activity level and the rate of productivity growth will bear upon the scope for and effectiveness of macroeconomic policies.

While conceptually it is easy enough to keep apart on the one hand the effects on the rate of growth of a *change* in the level of employment and on the other hand the long-run consequences for growth of the – high or low – *level* of employment at which an economy operates, in practice the distinction may prove quite difficult, because the effects of an employment change, even if completed within a short period, though transitional may extend over a considerable period of time. In any case, some of the statements most frequently encountered, though purporting to deal with the effects of the level of employment (and the pressure of demand) on the rate of productivity growth are really directed at the effects of a change in the level of employment and demand.

It is claimed for instance that a high level of employment, called forth by demand pressure, promotes growth by stimulating investment both in real capital and in research and development. In consequence the age structure of capital becomes more favourable and the introduction of new and improved techniques is promoted. Further, high levels of demand and employment are said to contribute to productivity in a purely mechanical way by raising the degree of utilisation of productive resources, while on the other hand strong demand pressures, by causing less efficient productive resources to be employed, may tend to hold down productivity.

All of these statements are beyond question in so far as they refer only to the level at which growth takes place and/or the transitional effects on the rate of growth of a change in the level of activity. But conceived as statements concerning the long-run effects on growth of the level of employment and demand they would be hard to defend.

For instance, it is probably quite true that in an economy where the level of unemployment keeps permanently at 3 per cent of the labour force, less efficient resources are utilised than if unemployment was steady at 4 or 5 per cent. But it certainly does not follow that at the lower unemployment level the rate of productivity increase would also be lower. (In fact, it might be higher if the improvability of low-quality resources surpassed that of high-quality resources.)

Similarly, though it is of course true that in a low-unemployment economy investment may be expected to be larger than in a high-unemployment economy, it does not follow that the *rate* of growth of capital will be higher and that in consequence the age structure of real capital will be more favourable. It is overlooked that in an economy characterised by a permanently relatively low level of employment the stock of real capital will be adjusted to the level of employment and that therefore the ratio of investment to capital and the age structure of capital may be invariant to the level of employment.

A closely related issue is raised by recent efforts (Barro and Grossman, 1971, 1976; Malinvaud, 1975) to supplement and perfect employment and monetary theory by generalising and extending the theory of non-market-clearing processes. Objection may be raised to what would appear to be a basic assumption of this approach, viz. that a position of excess supply in the labour market will as a general rule be accompanied by excess supply in the goods market appearing if not as excess stocks of unsold output then as excess production capacity and thus low rates of capacity utilisation.

Just as households supplying labour services are 'rationed' by the effective demand for labour services so firms are said to be rationed by the demand for their output. But in this sense price-setting firms are always 'rationed' by demand (and the prospects of price-takers by the market price) – except when in conditions of widespread excess demand availability of labour or other resources constitutes a narrower bottleneck than demand.

Of course, during and for some time after a decline in economic activity excess capacity will prevail. But it would be very peculiar indeed if when activity persists at a reduced level firms guided by the profit motive kept investment at a level maintaining excess capacity. Wicksell's *gedanken-experiment* may be illuminating here: in a world where workers were entrepreneurs who rented machines from capitalist owners excess supply of machine services could not exist at any stationary level of activity because machine-owners would adjust the stock of machines to the demand for machine-hours. This is not to imply that the machines would be literally fully employed, but rather that owners in deciding upon the stock of machines would take into account both the expected average level of demand and the variance of demand fluctuations around this level. If not for most, then certainly for many types of real capital idle capacity is deliberately maintained at average levels that would be considered intolerable as levels of unemployment in the labour market.

Some authors have been more concerned with the fluctuations of demand and employment and only indirectly with the average level of demand – in so far as the amplitude of employment fluctuations sets a limit to the obtainable average level. Schumpeter (1947), as will be recalled, viewed the business cycle as a necessary element in the capitalist growth process of creative destruction. Similarly, without entering into any extended discussion of the long-run effects of the level of activity on the rate of growth, Denison (1974) concludes tentatively that most favourable to growth is a generally high level of employment, occasionally interrupted by brief, but sharp, recessions which weed out inefficient producers. On the other hand several authors have put the blame for the relatively low rate of productivity growth in the British post-war economy on so-called stop–go policies. Dow (1964) thought that productivity growth would have been more rapid if demand had been steady, but at a moderate level. It may be added that without inconsistency the Schumpeterian view may be accepted at the same time as fluctuations in economic activity called forth by stop–go policies are considered detrimental to growth.

II. THE MECHANISMS RELATING DEMAND AND PRODUCTIVITY

Perusal of the literature uncovers only three important mechanisms thought to operate in the long run by which the level of demand and employment affect the rate of growth of productivity:

(1) Demand pressures and consequent high levels of employment leading to high wages and a squeeze on profits induce elimination of x-inefficiency;

promote adoption of labour-saving techniques and search for labour-
saving innovations – both by changing relative factor prices and through
direct scarcity of labour; and lead to the elimination of inefficient firms
and a shift of workers to more efficient firms.

(2) However, beyond some point the pressure of demand and lower
unemployment may hamper growth partly because the profit squeeze
proves a disincentive to investment, partly because inflationary
pressures lead to productivity losses from misallocation of resources.

(3) Historically probably more important than (1) and (2) has been that high
levels of demand and employment increase the mobility of both labour
and capital. It is well established that both international and
intranational migration are increasing functions of the level of economic
activity, and that in most countries where productivity has grown
rapidly the transfer of workers from low- to high-productivity sectors
has been an important factor.

It is an understatement – or overstatement – that our knowledge of the
various factors affecting economic growth and their relative importance is less
than complete. And, quite possibly, among important factors may be some
which are usually not included in economic analyses and which are difficult to
quantify. Further, it may well be the case that a factor which in some
circumstances or within a certain range of values promotes economic growth in
other cases or within another range of values proves detrimental to growth.
Thus the chance would appear slight of finding any significant, simple
relationship between level of employment and rate of growth, ignoring other
variables.

The experience of most industrial countries in the post-Second World War
period compared with earlier periods is certainly consistent with the hypothesis
that high employment promotes growth. Summary cross-section analysis of the
1950s and the 1960s would, however, appear only moderately favourable to
the hypothesis, partly for the reasons already indicated, partly because of the
insufficient comparability of national employment and other statistics. A recent
careful study (P. J. Pedersen, 1977) of average unemployment levels and
productivity growth in Denmark, covering the period 1911–70, finds positive
association between employment level and rate of productivity growth.
Reference has already been made to Denison's study (1974) of US growth
which again is consistent with the hypothesis, even though Denison explicitly
abstains from interpreting his results as a cause–effect relationship.

The recent study by Carré, Dubois and Malinvaud (1972, English edition
1975) discusses in considerable detail the effects of the pressure of demand on
French economic growth in the post-war period and arrives at a clear verdict
that growth would have been slower, in particular during the 1960s, if demand
had been weaker and in consequence employment lower. The conclusion refers
not only to the effects of demand on the supply and employment of labour, but
also to the effects on productivity increase.

III. THE PETTY EFFECT

Of particular interest is the early study by Denison (1967), which compares
developments 1950–62 in the United States and seven north-western European
countries plus Italy. In the present context it may be useful to take a closer look
at the analysis of the increase in output per unit of input. This productivity

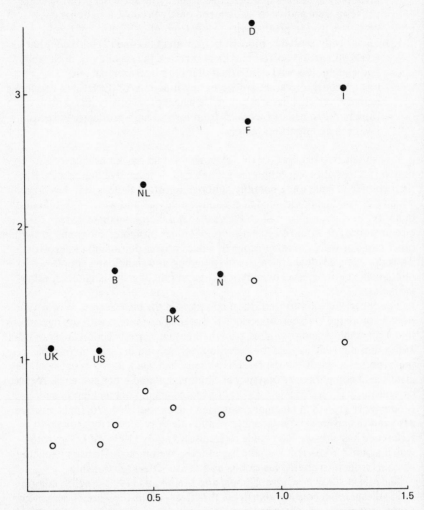

Fig. 2.1   Contributions to annual growth rates 1950–62 (output per unit of input)
Abscissa: Improved allocation of resources (excluding reduction of trade barriers)
Ordinate:
○ = Economies of scale
● = Total excluding improved allocation

increase is broken down into several main categories: advances of knowledge; decline in the lag in the application of knowledge and increase in general efficiency; improved allocation of resources; and economies of scale. Within the category 'improved allocation of resources' the contributions from the two sub-items 'contraction of agricultural inputs' and 'contraction of non-agricultural self-employment' may readily be assumed to depend upon the level of economic activity and the pre-existing economic structure of the country in question. In any one country the contribution to productivity growth from structural change will vary directly with the general level of economic activity (see, e.g., Okun, 1973; Slifman, 1976). On the other hand, comparing different countries, the contribution of the Petty effect[1] to productivity growth from the transfer of labour from low-productivity to high-productivity sectors, depends very much upon the economic structure of the countries being compared – a fairly obvious conclusion, which is confirmed by the development of the OECD countries in the 1960s (OECD, 1970).

However, the importance of the Petty effect would appear to be more pervasive than indicated by Denison's figures. Fig. 2.1 shows on the abscissa for the nine industrial countries the contribution to productivity growth from the Petty effect and on the ordinate that from economies of scale. A strikingly close correlation is immediately apparent. It is not too difficult to rationalise this relationship: in most of the countries activity levels have been fairly high, so that where scope has existed for sizeable intersectoral transfers of labour, the receiving sectors have expanded rapidly and thus been in a position to enjoy productivity gains from economies of scale. However, there are no obvious reasons why the remaining sources of productivity growth should have been strongly positively related to the gains from intersectoral shifts. Nevertheless, as is evident from Fig. 2.2, productivity growth from these remaining sources combined would appear to have been closely correlated with that from intersectoral shifts plus economies of scale and thus also with productivity growth recorded as due to intersectoral shifts only.

This is a rather odd result which – to judge from provisional estimates – would be produced also in a similar study of the developments of the same countries in the 1960s. The explanation is hardly to be found in any shortcomings of the methods applied by Denison (in any case the calculation of the gains from intersectoral shifts is a fairly straightforward matter), but rather – if not in a peculiar coincidence – in the nature of national accounts statistics, which are quite equal to the task of measuring the increase in a qualitatively unchanged output, but of very doubtful validity when it comes to the evaluation of improvements through qualitative changes. And the gains from the Petty effect are exactly the kind of productivity gains which may come about independent of any productivity gains and qualitative changes within any single sector and which therefore might be expected to stand out prominently in calculations of productivity gains based on national accounts.

[1]The expression Petty's law or Petty effect was coined by Colin Clark (1940).

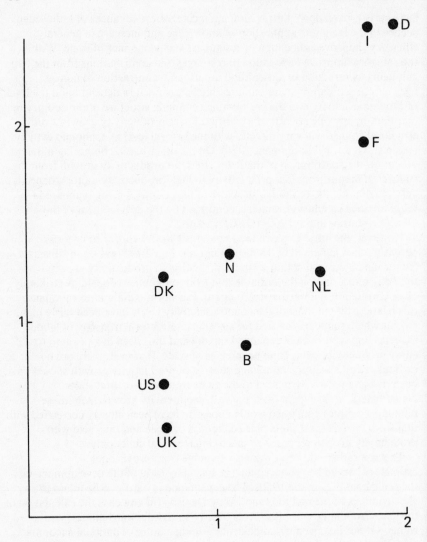

Fig. 2.2   Contribution to annual growth rates 1950–62 (output per unit of input)
Ordinate: Economies of scale plus improved allocation of resources (excluding
reduction of trade barriers)
Abscissa: Residual

Consider an extremely simple model of a two-sector economy: a low wage
sector A and a high wage sector I. The rate of migration from sector A, m_A, is
an increasing function of the wage ratio w_I/w_A and a decreasing function of

unemployment in sector I, $u_I = (L_I - E_I)/L_I$.[2] The flow of migrants per time unit being $m_A L_A$, the rate of growth by immigration of the labour force of sector I is $m_A L_A/L_I$. Taking as given the natural rate of increase n of the labour supply in sector I and the wage ratio w_I/w_A we have a flow balance characterised by constant u_I and absence of excess labour demand

$$g = n + m_A L_A/L_I \tag{1}$$

g being the rate of growth of demand for labour in I. Then, to each level of g consistent with (1) corresponds an equilibrium level of u_I such that

$$m_A(u_I, w_I/w_A) = (g - n)L_I/L_A. \tag{2}$$

At $g = n$ unemployment in sector I must be sufficiently high to prevent migration. (At a lower u_I migration would proceed until unemployment had increased enough to prevent further migration.) Evidently, the equilibrium level of unemployment is a decreasing function of g. However, if the elasticity of m_A in relation to u_I is (numerically) large, and in addition L_I/L_A is small, the impact of changes in g on the equilibrium level of unemployment will be relatively weak, the elasticity of u_I in relation to g, $e(u_I, g)$ being

$$e(u_I, g) = \frac{gL_I m_A L_A}{e(m_A, u_I)} . \tag{3}$$

It is expected then that in less developed countries characterised by a low L_I/L_A ratio (and a high w_I/w_A ratio) the level of unemployment in the high-income sector will be relatively insensitive to variations in the rate of growth of labour demand and employment in that sector. On the other hand in highly developed countries the schedule of u_I values corresponding to levels of g will be relatively low and the elasticity $e(u_I, g)$ relatively high. It would, of course, be rash to conclude merely from this that in general, because of a lower maximum level of g consistent with flow balance (1), highly developed economies will tend to be more prone to inflation than less developed economies.

However, in the context of the present paper the most important conclusion is that the contribution to overall productivity growth from a lower level of unemployment tends to decline at high levels of development characterised by relatively narrow intersectoral income differentials and a relatively small low-income sector. In short: the restricted scope for the Petty effect in highly developed countries reduces the impact on overall productivity growth from the level of unemployment.

---

[2]Further, m_A will depend upon, *inter alia*, the rules governing eligibility for unemployment assistance in sector I and the level of assistance, changes in which will, however, be ignored. It is unnecessary, and would in view of the results of several studies of interregional migration be unrealistic, to represent the income expected by migrants to sector I by $(1 - u_I)w_I$. What is required is only that the prospects of securing a job in sector I, as evaluated by members of sector A, moves inversely to u_I.

As the development process of dual economies is usually described, in the early stages of development productivity growth is largely confined to the high-income (modern) sector. Thus, in its early stages development is accompanied by a widening of income differentials. However, from a certain point, depending upon not only the level of development achieved but also the rate of expansion of the high-income sector, income differentials start narrowing as under the impact of intersectoral migration productivity growth of the low-income sector catches up with and subsequently overtakes that of the high-income sector. With the narrowing of intersectoral income differentials the overall growth rate of the economy may decline due to the decreasing scope for the Petty effect.[3]

IV. FEEDBACK FROM LABOUR SUPPLY TO DEMAND

In the simple and incomplete model on which the preceding discussion was based the rate of growth of demand for labour, g, was treated as exogenous. Presumably, however, in industrial countries a positive feedback from labour supply to demand operates. In support of this contention reference may be made, *inter alia,* to the studies by Kuznets (1961) and Easterlin (1968) (cf. also Abramovitz, 1968) of US growth in the decades up to the First World War: rising economic activity in the US called forth larger immigration which by providing the basis for larger capital-widening investments stimulated further expansion. Less intensively analysed, but no less interesting, were developments in European countries of emigration. Thus, during the US depression of the 1890s migration fell to a low level. In a number of European countries – Sweden and Denmark are obvious examples – the consequent more rapid growth of the domestic labour supply provided the basis for a strong expansion of economic activity which was accompanied – rather surprisingly – by an improvement of the balance of payments on current account and thus a decline in net capital imports. The main explanation for this is presumably to be found partly in a shift in the distribution of income from wages to profits, and partly in a systematic positive deviation of realised from expected profits as the course of prices shifted from a falling to a rising trend.

The feedback mechanism is presumably not that a larger labour supply automatically calls forth an increased demand (except slowly and indirectly by depressing the rate of increase of money wages) – children are not born with dollar bills in their mouths and new entrants to the labour market receive no

---

[3]In an important paper, so far unfortunately available only mimeographed and in Danish, M. Paldam (1977) has on the basis of IBRD data for 125 countries 1965–73 found a significant tendency for the rate of growth of per capita real income first to rise and later to fall with increasing real income levels, the growth rate reaching its maximum at about the real income level of the poorer West European industrial countries. The explanation suggested is – as in the text above – the changing weight of the Petty effect.

wages before they are employed – but rather that a growing labour supply allows an expansion – irrespective of how called forth – to proceed further than otherwise and thus gather momentum.

Also in accounting for the comparative growth experience of industrial countries, and in particular those of Western Europe in the post-Second World War period, several analysts have stressed the role of labour supply (Kindleberger, 1967; ECE, 1959, 1964). However, two of the countries – Germany and the Netherlands – which are prominent members of the group of countries in Kindleberger's analysis of the early post-war period with fast growth of labour supply and productivity stand out also as countries which entered the post-war period with – compared to pre-war – drastically reduced wage levels, relatively to wages not only in the US but also in the European countries whose growth lagged behind. Thus it may well be that a great part of the differences in economic experience ascribed to the development of labour supplies is properly to be accounted for by the very different initial competitive positions of the various countries and the consequent differences in levels of profits and investment.

The lower the degree of aggregation applied in the analysis the larger will obviously be the part of total productivity growth accounted for by the Petty effect. In his analysis of Swedish post-war developments E. Lundberg (1972) has pointed to the widespread existence of large intrasectoral differences in productivity levels and the implied scope for productivity gains from shifting workers and other mobile resources from inefficient firms and plants to best-practice units of production.

It is not immediately apparent, though, how a higher level of employment will secure such productivity gains. Indeed, in a closed economy the short-run effect of a higher level of employment must be – cf. the models of Salter (1960, 1966) and of Solow, Tobin, von Weizsäcker and Yaari (1966) – a postponement of the scrapping of older vintages of real capital and consequently a temporary fall in average productivity. In the longer run productivity will rise above the initial level only in so far as the share of investment in total income not only temporarily but in the long run is an increasing function of employment. Indeed, in the Salter–STWY model an increase in $S/Y = I/Y$ is the main route to higher productivity levels, but not a lastingly higher rate of growth of productivity, through accelerated obsolescence.

However, Lundberg's analysis is based on the EFO–Courbis model for an open economy which takes the domestic prices of internationally traded goods as exogenous variables. It is in the competitive (C-) sector that the productivity gains associated with accelerated obsolescence due to high employment are thought to be reaped. One possibility would be the case of export-led growth based on a highly competitive C-sector, high profits leading to a high rate of savings and investment and a correspondingly early scrapping of real capital, which in turn would tend to raise real wages. Thus the characteristics of the long-run growth path would depend upon the propensities to save out of profits and wage incomes and on fiscal policies – though recent research has tended to make light of the net contribution of public savings to total savings.

The other main possibility – of which Denmark in the 1960s provides a more striking example than Sweden – is that of S-sector-led growth, where the expansion of domestic demand by forcing up wages and squeezing profits in the C-sector accelerates the scrapping of older vintages of real capital in that sector. Temporarily, to be sure, the rate of productivity growth in the C-sector is raised, but at the cost of declining investment and employment in that sector and a deterioration of the balance of payments on current account.

The analysis of such a course of events was indeed the main point in Courbis' (1970) case against 'Keynesian' employment promoting demand policies. The analysis has subsequently been elaborated by Courbis and others and in particular combined with Mundell's analysis of the interaction between fiscal and monetary policies in open economies. As the experience of the aforementioned Scandinavian countries shows, the consequences of domestic demand pressures may be considerably delayed by the tenacity with which firms hang on to their export markets and by the increased scope for borrowing abroad provided by the growth of international capital markets.

The allocative gains in productivity based on intersectoral productivity differentials are once-for-all gains in the sense that in the process of reaping these gains the basis for further gains is eroded by the narrowing of intersectoral productivity differentials – though the process may extend over many decades. This once-for-all character is much more conspicuous in the case of intrasectoral gains based on productivity differentials between different vintages of real capital within the same industry, where in general the acceleration of productivity growth will prove short-lived, the lasting effect if any showing in an increase in the level along which growth takes place.

V. DEMAND PRESSURE AND PRODUCTIVITY GROWTH

There remains the possible stimulus to productivity growth from a state of excess demand pressure in the labour market. Whereas the theory of factor-price-induced innovations may rest on shaky ground it seems hard not to believe that a permanent scarcity of labour experienced by firms will provide a strong inducement to the search for labour-saving innovations. Thus, the very high levels of employment in many industrial countries during the 1960s may well have stimulated productivity growth through innovation, though it would appear impossible to give quantitative precision to this judgement.

Usually the natural-rate version of the Phillips curve is discussed on the basis of two – mostly implicit – assumptions:

(1) that the rate of productivity growth is unaffected by the level of employment, and
(2) that the economy in question is a closed economy.

Choosing suitable assumptions concerning expectations, and writing Dx for (dx/dt)/x, the 'natural' level of unemployment is defined as the value of u satisfying the equation (with traditional and obvious symbols) (cf. Artis 1971)

$$Dw - Dp = Dq = F(u) \tag{4}$$

It is no coincidence that, when in textbooks the implications of the natural-rate hypothesis are exemplified, almost invariably expansionary policies initially inducing a fall in unemployment are selected as illustration: hardly anybody could be led to believe that contractionary policies inducing a higher level of unemployment would call forth a spiralling fall in wages and prices. From which it would appear to follow that the natural-rate hypothesis is an – admittedly logical – theory of the permanently maintainable minimum level of unemployment.

What are the implications if the rate of probability growth varies inversely to the level of unemployment? The well-known fairly strong, but temporary, short-run effect of output and employment variations on apparent productivity presumably no more than delays the transmission of wage changes to price changes. Of greater importance might be a long-run positive effect from employment level to rate of productivity growth, which would tend to fortify the conclusion that the natural-rate hypothesis correctly interpreted specifies not a neutral unemployment level but rather an unemplopyment interval. However, the relatively best-established part of any positive long-run impact from the employment level on the rate of productivity growth is that based on the intersectoral Petty effect. But this is exactly the type of productivity growth which would *not* show in the relative movements of any fixed-weights indices of prices and wages, and which would presumably within any short period of time affect only a minority of the employed population.

In the nature of the case, the pure version of the natural-rate hypothesis does not apply to small, open economies operating under a regime of fixed rates of exchange. With part of the price system tied to prices abroad money wage changes imply – proportionately smaller – real wage changes. Equivalently: in a small open economy unemployment is never 'Keynesian', always 'classical' in the sense that in principle excess supply of labour could always be eliminated by a reduction of money wages relatively to international prices.

From the point of view of small, open economies the most important consequence of an inverse variation of the rate of productivity increase with the level of unemployment is the obvious one, that the effectiveness may be impaired of demand policies designed to improve the balance of payments and reduce the rate of increase of prices. Additional difficulties are created if the shape of the short-run Phillips curve tends to shift over time entailing a decreased sensitivity of wage inflation to the level of unemployment. On this, extensive recent research is as yet indecisive.

REFERENCES

M. Abramovitz (1968), 'The Passing of the Kuznets Cycle', *Economica*.

M. Artis (1971). 'Some Aspects of the Present Inflation and the National Institute Model', in H. G. Johnson and A. R. Nobay (eds) *The Current Inflation*.

R. Barro and H. Grossman (1971), 'A General Disequilibrium Model of Income and Employment', *AER*.

R. Barro and H. Grossman (1976), *Money, Employment and Inflation*.

J. J. Carré, P. Dubois, E. Malinvaud (1972, 1975), *French Economic Growth*.

Colin Clark (1940), *The Conditions of Economic Progress*.

R..Courbis (1970), *La Détermination de l'Equilibre Général en Economie Concurrencée*.

E. F. Denison (1967), *Why Growth Rates Differ*.

E. F. Denison (1974), *Accounting for United States Economic Growth 1929–1969*.

J. C. R. Dow (1964), *The Management of the British Economy 1945–60*.

R. A. Easterlin (1968), *Population, Labor Force, and Long Swings in Economic Growth*.

Economic Commission for Europe (1959), *Economic Survey of Europe in 1958*.

Economic Commission for Europe (1964), *Some Factors in Economic Growth in Europe During the 1950s*.

C. P. Kindleberger (1967), *Europe's Postwar Growth*.

S. Kuznets (1961), *Capital in the American Economy*.

E. Lundberg (1972), 'Productivity and Structural Change – a Policy Issue in Sweden', *EJ*.

E. Malinvaud (1975), *The Theory of Unemployment Reconsidered*.

OECD (1970), *The Growth of Output 1960–1980*.

A. M. Okun (1973), 'Upward Mobility in a High-pressure Economy', *BPEA*.

M. Paldam (1977), 'Bliver Verdens Indkomstfordeling skævere?' ('Is international income inequality increasing?'), mimeo, Economic Institute, Aarhus University.

P. J. Pedersen (1977), 'Inflation, Arbejdsløshed og Produktivitetsudvikling' ('Inflation, unemployment and productivity growth'), mimeo, Economic Institute, Aarhus University.

W. E. G. Salter (1960, 1966), *Productivity and Technical Change*.

J. A. Schumpeter (1947), *Capitalism, Socialism and Democracy*.

L. Slifman (1976), 'Job Mobility and Labor Demand', *Industrial Relations*.

R. M. Solow, J. Tobin, C. C. von Weizsäcker, M. Yaari (1966), 'Neoclassical Growth with Fixed Factor Proportions', *REStud*.

3 Macroeconomic Policy and Economic Growth

J. O. N. Perkins

University of Melbourne, Australia

I. INTRODUCTION

The purpose of this paper is to raise certain issues of macroeconomic policy that have an important bearing upon the rate of world economic growth. It has become clear over the last few years that one of the principal obstacles to achieving a high rate of world economic growth has been the twin problem of 'inflation with unemployment' or 'stagflation'; and, in particular, the evident willingness of many governments to tolerate, or actually to aim at, a lower level of real activity than could otherwise be achieved, in the belief that this is the best, or the only, way of reducing the rate of inflation.

It is therefore of crucial importance to see whether we can make recommendations to governments of policy measures that might reduce the rate of inflation without sacrificing real output in the process; or, to phrase it differently, to find ways of minimising the rate of inflation at a given level of activity, so there will be less need – or less temptation – for governments to try to reduce inflation by holding up the level of unemployment. This paper raises some questions that are designed to stimulate others to share the lessons that their countries have learned from trying to deal with these problems. The main part of the paper makes suggestions for varying the mix of macroeconomic measures in such a way as to reduce the price level or the rate of inflation, at a given level of activity; and to raise the level of activity without generating considerable inflation.

II. THE PROBLEM

The essence of the problem is to find ways of checking inflation, or at least to bring about a number of once-for-all reductions in the price level, without reducing the level of activity; so that a high rate of economic growth can be restored and maintained. Reductions in the level of activity may well check inflation, and it may be necessary or defensible to have recourse to this method if better ones cannot be found. At the same time, reductions in the level of activity have proved of late to be often a slow and inefficient way of reducing inflation, and the social costs of doing so by this means, especially for those least able to bear the sacrifices involved, may well be considerable. Whatever our views on the efficiency and costs of holding down demand as a means of restraining inflation, we can therefore all agree that we should make every effort to seek less costly ways of achieving that aim.

In discussing measures to hold down the rate of inflation it should be emphasised that we ought to pay due attention not only to inflation as measured by the available price indexes, but also to any concealed inflation resulting from controls over particular prices. These costs of concealed inflation take such forms as queues, rationing, and sales to favoured customers only; and the real costs they involve may often be significant. Furthermore, many types of controls over particular prices and incomes have adverse effects over the allocation of resources, and therefore reduce the available real output in the community at a given level of activity. Anything that reduces the efficiency with which resources are allocated will also tend to increase the price level. It would therefore be of general benefit for there to be an interchange of experience between economists from countries with varying types of controls about ways and means of minimising the adverse effects of any such controls, and of seeing that they – or any other form of prices and incomes policy – make as large a contribution as possible towards restraining inflation (measured in an appropriate and meaningful way, so as to include concealed inflation).

Whatever the contribution that can be made by such measures in any particular country, their chances of success will be the greater, or the damage they do will be the less, if the combination of macroeconomic measures chosen is also one that will help to hold down the general price level at a given level of activity. Furthermore, the greater the success we may have in holding down prices by means of an appropriate mix of macroeconomic measures, the less will be the need, or the temptation, for governments to resort to trying to check inflation by holding down the level of activity in their economies well below capacity. Can we reduce the price level by changing the mix?

Our aim in macroeconomic policy should be to try to find ways of reducing the rate of inflation, or at least of bringing about a series of once-for-all reductions in the price level, without reducing the level of activity below what would be feasible and desirable from other points of view.

Let us first ask whether a change in the mix of monetary and budgetary measures might be made in such a way as to reduce the price level but keep activity constant. The principle of a change in mix by which this might be done is that monetary policy should be tightened – by such a measure as open-market sales of bonds by the government – whilst a more expansionary budget would be simultaneously introduced, but without any addition being made to the money supply; that is, there would be a rise in government outlay financed either by extra taxation or by borrowing more from the public. The net result would be less money in circulation, the same amount of goods, and a lower price level.

The half of this package that consists of a monetary contraction would tend to reduce the prices not only of financial assets (which would be immediately affected by the bond sales that initiated this part of the operation) but also the

prices of those real goods that were fairly close substitutes for financial assets –
most obviously real estate and stocks of commodities, but also the prices of
such items as paintings and antiques (and of any other real assets that people
became less inclined to hold as assets when the rate of interest on financial
assets became more attractive). For as the sale of bonds by the government
makes financial assets more attractive than they would otherwise have been,
people became less ready to buy real assets, whose prices would therefore tend
to fall (even if there was no immediate change in activity). As people's holdings
of money would have been reduced by the operation, they would try to
economise in money balances held, but the resulting rise in the velocity of
circulation could not normally be expected to offset fully the reduction in the
money supply. People would also try to sell some of their real assets to one
another in the hope of replenishing their stocks of money, and this would
reduce the prices of goods.

The monetary contraction would also tend to reduce the level of activity as
soon as the effects of the contraction spread from asset markets to the markets
for currently produced goods and services. This is why the part of the package
consisting of a budgetary expansion would be required. Provided that the
government can prevent any fall in the level of activity by introducing a
budgetary measure that does not reverse (or at least not fully reverse) the fall in
the money supply, it should be possible to hold activity at the same level as it
would have been if the package had not been introduced. The most promising
form of budgetary expansion would be a rise in government spending on goods
and services, financed by extra borrowing from the public. The extra
employment provided by the government spending would come about directly
and immediately, and it would have a net upward effect on the level of demand
provided that the extra borrowing by the government did not have a fully
offsetting downward effect on private expenditure. If one takes an extreme
monetarist view, one would say that a government cannot stimulate activity by
a budgetary measure that is not accompanied by a rise in the money supply.
But the vast majority of economists would argue that this is far too extreme a
view, and that a purely budgetary measure (that is, a rise in government
spending that is *not* financed by a rise in the money supply) can in fact, do
something to raise demand. Provided that this is so, the expansionary
budgetary measures in the package can in principle be arranged in such a way
as to offset any unwanted downward effect on activity that would otherwise
have resulted from the tightening of monetary measures that constitutes the
other half of the package.

If the rise in government spending is financed by additional taxation one
could feel less confident that the budgetary element in the package would result
in a net stimulus to activity. But one would expect a rise in government
spending on goods and services to add to activity to the full extent of the rise in
this expenditure if the people employed in this way spent about the same
proportion of any change in their disposable incomes as did the people whose
taxes were raised (the so-called 'balanced-budget multiplier'). If the extra

governmental outlays were on transfer payments, such as pensions, the outcome would depend on whether the proportion of this additional income spent by the recipients did or did not exceed the change in their expenditures made by taxpayers as a result of the extra tax payments; but if the transfers went mainly to the poor and the taxes were paid mainly by the rich one could expect there to be some net rise in the level of activity. It is also likely that a tax cut whose monetary effects were offset by extra governmental borrowing from the public would on balance add to the level of demand, provided that the tax cuts were chosen appropriately.

The central principle of the macroeconomic policy mix to reduce the price level at a given level of activity is, then, that there should be a simultaneous tightening of monetary policy and the introduction of a budgetary policy that will raise demand without adding to the money supply. One would expect this package to result in some rise in interest rates in the short run; but so far as it succeeded in holding down the price level (at the given level of activity) one could expect interest rates to fall in future.

A once-for-all switch of monetary and budgetary policy in these directions could at any rate be expected to have a once-for-all effect in reducing the price level. But it will be possible to repeat the measure so as to effect a series of price reductions; and any check to rising prices in an inflationary period may help to arrest the expectation of inflation, and so inflation itself. Those who like to think in terms of an 'expectations-adjusted Phillips curve' may think of the proposed change in mix as operating by lowering the general expectation about the rate of inflation at any given level of activity, and to that extent making it unnecessary to hold down the level of activity so far or for so long as would otherwise have been necessary to have a similar effect in moderating people's expectations about the future rate of inflation.

III. A PACKAGE TO OVERCOME 'STAGFLATION'

The foregoing proposals can be adapted to give a net expansionary effect, whilst minimising or avoiding any inflationary effect, in an economy suffering from 'stagflation' (inflation at less than full employment). The level of activity should be raised by an appropriately expansionary budgetary policy, but monetary policy should be kept sufficiently tight to see that any rise in the money supply is not so great as to accommodate an unwanted rise in the price level as activity rises. But in this case some expansion of the money supply will be consistent with price stability, as real output will be rising.

The nearer the economy is to full employment, however, the more likely is it that the expansionary effects of the budgetary measures on the level of activity will be offset by the depressing effects on activity of the tightening of monetary policy; and at full employment resources would have to be released from some other form of activity in order to make possible any real expansion in the forms of expenditure stimulated by the budgetary measures. But when an economy is operating well below capacity it is not to be expected that expansionary budgetary measures will 'crowd out' a comparable amount of other forms of spending. Indeed, the improved business prospects that will result as the net stimulus to activity takes effect should encourage investment, which in such circumstances is usually being restrained by poor sales prospects, rather than by any difficulty in raising capital. Even the view that some businesses may be so concerned about inflation in such conditions that any expansionary policy measure will cause them to invest less (in the expectation that it will make inflation worse) cannot be seriously maintained in the context of the proposed package; for the monetary element in it will be designed to hold down the price level. To that extent it should stimulate investment so far as it is indeed being held back by fears about inflation.

In short, provided that governments try to stimulate activity primarily by budgetary rather than monetary measures they should be able to overcome stagflation without serious upward pressure on the price level.

IV. REDUCING COST-PUSH TAXES

There is now fairly widespread acceptance of the view that many taxes (perhaps all taxes) may have some degree of cost-push effect. Most economists would now acknowledge this, whilst still maintaining that a tax increase, taken alone, will on balance probably tend to reduce the price level by reducing demand. But it is possible that some types of taxes, in some circumstances at least, may have such a large upward effect upon wage settlements, or upon the prices of firms whose costs are raised by them, that a tax increase could sometimes actually tend to raise the price level, even after allowing for its demand-deflationary effects on the price level.

If we accept that there is some cost-push or wage-push effect from some taxes, this means that there is to that extent a stronger case for reducing government spending rather than raising tax rates when demand is too high. By the same token, when a stimulus to demand is required this consideration of tax-push inflation strengthens the case for providing it by tax cuts rather than by increases in government spending. If we believe that some forms of high taxes reduce economic efficiency in various ways, especially by reducing incentives, and that this makes it harder to restrain inflation, the case for keeping taxes low is to that extent stronger.

If, therefore, we have the choice between a 'high-level budget' – one with high levels of both government spending and tax receipts – and a 'low-level budget', considerations of the possible cost-push effect of taxes would incline us towards a budget that would achieve the desired effect on demand at a low figure on both sides of the budget. This places on one side the question of how far borrowing from the public can and should be used to finance a high level of government spending. But it will certainly be both easier and more desirable to reduce taxes if government spending is at a relatively low level.

But this principle should not be allowed to give rise to a prejudice against government spending in general. If government spending is absorbing real resources that would be better employed elsewhere in the economy obviously these least desirable forms of government spending should be reduced or eliminated and steps taken to ensure that the resources so released are used in those parts of the private sector (or the public sector) where they can be used to better effect.

But this is true quite apart from any question of macroeconomic policy, though a better allocation of resources of any sort will help to restrain inflation by making available to the community higher real income from a given level of production, and so make a given money income consistent with a lower price level or a lower rate of inflation.

It is, however, essential not to club together all forms of government spending in a blanket approval or condemnation; for otherwise good and bad forms of spending may both be raised or reduced together. There is, unfortunately, a disposition on the part of some politicians and journalists to advocate cuts in government spending in general, simply because some forms of government spending are believed to be wasteful of resources. If this 'blanket' approach is taken, it may be that governments will find that it is politically easier to curtail some forms of government spending that are in fact among the socially desirable ones, whilst allowing many of the more wasteful forms of spending to continue unchecked. (It should also be emphasised that among the most wasteful uses of resources are often those forms of private activity that are enabled to continue only because of government subsidies or other forms of official assistance.)

Provided that government expenditures are all in socially defensible directions, the case for holding them down further on grounds that they tend to raise the rate of inflation is not generally valid, unless the only way of financing them is by taxes that have cost-push effects. But in fact it may be both feasible and desirable to finance the expenditures by making available to the public attractive securities issued by the government.

V. OBJECTIONS TO HIGH NOMINAL INTEREST RATES

One reason why governments have often not moved far enough in the direction of high nominal interest rates to hold down the rate of inflation is that they have been reluctant to impose on borrowers the very high real level of payments that are required in the near future under most long-term loan repayment arrangements in periods when very high nominal interest rates are payable. If a high rate of inflation is expected at the time the loan is made, high nominal interest rates are necessary if the lender is to be compensated for the expected fall in the real value of the money in which he will be repaid in future: yet where long-term contracts provide for the same nominal amount to be repaid each year by way of interest and principal (as under most mortgage contracts) in a period during which there is a high rate of inflation, this means that the borrower has to make a very high level of real payments in the immediate future, and only in the very long run, if inflation continues at the expected rate, will the real level of his annual repayments fall sharply. In this situation it is not surprising that governments have been reluctant to see nominal interest rates rise to the high level that would have been appropriate in order to reflect existing expectations about the rate of inflation. But the appropriate remedies for this problem are either to arrange for the interest and principal of the loans to be indexed by some appropriate indicator of the rate of inflation; or for the rate to be varied at regular intervals over the term of the contract according to some short-term rate of interest that varies with market conditions (including expectations about the rate of inflation); or to make some arrangement for spreading the real value (as distinct from the nominal value) of the annual repayments of interest and principal more evenly over the life of the loan.

It is, however, a counter-productive policy to keep nominal interest rates artificially low, as that further exacerbates the problem discussed in the previous paragraph. For if governments are reluctant to let nominal rates rise (either by indexing bonds, or issuing them with floating rates of interest, or at high nominal rates) to accord with people's expectations about inflation, people will try to shift their holdings of assets towards goods, and this will raise the prices of the latter (especially such durable assets as real estate, but ultimately all goods and services). Each successive shift in people's preferences towards goods and away from money (and often out of other financial assets) makes inflation worse, and so ultimately raises nominal interest rates still further.

Perhaps the most serious practical obstacle to changing the policy mix in the direction suggested above is that even a temporary rise in nominal interest rates may elicit widespread opposition from industry at a time when there is widespread agreement that investment is too low. It should therefore be emphasised that the budgetary element in the package suggested could be wholly directed (if that were desired) towards reducing these taxes that hold back investment, or to directly subsidising it. In any event, the whole purpose of introducing the policy mix in question is to enable the economy to be operated at a higher level of activity than will prevail if governments continue to rely on holding down activity as a means of restraining inflation: and if the policy succeeds in thus making possible a higher level of activity and economic growth this would be the best possible stimulus to investment.

VI. INTERNATIONAL ASPECTS

We have so far considered the macroeconomic policy mix in the context of a closed economy. This is an appropriate starting-point in a discussion of the global problem in a world in which so many governments have been resorting to unemployment as a means of trying to check inflation. From the viewpoint of the world economy as a whole, the conclusion should be that the aim should be to persuade as many governments as possible to adopt a mix of macroeconomic measures that will be most likely to hold down the price level at any given level of activity, so that they will be correspondingly readier to operate their economies at near to full employment than they would if they were trying to check inflation only by operating on the real level of activity.

But each individual government is normally most concerned with the feasibility of a policy from its own immediate point of view. We have therefore to ask whether there are any complications in applying a policy mix with the suggested features in an individual open economy.

If a country adopts expansionary budgetary measures coupled with a tightening of monetary policy one would expect this to result in a net improvement in its capital account, which may be on a substantial scale if the international flow of capital is very responsive to interest-rate differentials. Provided this improvement in the capital account is allowed to have its natural effect on the exchange rate (rather than add to the country's reserves) the consequent appreciation will be a factor tending to hold down the price level of the country applying the policy. At the same time, the more quickly the flow of capital responds to interest rate changes, the less will be the rise in interest rates within the country applying the measure, and so the less the scope for the monetary measures to reduce the prices of real assets through this channel. The downward impact on prices will therefore be greatest through the exchange rate in circumstances where there is least effect through the market for domestic assets.

There will, however, be a subsequent effect on the exchange rate of the country applying the policy that will be the reverse of helpful. The extra payments of interest going to other countries as a result of the rise in interest rates that started the process (and as a result of any tax deductions affecting interest payments for non-residents, which may be part of the expansionary budgetary measures in the package) will be tending to make its exchange rate depreciate; and after a time this effect will tend to exceed that of any rise in net capital inflow (or fall in outflow) resulting from the change of mix. But as its price level comes down, so will its nominal interest rates, so that this should not be a long-term problem. Obviously if other countries are simultaneously following similar policies these two effects – the helpful one through the capital account and the possibly unhelpful one through dividend and interest payments in the current account – will not occur. If one country operates the policy alone, therefore it will in the short run find that it is not handicapped by the failure of other countries to do likewise; but over the medium run it may for a time be the outside world (whose rate of exchange will at that stage tend to appreciate) that will benefit (in the sense of suffering less inflation), rather than the country whose government is following the policy. It will therefore be easier for a country to implement the suggested policy if other countries are simultaneously pursuing a similar policy.

The other principle of budgetary–monetary mix that has been suggested above is that governments should try to reduce tax rates wherever they have reason to believe that the taxes have a cost-push effect. If both government spending and taxes are reduced in one country, in such a way as to keep activity constant but at a lower price level (as a result of reducing the cost-push inflation generated by high tax rates), this may be expected to result in some appreciation of its currency, and a consequent reinforcement of the downward effect on prices resulting from the change of mix there.

From the viewpoint of the world as a whole it is obviously helpful if as many governments as possible are simultaneously trying to apply the suggested principles directed at holding down the price level without resorting to lower levels of activity. It is therefore of some importance to see that any pressures placed upon governments from outside, including especially those placed on countries borrowing from the IMF, should be in directions that will encourage the reduction of inflation and the improvement of their balance of payments in ways that do not (so far as possible) sacrifice real economic growth.

In this context the aim of restraining the growth of the money supply scores well, as this should constitute one element in a package designed to hold down the price level – though it may need complementing by measures to restrain the growth of a wide range of liquid assets, implemented by means that do not encourage the expansion of alternative forms of liquid assets. But the simultaneous adoption of targets for the budget that result in a net contraction of activity below full employment is not consistent with the aim of trying to hold down the price level without sacrificing output. The sort of budgetary measures that do deserve encouragement, however – if the principles of the suggested mix are accepted – are ones that will sustain or raise the level of activity without adding to the rate of growth of the money supply, and ones that hold down the level of tax rates at a given level of activity.

Emphasis has in recent years been placed upon holding down the net *difference* between government outlay and its current receipts from taxes (and revenue) – which is sometimes known as 'the budget deficit' (though the usage of this term varies from country to country, and it is therefore probably best avoided in international discussions), and sometimes as the 'public sector borrowing requirement'. The use of any such net figure as a guide to policy should, however, satisfy no one, and is certainly not likely to do much to ensure that a country will follow a policy mix on the lines suggested. It will not satisfy those who place emphasis on the need to control the rise in the money supply, for a given public sector borrowing requirement can be consistent with a wide range of different figures for the effect of government finances on the money supply, as that depends also on how far the government is borrowing from, or repaying loans to, the public.

Nor should the use of a target for the public sector borrowing requirement satisfying those who are concerned to maintain the economy as close as possible to 'full' (but not to 'overfull') employment; for any particular figure for the difference between government outlay and revenue may be struck at many different levels of total spending and taxation, and so at many different levels of activity.

Furthermore, the aim of keeping the borrowing requirement within a certain figure does nothing to help to restrain the growth of taxation, which may have considerable cost-push effects when tax receipts are high in relation to total output. Indeed, governments may even increase taxation (especially when reductions in their spending are politically difficult) when they are trying to hold down their borrowing requirement. If one aim is to reduce taxes, this should be done by accepting stated targets for reducing the ratio of taxes to total output.

A target that may well be useful in an open economy is one for Domestic Credit Expansion – 'DCE' – rather than for the money supply alone; for DCE is defined as the growth of the money supply less any balance of payments deficit (or plus any surplus). The adoption of this target therefore discourages governments from trying to reduce the rate of growth of the money supply by adopting policies that result in a balance of payments deficit. This is a worthwhile aim if the external deficit results from the country concerned permitting excess demand; but if the external deficit occurs as a result of external influences beyond its control the consequence of adopting such a target may be to make the country pursue a more contractionary policy than would otherwise have been necessary. If the consequence is that it operates its economy at a lower level of activity than would otherwise have been feasible, this obviously does not contribute to the aim of trying to maintain a high rate of growth of the world economy. On the other hand, if the main impact of the contractionary measures is in the direction of improving the balance of payments, rather than in reducing the level of domestic activity, the use of such a target would not be open to this objection.

But none of these targets fully embody the principles of macroeconomic mix suggested in this paper. A more complex interrelated set of targets would be required to achieve this, including not only one for restraining the growth of the money supply (and of liquid assets generally) or for DCE, but also one for ensuring that the overall effect of the budget on activity (which is not easily measured by any particular financial magnitude) is expansionary enough to maintain activity in the face of the contractionary monetary measures; and at the same time a target to hold down tax rates where they are thought to have cost-push effects.

VII. CONCLUSION

The main contention of this paper has been that there is a way of holding down the price level without accepting the very considerable loss of potential output that the world has been suffering during the past few years largely because of the efforts of governments to overcome inflation by deflationary policies. It is true that some types of measures to restore something like full employment growth for the world economy could lead to a substantial revival of inflation, but if that occurred it would be primarily because the wrong combination of macroeconomic measures has been used to provide the stimulus. If a tight rein is kept on the expansion of the money supply, and of the stock of close substitutes for money, there is no evident reason why expansionary budgetary policies, including a substantial reduction in real tax rates, should not be used in such a way as to promote a revival of a high rate of world economic growth without serious inflation. The main obstacle to doing this seems to be a widespread belief that any form of expansionary measure *must* precipitate rapid inflation, together with an unwillingness of governments to adopt a mix of measures that includes high enough nominal interest rates – which would almost certainly need to be done by way of indexed or floating rate bonds – coupled with low enough tax rates to enable the price level to be held down when output recovers.

One cannot, admittedly, be sure that the use of a mainly budgetary stimulus combined with a tight monetary policy would succeed in restoring the world to full employment growth without serious inflation; but the strong presumption is that it would succeed. The real costs to the world economy in terms of economic growth, and so of economic welfare forgone, if some such policy is not attempted make the case for trying it a very powerful one.

ADDENDUM

Since this paper was written I have seen the published proceedings of the IEA Congress on *Economic Integration, Worldwide, Regional, Sectoral*, edited by F. Machlup (Macmillan, 1976), on p. 203 of which is the only published reference I have been able to find to the basic suggestion contained in the present paper. It occurs in the course of Comments made by Robert A. Mundell on the paper of Peter B. Kenen, on 'International Capital Movements and the Integration of Capital Markets'. I quote the passage in full: 'The appropriate policy mix for inflationary recessions requires a split of our monetary and fiscal instruments, using expansionary fiscal policy to cope with excessive unemployment, and monetary restraint to curb excessive inflation. Tight money and fiscal ease lower both inflation and unemployment, and tend to improve the capital account of the balance of payments more than they hurt the balance of trade. The two financial instruments have differential effects on inflation and unemployment. The differences arise because of the homogeneous character of wage, price and money changes, differences between national and international impacts, aggregate supply *versus* aggregate demand changes and even expectational effects. And just as monetary and fiscal policies are totally different instruments, so the rate of inflation and the level of unemployment are differential targets. Tax policy has a comparative advantage in altering the equilibrium level of unemployment and the rate of monetary expansion on the rate of inflation.' Although Mundell does not spell out the nature of the differential effects to which he refers, some of them at least appear to be those on which the arguments of the proposals in the present paper are based.

4. Can Changing Consumer Tastes Save Resources?

Tibor Scitovsky

London School of Economics, United Kingdom

I. THE NEED TO SAVE RESOURCES

In the past, economic progress has mostly taken the form of a rise in labour productivity based on the substitution of mechanical for muscular energy and of material for human resources. The automatic forces of the market reinforced and speeded up that trend by raising the prices and so discouraging the consumption of all those sources of satisfaction that depend solely or mainly on human interaction. An example of these is the performing arts, whose prices rose and use declined with the rise in wages, except where public policies and subsidies slowed or arrested the process.

The spectacular mechanical and material development of the West was a welcome and necessary phase, which paved and showed the way that others are still following and are likely to follow for a long time yet. But as far as the developed countries themselves are concerned, their material development may well be close to having run its full course. For one thing, even as we continue our materialistic pursuits, we seem increasingly to reach out for their non-material rewards – a trend I shall deal with in the following. For another thing, the great increase in world population has made us realise that nature's bounty is not quite as lavish as it once seemed; moreover, as the poor nations of the Third World increasingly assert their claim to the same life-style that today is the privilege of a small minority, the globe's exhaustible resources appear not only exhaustible but insufficient.

The US share in the world's consumption of energy and mineral resources is six to seven times as great as her share in the world's population. If the remaining 95 per cent of the world's population raised their consumption to the US level and pattern, the globe's known fuel and mineral deposits would be used up in a single generation. Calculations of that sort, of course, are notoriously treacherous, because they assume too many factors as given. But they do indicate orders of magnitude and also serve to warn us that many of those givens will have to give. We will have to develop new sources of energy, new ways of saving energy and other resources, as well as ways to eliminate waste and wasteful life-styles. This paper focuses on the problem of wasteful life-styles.

Our present consumption pattern was moulded by very different scarcities and price ratios from those likely to prevail in the future. Already in the light of today's much higher energy prices, it seems to provide consumer satisfaction in a wasteful way. It is wasteful, not only in that the productive system uses up too many resources to produce what consumers want, but also in the sense that consumers choose an excessively expensive life-style to achieve satisfaction. Changing prices and scarcities can be counted on to change consumption patterns; but the process is sluggish and painful, partly because the automatic forces of the market are sluggish, partly because consumers get addicted to their accustomed ways, and partly also because the accumulated stock of still usable producers' and consumers' durables imparts a lot of rigidity to our life-style. That raises the question whether policy, and what kind of policy, could speed and facilitate matters by inducing the public to change its expenditure pattern in ways that would reduce resource costs without reducing consumer satisfaction.

II. CAN RESOURCE COSTS BE REDUCED WITHOUT REDUCING CONSUMER SATISFACTION?

That is a delicate question, which economists are not in the habit of asking, let alone answering. The following argument therefore is highly tentative and speculative – put forward with great caution and humility, but in the hope that it will stimulate more thinking on the subject and ultimately lead to more and better answers than I can hazard at this early stage.

Economists have rightly been reluctant to engage in social engineering and tamper with consumers' preferences; yet it ought to be possible to save material resources while detracting neither from the consumer's satisfaction nor from his sovereignty. After all, the input of exhaustible resources, though correlated with the level of living, bears no fixed relation to it. There are tremendous differences in different countries' consumption pattern and resource utilisation that have nothing to do with differences in their levels of living and seem fortuitous or due to differences in national tradition, explained in turn by historical accident. Sweden, Switzerland, Western Germany and Norway, for example, are countries whose standard of living is estimated to be higher (certainly no lower) than that of the United States, yet their per-capita consumption of energy is less than half that of the United States – as is also their per-capita generation of household waste, a good index of the consumer's use of exhaustible materials other than energy. To compensate, those countries consume twice the quantities we Americans consume of such other good things of life as vacations, active sports, the performing arts, whose input of exhaustible resources is small. I am not advocating the forcible imposition of one country's expenditure pattern on another; but the persuasive force of market opportunities and prices is surely a permissible weapon, and the example just given illustrates the scope for change, which ought to be achievable by persuasion.

For a more rigorous discussion of the scope, nature and means of change, it is useful to subdivide the consumer's needs and sources of satisfaction into three categories. First, one can distinguish between comforts and stimuli. Stimuli are anything the consumer values for the novelty, variety, excitement, challenge, surprise, or stimulus interest it provides. Comforts are whatever eliminates, relieves or prevents pains and discomforts, or anticipated pains and discomforts. Comforts may further be subdivided into personal and social comforts. Personal comforts cater to biological needs, make one physically comfortable, save time and effort in the performance of various chores, or provide for the future satisfaction of such needs and desires. Social comforts are satisfactions derived from one's membership and standing in society, in professional and social organisations, in one's workplace, and in any other formal or informal, permanent or *ad hoc* social group, as well as from whatever titles, objects, possessions and activities symbolise such membership or standing.

That classification into personal and social comforts and stimuli is comprehensive, comprising all forms of human satisfaction; and it classifies satisfactions, not goods and services. For many satisfactions, including some of the most important, do not depend on economic goods and services for their fulfilment; and many economic goods and services yield more than one of the three types of satisfactions listed. Let me stress that man's need for social comfort and stimulation is no less essential and no less urgent than his need for personal comfort. That fact needs stressing, because consumers and economists alike focus their attention on personal comforts and barely give grudging recognition to man's other needs. The probable reason is that, while the need for each of our personal comforts is highly specific, the need for social comfort and for stimulation can be filled in many ways by a great variety of activities and objects. As a result, none of these is indispensable, any one of them can easily be given up in favour of one of the many available substitutes; and that makes the need for all of them seem unimportant, however essential the need for *some* social comfort and *some* stimulation. Also, personal comforts are generally the most expensive in terms of economic goods and exhaustible resources, which is a further reason for their claiming the centre of attention. Indeed, with so much attention lavished by the consumer on how best to obtain his personal comforts, and by the economist on analysing the rational budgeting of resources needed to provide them, one wonders why their consumption and use should have become quite so wasteful in the developed countries.

One reason, much discussed and well known, is external diseconomies, the incidence of which has greatly increased with the increasing density of population and the rising standards of personal comfort. The production and consumption of many personal comforts generate pollutants, causing discomfort to others or necessitating the use of further resources to eliminate those pollutants, prevent their generation, or offset their harmful and unpleasant effects.

Other reasons, no less important, for the seemingly excessive cost of our personal comforts have to do with our failure to face up squarely to our need for the other satisfactions, social comfort and stimulation. As a result, we tend to be less rationally calculating when we cater to those needs – we obtain most of them jointly with personal comforts, in ways that add, often substantially, to the cost of our personal comforts.

An obvious example is conspicuous consumption: the acquisition of goods and services ostensibly for personal comfort but in quantities and at prices geared not so much to our need for personal comfort as to our desire for the status their use or ownership secures. One must accept man's need for status, recognition, and other people's respect, as an essential human need; and conspicuous consumption is just one, an expensive but not the most expensive way of satisfying that need. Titles, decorations, medals, citations are another, virtually costless, way of catering to some of that same need; and they are much used in the communist countries, somewhat less in Britain and France, and hardly at all in other Western democracies, which seem unable to forget and forgive the system's feudal origins. Our faith in market selection makes us seek social comfort in conspicuous consumption, already mentioned, and in that potentially most expensive source, job importance.

III. SOCIAL COMFORT AND JOB IMPORTANCE

Most people's main source of social comfort is the importance or seeming importance and usefulness of their job, its place in the economic or political hierarchy, the title it confers, the functions it involves, the number of people over whom it gives control, and the extent of that control. People's demand for job importance rises with the rise in their real income; hence the rising demand for education, which is, or seems, the prerequisite for the more prestigious jobs. The proportion of such jobs, however, does not increase just because the supply of education and the proportion of highly trained people in the labour force are increasing; it depends mainly on the hierarchical organisation of society and the economy. That is why the rises in incomes and education in the developed economies are increasingly creating an excess demand for job importance. That excess demand is relieved to some extent by the inflow of foreign labour, willing to take the more lowly jobs for which the indigenous labour force considers itself overtrained; it is also being filled to some extent by the creation of top-heavy hierarchies and an ever-increasing proportion of administrative positions. Even so, part of the demand for job importance seems to remain unsatisfied. Witness the frustration, amply documented in the United States, of the many highly qualified people placed in positions that provide insufficient outlet for the exercise of their qualifications yet unable to find more suitable jobs. Witness also the high unemployment rates of professionals and highly skilled workers, which so often exist side by side with staff shortages and unfilled positions on lowly levels, so that many humble but necessary jobs never get performed, because most people prefer unemployment to work beneath their station if unemployment compensation or accumulated savings give them the choice.

That the existence of excess demand for job importance is harmful and costly is obvious enough; but the remedies so far mentioned are also costly. The least so, perhaps, is the influx of foreign workers, though it creates social and political problems and is at best a temporary remedy, because once the immigrants get assimilated, they soon acquire the skills, preferences and expectations of the indigenous labour force. More costly is the direct catering to the demand for job importance: the creation of professional and administrative positions in government, education, the social services and the administration of private business beyond the requirements of efficient organisation. In Britain and the US, there has been a great redistribution of manpower in that direction for several reasons, of which the increased demand for job importance is only one. Whether that redistribution has gone beyond the requirements of efficiency, if so, how far it has gone and at what cost to society is difficult to estimate. In a formal sense, the marginal social cost of creating job importance is the excess of a person's wage or salary over the value of his or her contribution to output: the difficulty lies in estimating that contribution and its value. Britain's great economic problems are increasingly attributed to the shift of manpower away from the more productive down-to-earth occupations; and if that is a correct diagnosis, then the cost of that shift is enormous.

That raises the question how, and by what kind of policy, could people be helped to obtain at lesser cost the social comfort of regarding themselves and being regarded by others as important and useful members of society? The first and obvious answer is educational planning: the better matching of the number of people who acquire given productive and administrative skills with the foreseeable number of positions that will require those skills. I am not for providing less education than the public wants, only in favour of its better distribution and possibly also (in some countries) of channelling people away from production skills, towards more consumption skills. An additional reason for that will become evident later.

Secondly, policies designed to give production workers more initiative, more challenge, as well as more responsibility and sense of responsibility ought to diminish both the frustration and the striving for higher positions so prevalent at present. Several countries are currently experimenting with such policies.

Finally, the overwhelming importance people attach to their job and its place in the hierarchy as a source and token of status is likely to diminish if consumption skills get more attention and become more prevalent. That brings me to the next subject, our tendency also to obtain stimulation jointly with personal comforts and at high cost.

IV. STIMULATION AND HUMAN SATISFACTION

Stimulation as a source of human satisfaction is, at least from the economist's point of view, a new and largely unexplored subject. Psychologists have clearly established the essential nature of man's need for stimulation and studied the additiveness of stimuli from different sources, the satiability of man's need and desire for stimulus, as well as the pathology of stimulus deprivation. They have also gained some understanding of the nature of the stuff that provides stimulus, and have begun to quantify it.

The number and variety of sources of stimulation is tremendous – as one would expect, considering man's almost continuous need for stimulation during most of his waking hours. Many are free, such as conversation, games, physical exercise and most active sports, while others, such as spectator sports, commercial entertainment, performing arts, art objects and vacation travel, are economic goods produced and sold expressly for the stimulus they provide. TV and radio programmes are public goods, whether public corporations or private advertisers provide them. The stimulus and satisfaction of work is the free by-product of creative and productive activity; many others are by-products or joint products of goods and services that also provide personal comforts. Obvious examples of the latter are window-shopping, the acquisition of new possessions, driving for pleasure, the plaything aspect of many consumer durables, and the novelty of fashion, new gadgets, and new models of old gadgets and consumer durables.

With so great a variety of stimuli, some free, others costly, some available by themselves, others only as joint products or as part of package deals, the resource cost of obtaining a desired amount of stimulation varies tremendously with the source or sources from which it is obtained. It makes a great deal of difference therefore how, where, and in what form people get their stimulation, whether they get what they want, and whether they get it in optimum quantities, at minimum cost. We know that differences in different people's freely chosen stimulus patterns can be enormous, and differences in the resource cost of those different stimulus patterns are just as great. Why is there quite so great a variety of choices?

A basic postulate of economics is that the individual is the best judge of what gives him satisfaction and a pretty good judge also of how best to obtain that satisfaction. With minor qualifications, that postulate is generally accepted in the realm of personal comforts; but when it comes to stimulation as a source of satisfaction, there arises a logical difficulty which seems to rule out consumer rationality in the sense in which we know and accept it as the governing principle of consumer behaviour in other areas of consumer choice.

The stuff of mental stimulation – the main form of human stimulation – is novelty. It is the mental processing of novelty we enjoy, provided it comes in the right quantity, with neither too much nor too little redundancy, i.e. relatedness to the familiar. Now rational consumer choice depends on knowledge, advance knowledge of the nature and amount of satisfaction that can be expected from the various alternatives available. But knowing in advance how much stimulation to expect from a particular source of novelty inevitably destroys some of its novelty and reduces its ability to stimulate. Moreover, acquiring the knowledge necessary for informed consumer choice is inseparable from acquiring or increasing the redundancy needed for enjoyable stimulation; and that too creates a problem, related to, though different from, the previous one. This second is much the more serious of the two problems; but I shall illustrate both, with two simple examples.

The enjoyment of a detective story depends on the suspense and surprise it provides. But to make an informed choice and select from among several detective stories the one I would most enjoy reading is virtually impossible, because such choice would have to be based on information whose very acquisition would diminish the suspense and surprise. I am better off if I choose to remain ignorant of the contents and make my choice by trusting friends' advice, reviewers' judgement, or authors' reputations.

My other example has to do with music. To enjoy music one must know something about it and that something has to be learned. Ideally, the learning process itself could be enjoyable, but mostly it is not, because inspired teachers are rare and because part of the learning process consists in listening *before* having learned to enjoy what one is listening to. That is why acquiring a musical education is usually as dull and strenuous as most other learning. One is tempted to liken the strain (and cost) of one's initiation to music to the cost of an investment, incurred for the sake of the future returns it is expected to yield. The two cases, however, are fundamentally different. An entrepreneur can estimate investment costs and expected future profits with some degree of confidence, calculate the probable rate of return, discount for risk, and make a reasonably rational decision. By contrast, the would-be music lover, who is trying to decide whether to acquire a musical education, cannot make an equally informed decision, because he would need to have that education not only to enjoy music but even to judge the nature and desirability of musical enjoyment. In other words, he is in the impossible situation of having to have musical knowledge to be able rationally to decide whether that musical knowledge is worth acquiring. Nor is that problem confined to music; it is common to all forms of stimulus consumption that require a skill for their enjoyment.

Those examples illustrate the insuperable difficulty that confronts the consumer in the realm of stimulus satisfaction when he wants to make an informed, rational choice. In the usual sense of the term, therefore, consumer rationality with respect to stimulus satisfaction is impossible. Possible, though of limited usefulness, is retrospective consumer rationality. After the event, with the benefit of hindsight, one can judge which story was the best and whether it was worth investing the time, pain and money into learning to appreciate music. Before the event, the best one can do is to follow the judgement of others who have the benefit of hindsight, in the hope that one's own retrospective judgement will coincide with theirs. ·

V. THE ORIGIN OF DIFFERENCES IN TASTES

The above argument throws new light on the origin of differences in tastes. In the past, economists accepted these unquestioningly and considered them sacrosanct. In the realm of personal comforts, however, where rational consumer choice is possible, tastes vary but little and most differences in consumption patterns are explained by differences in income and relative prices. What these fail to explain are differences in different people's patterns of stimulus enjoyment; and in that area, the impossibility of rational consumer choice is by far the simplest explanation. In other words, variety of tastes, confined as it is to sources of stimulation, is best explained by the difficulty of using prospective rationality with respect to stimulus satisfaction.

National differences in living habits and consumption patterns, where not due to income differences, are also largely confined to differences in patterns and sources of stimulus enjoyment; and those differences are again best explained by the impossibility of rational consumer choice in that area. But, while national characteristics differ greatly between countries, they are quite stable and persistent within each country, owing, probably, to what I called retrospective rationality. Each generation knows, with the benefit of hindsight, the advantage of possessing its own consumption skills; and the next generation benefits by that knowledge and acquires the same consumption skills if it respects tradition or submits to the authority of its elders.

Indeed, the paradox I am discussing, the logical impossibility of rationally choosing the best pattern of stimulus enjoyment, must seem a tame and largely academic paradox to many people, because it is so very easy to resolve by providing a humanistic education. A humanistic education is mostly training in consumption skills, which prepares people for the enjoyment of a variety of stimuli; and by making it a compulsory part of the school curriculum, we can save our children the ordeal of an impossible choice. That solution, however, is better at preventing regress than at promoting progress; and besides, it is often not practicable.

In the US, the requirements of imparting production skills and a good grounding in science and technology have largely crowded out the humanistic and cultural part of the curriculum. Also, the individual's freedom of choice is an article of faith with us, which has kept the influence of tradition to a minimum and has even led to children being allowed freely to choose a large part of their school curriculum. That explains why we have few characteristic national pastimes; but it does not mean that our choice of sources of stimulation is random. The impossibility of rational choice means that one cannot weigh the benefits of having, against the costs of acquiring each consumption skill and then choose those with the most favourable benefit/cost ratios, because one cannot ascertain the benefits. In such a situation, it is reasonable to minimise one's investment in consumption skills; and that is exactly what happens. Many stimuli require for their enjoyment little or no consumption skills or skills already acquired for some other purpose; and it is natural for the unskilled consumer to seek stimulation from these. If that proves costly or yields less stimulation than he wants, he will never know it, unless by chance he later acquires some of the consumption skills he has spurned in the beginning and so can exercise retrospective rationality.

VI. THE UNITED STATES CONSUMPTION PATTERN

How can we, as outside observers, judge the US consumption pattern and tell whether it provides the desired amount and kind of stimulus, and whether it provides stimulus at minimum cost? The first is too complex and difficult a question to deal with here,[1] but something can be said on the second.

The sources of mental stimulation whose enjoyment requires the least skills are shopping, window-shopping and otherwise learning of market opportunities, following and keeping up with changing fashions, using as playthings and sources of variety vehicles,[2] appliances and other aids to personal comfort, light entertainment, and spectator sports. Those that involve the most skills are music, literature, the arts, conversation, and problem-solving, which last ranges from puzzles and bridge to scientific inquiry. Those in the latter group require labour inputs and little else; those in the former have other inputs as well and, when they are by-products of or joint products with personal comforts, can be inefficient and costly sources of stimulation.

Unfortunately, we have no estimates of the cost of stimuli that are jointly produced with personal comforts, except for a single study of the cost of annual model changes in the US automobile industry.[3] That study has estimated the annual extra cost to society of cars following fashion in appearance, size, power, and gadgetry, over and above what producing and running the same number of cars would have cost had they merely 'been built with the developing technology.' Over the period 1956–60, that extra cost is estimated to have averaged $4845 million p.a., 1.3 per cent of the net national income and well over a quarter (28.1 per cent) of total consumers' expenditure on conventional recreation. Since all it paid for is the stimulus of variety in the appearance and gadgetry of cars, it well illustrates the high cost of stimulation when that comes in a package deal jointly with personal comforts. The remedy is not, of course, to deprive consumers of a stimulus they opted for but to put them into a position where they can opt for something better.

---

[1] I have tried to deal with it in my *The Joyless Economy*.
[2] Cars are aesthetic objects and a complex of gadgets to play with, additional stimulus stems from driving for the exhilaration of speed, for exercising one's skill, and for the fast-changing visual image one gets from being on a moving vehicle.
[3] Cf. F. M. Fisher, Z. Griliches and C. Kaysen, 'The Costs of Automobile Model Changes since 1949', *Journal of Political Economy*, Oct 1962.

If retrospective choice is to be trusted, consumption skills are worth having, and the satisfactions they render accessible are greater and longer-lasting than most of those unskilled consumers have access to. Yet such skills and satisfactions seem confined to a minority, which is very much smaller in the US than it is in most of Europe, although the average American has more education than the average citizen of any European country. The reason, almost certainly, is that our educational superiority is confined to production skills and does not extend to consumption skills. Our predicament in this respect is cause for concern not only to us, because the pattern we set is widely followed by others. The supply of education is rapidly increasing everywhere and the stress is always on production skills. I am pleading for an increase also of consumption skills, both because it would increase satisfaction and because it would lower the cost of satisfaction.

Education is cheapest in schools, which ought to exploit the increased demand for schooling, however much that is focused on production skills. Just as effective, however, and just as important, is informal learning by doing, trying, experimenting. That is the justification for subsidising the arts. But to get the public to learn consumption skills by practice is a lengthy and difficult process, whose success depends on ease of access not only in terms of cost. The price elasticity of demand for the performing arts is very low – estimated at 0.25 in the US. That is supposed to measure the response of consumption to a price, *given people's preferences*; but it also gives an inkling of the difficulty of changing those preferences – at least of changing them by price change alone. Yet the difficulty can be and has been overcome. The demand for theatre and music is three to four times, perhaps even five times as great in the countries of Eastern and Northern Europe, where the price of admission covers 30–40 per cent of cost, than it is in the US, where the ticket price pays for 60 per cent of expenses. So great a difference in demand clearly reflects a difference in tastes much more than in price, probably explained by the communist and Scandinavian countries' greater success in making the arts popular. Credit may be due to the much longer period over which they have subsidised the arts or to the way they have done it.

The US subsidy programme has not been too successful so far in enticing the wider public into appreciating the performing arts; and while it is too early to pass judgement, two likely reasons for its failure are worth mentioning. One is the desire to minimise losses by selling every seat. That has led to so great a reliance on subscribers that, today, access is mostly limited to old-established enthusiasts, who alone are willing to plan and buy subscriptions weeks ahead; and access is denied to those who merely want a taste to find out if they like it. The other reason is that subsidisers take serious art, and the limiting of subsidies to serious art too seriously, and tend to sharpen the dividing line between it and light entertainment. That renders it that much the harder for the public to stray across that line. It is so much easier to pick up a liking for the arts by trial and experiment in, say, Copenhagen, whose main concert hall is in an amusement park, next door to the roller coaster, with tickets usually available at the entrance when you want to go in.

This question posed in my title was raised more than answered in this paper. That was the easier part but it, too, had to be done. I am content to leave the difficult part to others.

ANNUAL ADMISSIONS TO THEATRES AND CONCERTS PER HEAD OF THE
POPULATION

	Theatres	*Concerts*	*Total*
German Democratic Republic	0.73	0.25	0.98
Czechoslovakia	0.71	0.16	0.87
Austria[1]	0.66	0.22	0.88
Roumania	0.65		
USSR	0.64		
Bulgaria[2]	0.58	0.15	0.73
Hungary	0.58	0.09	0.67
Sweden[3]	0.53	0.14	0.67
German Federal Republic[4]	0.43	0.16	0.59
Poland	0.41	0.16	0.57
Finland	0.41		
Italy	0.34		
Norway	0.30		
Switzerland[5]	0.26	0.13	0.39
UK[6]			0.27 – 0.34
Netherlands	0.09	0.14	0.23
USA[3,7]	0.11	0.07	0.18

[1] Admission data for concerts are available only for Vienna. This estimate assumes that the ratio of concert to theatre admissions is the same for the whole country as it is for Vienna.
[2] Estimated from number of concerts given, on assumption that average attendance was 300. Probably an underestimate.
[3] Data are available for orchestral concerts. This estimate assumes that attendance at vocal, solo-instrument and chamber-music concerts equalled that at orchestral concerts.
[4] Data are available for concerts only in regular concert halls and theatres. This estimate assumes that concerts held elsewhere (whose number is known) had the same attendance on average as regular concerts.
[5] Admission data to concerts are available only for Zurich. This estimate assumes that the ratio of concert to theatre admissions is the same for the whole country as it is for Zurich.
[6] Estimated from data on consumers' expenditure on theatres and concerts.
[7] Data for Broadway, 'the Road', non-profit opera ballet theatre and modern dance, and college- and university-sponsored events, supplemented by estimates of 'off Broadway' and summer theatre (20 per cent of Broadway admissions) and of semi-professional theatre staged by college and university drama departments (200 per cent of admissions to college- and university-sponsored professional events).

SOURCES The latest Statistical Yearbooks of the German Democratic Republic, Austria, USSR, Hungary, Sweden, Poland, Italy, Switzerland, Netherlands, the cities of Vienna, Zurich, and the 1972 and 1973 Statistical Yearbooks of (West) German municipalities; UNESCO's *Cultural Policy* series for Roumania, Bulgaria, Czechoslovakia, Finland; U.K. estimate obtained privately; for US, *Variety*, 2 June 1976, Ford Foundation, *The Finances of the Performing Arts*, and Association of College, University and Community Arts Administrators, *Profile Survey*.

5 Growth Factors and Strategy Choices in a Semi-developed Situation

Marian Ostrowski and Zdzislaw Sadowski

Warsaw, Poland

I. THE PROBLEM

The basic idea of this paper was born from a feeling that traditional approaches to economic growth theory tend to neglect an important constraint which – though not necessarily restricted to any particular level of development – seems to be having a most serious effect on the interplay of growth factors in semi-developed economies. This constraint results from the very high and quickly growing level of consumers' aspirations which enters into contradiction with the not-so-high level of productive capacities.

One reason for this apparent neglect of growth theory is that its main attention has long been focused on two extreme cases: on the one hand the functioning of growth mechanism in highly developed economies, and on the other hand on setting it into motion – and sustaining this motion – in economies developing from lower levels. This dichotomic approach is understandable: it reflected what was considered most pertinent to the world economy; it was also easier to deal with clear-cut cases.

Semi-development admittedly does not present a clear-cut case. In fact all we can say for sure is that it encompasses all cases between the two extremes. But where are the dividing lines?

For general orientation we may adopt a crude assumption that semi-development – and the corresponding phenomena which we intend to study – is linked to a level of income of the order of $1000–2500 per caput. But even some countries that are well below these brackets should perhaps be considered as semi-developed, particularly when they are large enough to include important areas or centres well advanced in the economic sense of the word. Rather than trying to enumerate countries which should or should not be included, we therefore prefer to speak of a semi-developed situation, which is defined as that of a country facing problems of the nature described in this paper. If these problems are really of such importance as we attach to them, it implies that, in the semi-developed situation, growth mechanisms work in a different way than in either the highly developed or the less developed countries. This would then explain the need for abandoning the dichotomic approach and distinguishing a third area of investigation. It may well be that, in the present world, it is more 'normal' than any other one.

Semi-development is not linked to any particular form of socio-economic organisation of the society. In saying this we want to point to our intention of avoiding another type of dichotomy in the assessment of growth problems, i.e. that which consists in drawing a dividing line between market economies and centrally planned economies. We feel that the nature of problems involved in the growth mechanism may be similar; what is different is the machinery through which the mechanism works, and hence some forms of the solutions which are, more or less temporarily, arrived at.

II. THE GOAL FUNCTION

Consumers' aspirations – though always recognised in theory through assumptions concerning tastes and preferences of consumers – were never included as an autonomous factor in the theory of growth rate determination nor in the principles of economic planning. Macroeconomic theory is founded on the notion of a society striving to maximise a certain goal function, given the physical constraints in the form of factor endowment. Hence models of economic growth are based on a production-function approach. Consumption is shown as dependent on the level of output and the resulting income. A similar approach is adopted by the practice of macroeconomic planning. The social aspect of development is taken care of by the possible inclusion of ideas and assumptions concerning the distribution of income.

The question of the goal function has, of course, long been a controversial issue. Among the macroeconomic magnitudes which could best be used to represent the totality of socio-economic goals, choice was in fact between a measure of the total output – whether net material product or gross national product or any possible variations of either – and a measure of 'final' satisfaction expressed in terms of total consumption expenditure – whatever its precise statistical interpretation.

Neither of these two measures could be treated as satisfactory in terms of their ability to reflect the complexity of socio-economic development objectives. Hence it was widely agreed that economic calculation cannot be expected to bring about comprehensive results. In theory this led to the recognition of the need for widening the notion of growth effects. In practice any economic calculation had to be supplemented by more or less arbitrary decisions concerning those growth effects which could not find reflection in economic measures.

But striving to include in economic calculation all possible effects is condemned to failure, not only for technical reasons: for social reasons many of them cannot be unambiguously defined and measured because of differences in the viewpoints taken by various participants in the growth process. This observation points out the need for some kind of decomposition of the aggregate goal function, not in the well-known sense of material disaggregation but in order to reflect the attitudes of various agents.

III. DISAGGREGATION OF THE GOAL FUNCTION

In what follows we try to make a step in this direction by means of a highly simplified model of those principal agents and their interaction. We shall distinguish in any national economy only three principal groups of agents which can be considered sub-systems of the whole system: the Public, the Enterprises, and the Decision-making Authority.

The DMA is the body responsible for shaping the economic development policies. A body of this kind exists nowadays in every country, whether socialist or capitalist, although its scope of authority, its influence, and its internal constitution may differ. In a socialist society it embraces government bodies responsible for central planning and management of the national economy. In a capitalist society, it is a part of the government responsible for dealing with the performance of the economy. What is important is that, even in a highly market-oriented economy, the growth processes are no longer the outcome of free play of market forces but are influenced heavily by government policies, whether using monetary or fiscal measures or direct controls.

'The Enterprises' is a non-homogeneous complex comprising industrial organisations of all possible sizes and areas of activity. In a socialist society they are either state-owned or co-operative organisations. In market economies both private and publicly owned enterprises are included. It is clear that vast differences exist between various components of this sub-system in respect of their particular interests. But we are not concerned here with the differences, but rather with what is common to them. The Enterprises are understood in a techno-organisational way and not as grouping of individuals.

Finally, 'the Public' stands to denote all members of the given society both as consumers and contributors to the joint output.

It is believed that a semi-developed situation is characterised by a higher intensity of development aspirations of all the three agents than any other situation. So to speak, everybody wants growth, although they may mean different things by this. A semi-developed society is totally growth-oriented.

The high intensity of growth aspirations on the part of DMA is due to two main factors: (i) it is keenly aware of the distance between the economic level of its country and that of the highly developed economies; and (ii) at the same time it works in a country in which the socio-economic environment is basically favourable to growth, so that high levels of economic development are already within reach – which gives an extra boost to aspirations.

The objectives of DMAs in determining policies with regard to the rate of growth are by no means the same everywhere. The distinguishing feature of semi-developed countries *vis-à-vis* the more developed ones is that DMAs in the latter groups are more concerned with stabilisation than with speedy growth. Less developed countries logically should pursue the goal of growth maximisation, but they are not well enough equipped in growth machinery to be able to do so.

The high intensity of growth aspirations on the part of the Enterprises may not be a particular feature of the semi-developed situation as compared with highly advanced countries. It is, however, important to note as a factor adding still more strength to the growth-drive of the DMA. But it will be assumed here that 'Enterprises' in a typical semi-developed situation do not represent any special position with respect to the growth drive in the macroeconomic sense. Their action is parallel to that of the DMA. If they are mentioned at all as a separate agent, it is because a more detailed investigation than is possible in this paper would have to take into consideration the consequences of differences between the DMA and the Enterprises.

The Public is also very conscious of growth aspirations (which is not the case in a less developed country). These aspirations, however, clearly take a different turn from those of the DMA (and the Enterprises). While the aspirations of the DMA are orientated rather towards production those of the Public are biased towards consumption.

It is worth stressing that the ways in which the world economy evolves are not neutral to the attitudes taken by the three agents towards growth. One can hardly deny that a main feature of our times is the growing interdependence between all the national economies (as well as other important sub-systems such as transnational corporations). This growing interdependence can be seen not only from the world trade figures, but also from the enormous increase in direct ties and linkages which can be seen, among other things, in the spectacular growth of individual international travel, whether for business or for pleasure. The direct result for those less and semi-developed is visible in the spread of all kinds of demonstration effects, i.e. of various forms of imitation, leading to increased aspirations of people and groups. Imitation finds its expression in attitudes both to consumption and to production.

IV. GROWTH RATE DETERMINATION

Because of its preoccupation with the logic of growth rate maximisation, i.e. with determining the relationships and constraints in terms of some assumed types of production functions in macro-terms, the theory of growth serves in its way the purpose of instructing the DMA on the economic (and technical) constraints against which it has to make its decisions. Indeed, the essence of strategy choices in any society is connected with the rate of economic growth. The determination of this rate is the central macroeconomic problem which – in one form or another – emerges in every country, whatever its system. It is, by its very nature, a problem for DMA.

The logic of choice of the growth rate by the DMA can be described as follows.

A certain assumption must be made as to the time horizon for growth rate determination. The practice of development planning in various nations seems to indicate that, for pragmatic reasons, real choices are usually made for a medium term of several – say – five years.

Given the time horizon, the DMA striving at growth rate maximisation should operate so as to try to equilibrate the social benefits of accelerating growth with the social costs of so doing. This is graphically represented in Fig. 5.1.

The shape of the benefit curve OA may be debatable, but it does not affect reasoning as long as this curve does intersect the cost curve OK which can be defended as the normal case. The shape of the curve OK is self-explanatory.

We want to focus our attention on the lines MM and NN.

The line MM represents the maximum growth rate attainable by the national economy, given the physical constraints resulting from available resources. The notion of such rate is well known in literature. It is often interpreted as

$$r_{max} = a + b$$

where a is the rate of growth of labour supply and b is the growth rate of labour productivity. This is a convenient, though not the only possible, way of visualising this rate.

The striving of DMA to maximise the rate of growth means in effect that the shape of its assessment of social benefits of growth acceleration (and hence the shape of OA curve) is such that the point P will tend to lie rather close to the line MM. There is a host of problems involved in the actual determination of

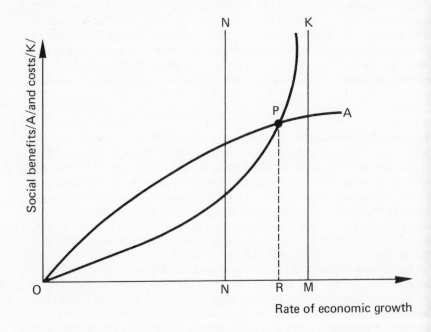

Fig. 5.1

point P in view of the limited knowledge about the costs, the benefits and the position of the MM line. But this is not our concern here.

Our problem is related to the position of the line NN, which we shall introduce as representing what we call the 'expected rate of growth'.

V. THE EXPECTED RATE OF GROWTH

The concept of the expected growth rate is introduced to represent the desires of the Public. It is, in fact, a measure of the consumption-oriented growth aspirations of the Public. The consumption-growth expectations of the Public imply a certain expected overall rate of growth as measured by national income or GNP.

A technical way of determining the expected rate of growth is through a 'coefficient of income requirement'. A given expected growth rate of consumption of C per cent per annum implies a requirement with regard to national income to grow by kC per cent, where k is the coefficient in question. It seems that k may be relatively stable over the years if the composition of consumption expenditure and the structure of the productive apparatus of the country do not undergo revolutionary changes within the period under consideration. As we deal with the medium term, this seems to be a legitimate assumption.

The concept of the expected rate of growth is not needed as long as the rate may be considered constant. But this is exactly what we believe is no longer true of a semi-developed situation.

The way in which the growth mechanism actually seems to work is such that the maximum-growth aspirations of DMA supported by the Enterprises contribute gradually towards raising the consumption aspirations of the Public and hence the expected growth rate.

But the expected growth rate sets a kind of minimum level below which the actual growth rate should not fall because of the expectations of the Public. This minimum is in no way absolute; it is determined for a given period by the prevailing social moods and attitudes.

The expected rate is not just a product of imagination. In making its strategy choices the DMA must have an idea – even if only implicit – of a minimum social requirement for the growth of consumption. This is taken care of in its development plans by assuming certain target figures for the growth of consumption.

But the DMA is always confronted with an uneasy choice between the option of raising these target figures for current consumption and that of raising the rate of overall growth in the longer run. This is in fact its crucial policy decision which is well recognised under different names, such as the choice of the rate of accumulation, influencing the savings rate, or determination of the rate of capital formation.

Naturally enough, the DMA makes its decisions in the context of definite social moods and attitudes, determined by – or perhaps only connected with –

the already attained level of development. These moods find their expression in what the Public expects from the growth process. Current consumption may be treated as an aggregate measure – admittedly imperfect – of these expectations. Through these expectations the Public sets a minimum social requirement for the growth of current consumption.

Of course, any such requirement can temporarily be met by reducing the rate of accumulation. But this is no good, as it would reduce future growth rates of both national income and consumption. The growth aspirations of the Public are not aimed at a one-time increase of consumption: what is really wanted is a continually growing stream. Therefore the expectations of the Public with regard to current consumption have to be reinterpreted into what they really mean in terms of an implied rate of growth of national income over a longer period. This is what we mean by the 'expected rate of growth'.

The importance of the expected rate of growth results from the social consequences of not meeting the expectations by the actual growth process. Every human society, having definite expectations with regard to growth and development, has also its own ways of reacting to their non-fulfilment. The reaction need not necessarily be violent. What may often be much more serious is that it may take the form of a change in the productive attitudes of the people, including loosening of work discipline and reduced productivity of labour as symptoms of social frustration.

As long as the position of line NN remains as presented in Fig. 5.1 it creates no problem for the growth process. The problem appears when it shifts to the right, reflecting rising expectations on the part of the Public. A particularly grave problem may arise, if at the same time the maximum rate tends to fall, i.e. the line MM is shifted to the left. We may logically expect that a situation may arise in which the actual growth rate cannot meet the minimum requirement set by the expected growth rate because this requirement surpasses the ceiling set by the maximum rate.

VI. THE MAXIMUM AND EXPECTED RATES OF GROWTH

The phenomenon of the increasing expected rate of growth is, in our view, particularly important in semi-developed countries which have been able to maintain high growth rates over a longer period of time and have a relatively egalitarian pattern of income distribution. High growth rates lead to quickly rising aspirations on the part of the Public, while the equity of distribution helps spread these aspirations more or less evenly among all the layers of society. A similar effect on the rise of aspirations can result, e.g. from the adoption of a broad and quickly expanding system of free social services to which the Public gets quickly used and expects more.

All such phenomena can (and do) arise in countries at various levels of development.

But at the very low levels their impact tends to be neutralised by the existing disparities of income distribution between social groups. In other words, it does arise only within relatively higher income groups while those who are really poor are not yet in a position to develop the rapidly growing aspirations drive, if only because of limited exposure to the demonstration effect, e.g. typical peasants in the African interior.

On the other hand, in the highly developed market economies income distribution may also count as a neutralising factor, though maybe rather on the opposite side: those well off are perhaps less 'growth-thirsty' and hence do not present the kind of drive we are talking about.

But in both cases the future may well bring substantial changes in growth conditions. In less developed countries, there is the hope and the will to arrive sooner or later at a semi-developed situation. In advanced economies, a gradual reduction of attainable growth rates may well bring one day the maximum rate below the expected one. Thus, the semi-developed situation may be more general than it would seem.

As was mentioned earlier, the phenomenon of the increasing expected rate of growth acquires particular importance when the maximum rate (as determined mainly by physical constraints) tends to become lower. This may well be quite pertinent in the world of increasing scarcities of basic products. But what is also important to underline is that the increasing expected growth rate may itself eventually become a powerful factor working towards reducing the potential maximum rate of growth through its adverse effect on labour productivity. Thus DMA may find itself in an increasingly difficult situation with regard to strategy and policy choices.

It is therefore essential for strategy decisions in any country to arrive at a clear diagnosis of what is the actual position of the lines MM and NN and what are the directions of its change in given circumstances.

Some possible relationships between the two growth rates are shown in Fig. 5.2 where the convention of relating them to time was used. The diagram helps distinguish five basic situations which are marked by letters from A to E.

Situation A may be interpreted as that of a country at a very low level of development which has not yet taken off for sustained growth. Because of a very low ceiling for the growth of employment and labour productivity growth aspirations are higher than possibilities. The situation is unfavourable to growth. The main challenge for development policy is to create growth-promoting conditions, mostly through some socio-political readjustments helping to liberate development forces.

Situation B is that of a developing country which finds itself in a position to raise its growth rate steadily owing to the successful removal of some growth barriers. The maximum rate is growing and surpasses the expected rate. The situation is favourable to development and the main challenge to policy is to further accelerate growth.

Situation C is an extension of what was arrived at in B but the expected rate has already begun to rise. The main challenge is to maintain the continuity of rapid growth. Basically, this is a situation of semi-development in its earlier stages.

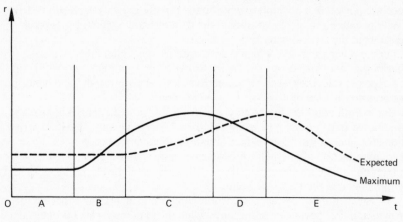

Fig. 5.2

Situation D reflects a further increase in the expected growth rate, resulting mainly from the fact of sustaining a high actual rate over a longer period of time. This is what we believe is a typical semi-developed situation. At the same time, due to external factors such as resource scarcities the maximum rate may tend to fall, which may accentuate the difficulties. But even without that the situation is becoming increasingly unfavourable for continued growth. The main challenge to policy is to find ways of restoring the previous relative position of the two rates.

Situation E reflects the possible – at least temporary – result of not finding satisfactory policy solutions in situation D. The expected rate is well above the maximum one. The situation is again unfavourable to growth, as it is loaded with social tension. Only after a considerable time-lag can one expect an automatic downward adjustment of public aspirations to real possibilities of growth. The challenge for policy is to shorten this time-lag though without giving up endeavours to push the maximum rate upward.

VII. CONCLUSIONS

It is clear that the above presentation gives nothing more than a suggested approach. If found promising and defensible on general grounds, it would call for further work leading to its verification and the elaboration of policy implications. So far the present authors have not been able to do much more than to work on some crude estimates related to the experience of their own country.

The policy implications of the described phenomenon must be analysed in terms of the feedbacks between the expected and the maximum growth rates. The crucial thing is that in the semi-developed situation where it emerges the

OMA must include among its policies ancillary policies aimed at containing the spontaneous consumption drive of the Public.

We do not want to enter into any closer discussion of such policies in the present paper. It would seem, however, necessary to point to one important direction in which they should perhaps be looked for rather than anywhere else. We found earlier a significant factor responsible for the consumption drive of the Public in a semi-developed situation in the tendency towards imitation of the consumption patterns of highly advanced societies characterised by acquisitive attitudes towards life. The conclusions which we are able to draw from our reasoning at this stage seem to give much strength to the idea that endeavours to find the right substitutes for acquisitiveness are needed not only because such postures may be considered morally unhealthy but also – and perhaps primarily so – because in the present world they set in motion a socio-economic mechanism adverse to the economic growth of societies.

6 Development Ideas in Historical Perspective: the New Interest in Development

Paul Streeten*

World Bank, Washington USA

I. DEVELOPMENT AS A NEW BRANCH OF ECONOMICS

Development Economics is a new branch of economics. There was little that
went under this name before the Second World War, though many of the same
problems were dealt with by members of the colonial services, anthropologists
and others. Since much of economics is a response to current political and
social problems, it is pertinent to ask what new conditions gave rise to the new
and rapidly growing interest in development.

First, there was a new awareness that poverty is not the inevitable fate of the
majority of mankind. This awareness was itself the result of the achievement of
affluence for the masses in the West, the high economic growth rates of
countries in Western Europe, of North America, of the Soviet Union and of
Japan, and the improvement in mass communications which brought events in
the rich North to the consciousness of the poor South, and more specifically to
the consciousness of the new elites there. As a result of the propaganda of
politicians and economists, aided by the transistor radio, television and jet
planes, economic growth came to be regarded as a human right.

A second source was the Cold War, in which East and West, the Second and
First World, competed in attracting the attention of the Third World. Both the
capitalist, mixed economies of the West, and especially the US, and the
planned economy of the Soviet Union attempted to win friends and influence
people by showing that their economic performance was superior, by holding
up their respective regimes as ideals to be imitated and by giving development
aid. It is interesting to note that with the thawing of the Cold War (if this is the
right metaphor) and with the relatively reduced significance of military
expenditure, the expectations of those who thought that this would make more
resources available for international aid were disappointed: the flow of aid

* I am grateful to Ajit Ghose and Jeffrey James for assistance in preparing this paper,
and to Albert Hirschman, Dudley Seers, Karsten Laursen and J. C. Voorhoeve for
helpful comments. The paper forms part of a larger study, undertaken for the Rothko
Chapel, Houston, Texas.

levelled off and shrank as a proportion of national income.[1] It not only shows up the limits of economics but illustrates the principle of the irrelevant alternative, according to which a boy comes home and tells his father proudly that he had saved tenpence by walking and not taking a bus. To this the father replies contemptuously: 'You fool; why did you not save £1.00 by not taking a taxi?'

A third factor was the population explosion. When population was kept at a fairly constant level as a result of high mortality rates, poverty was bearable. There was no growing pressure on scarce resources, son followed father in his occupation and traditional ways continued. But a growing population requires production increases simply in order to maintain the level of living. The maintenance of 'traditional ways' and freedom from the pollution and rapaciousness of modern civilisation presents an attractive, romantic picture, but it is unrealistic. Admittedly, it was the introduction of modern medical and other scientific technology that reduced spectacularly mortality rates, while no equally cheap and effective method to reduce traditional high birth rates was available. But it remains true that, without development and the disruption it brings, societies could not continue to enjoy the happy existence presented by some romantic anthropologists, but would be faced with growing misery.

The fourth source is the large number of countries that attained independence after the war. Decolonisation is the most important effect of the last war. In the last thirty years 102 countries have achieved independence. Membership of the United Nations has increased from 51 to 147 (and the total number of countries is 153). Development and planning for development were written on the banners of the governments of these countries.

An understanding of the reasons for the rapid growth of interest in development economics is both interesting in itself, and helpful in identifying possible biases and omissions in our work. Gunnar Myrdal, who has consistently tried to remain aware of these influences wrote:

> For social scientists it is a sobering and useful exercise in self-understanding to attempt to see clearly how the direction of our scientific exertions, particularly in economics, is conditioned by the society in which we live, and most directly by the political climate (which, in turn, is related to all other changes in society). Rarely, if ever, has the development of economics by its own force blazed the way to new perspectives. The cue to the continual reorientation of our work has normally come from the sphere of politics; responding to that cue, students are launched, data collected, and the literature on the 'new' problems expands. By its cumulative results, this research activity, which mirrors the political strivings of the time, may eventually contribute to a rationalization of these strivings and even give them a different turn.

[1]See Tables 1, 2 and 3 in Appendix.

So it has always been. The major recastings of economic thought that we connect with the names of Adam Smith, Malthus, Ricardo, List, Marx, John Stuart Mill, Jevons and Walras, Wicksell and Keynes, were all responses to changing political conditions and opportunities.[2]

II. THE FERMENT OF NEW IDEAS

It is not easy to convey, in the present atmosphere of gloom, boredom and indifference surrounding discussions of development problems, what an exciting time of ferment these early years were.

The excitement arose both from the challenge and the vision of the task of eradicating poverty and opening up new lives and opportunities for self-fulfilment to hundreds of millions of people, and from the new ideas to which this challenge gave rise. These ideas were a revolt against the traditional, conventional views of the profession.

Albert Hirschman recently pointed to the importance, in the history of development economics, of Samuelson's proof of factor-price equalisation in 1948–49.[3] The articles proved that, on certain assumptions conventionally accepted in the theory of international trade, free trade would equalise absolute factor rewards, and trade could therefore perform precisely the same function as free international movement of factors. In a world in which people became increasingly aware of wide and widening international income gaps, this was a brilliant and startling conclusion. As Albert Hirschman says, here the neoclassical paradigm was not undermined by the accumulation of contradictory evidence, as Thomas Kuhn's scientific revolutionary sequence would lead us to expect, but 'the theory contributed to the contradiction by resolutely walking away from the facts.[4]

Raúl Prebisch, Hans Singer and Gunnar Myrdal, less elegantly but more realistically, challenged not only Samuelson's findings but the more general view that equilibrating forces showed a tendency for the fruits of economic progress to be widely and, after a time-lag, evenly shared.

At the same time, the Harrod–Domar model, though formulated for different conditions than those of underdevelopment, added output-generation to the Keynesian income-generation of investment, and thereby provided the principal pillar for the analysis of development and for many development

[2]Gunnar Myrdal, *Asian Drama*, Vol 1 (Penguin Books, 1968) p. 9.

[3]Albert O. Hirschman, 'A Generalized Linkage Approach to Development, with Special Reference to Staples', *Essays on Economic Development and Cultural Change in Honor of Bert F. Hoselitz, Economic Development and Cultural Change*, vol. 25, Supplement, 1977, ed. Manning Nash. The two articles by Paul A. Samuelson were 'International Trade and the Equalisation of Factor Prices', *Economic Journal*, 58 (June 1948) 163–84, and 'International Factor-Price Equalisation Once Again', ibid (June 1949) 181–97.

[4]Ibid., p. 68.

plans.[5] Capital accumulation became, if not the necessary and sufficient condition for development, at any rate the main strategic variable, and the propensity to save and the capital/output ratio became the basic equipment of development analysts, planners and aid officials. The notion that capital was scarce and savings difficult to raise in poor countries was qualified by pointing to the opportunities of attracting it from abroad, from the capital-rich countries, which would find new profitable investment opportunities in the countries to be developed. Notions like those of Balanced Growth (Ragnar Nurkse), the 'critical minimum effort' and the Big Push (Paul Rosenstein-Rodan) threw new light on the role of market forces and planning.

From the beginning there were critics. Paul Baran argued that the political power structure in the poor countries prevented adequate and productive investment and that foreign investment and aid reinforced social and political systems hostile to development.[6] And between the position that development was ensured by adequate amounts of capital accumulation, and the conviction that the political power structure made development impossible, there were many intermediate positions. It soon became evident that some development was taking place in some places, but that it was not always simply a matter of capital.

The analysis was refined, qualified, criticised. Albert Hirschman emphasised entrepreneurial incentives, appropriate sequences of motivational pressures and linkages. Other writers attempted to introduce in addition to total income the distribution of this income as an important force determining subsequent investment. A more equal distribution was thought to be necessary in order to generate the mass markets which could exploit economies of scale; a less equal income distribution was thought to be conducive to higher savings. The choice of techniques was discussed in both its productive and distributional aspects.[7] What is remarkable about these early discussions is the proliferation of ideas, criticisms and qualifications, which contrasts sharply with the monolithic view of a single paradigm. The early days of development economics were a time of intellectual pioneering, of considerable excitement, of the opening of new geographical and intellectual frontiers, of optimism and confidence.

> Bliss was it in that dawn to be alive,
> But to be young was very heaven!

[5] Paul Streeten, 'A Critique of the "Capital/Output Ratio" and its Application to Development Planning', chapter 6 in *The Frontiers of Development Studies* (Macmillan, 1972).

[6] Paul A. Baran, 'On the Political Economy of Backwardness', *Manchester School of Economic and Social Studies* 20 (January 1952) 66–84.

[7] Walter Galenson and Harvey Leibenstein, 'Investment Criteria, Productivity and Economic Development', *Quarterly Journal of Economics*, 69 (August 1955) 343–70.

III. DISCARDED IDEAS

Before distilling the ideas that survived the test of time, it is useful to summarise the elements in earlier thinking on development which have largely been discarded.

(1) Analysis and policy were dominated by the then recent experience of the rapid recovery from the war, supported by Marshall Aid, of the industrial countries of Western Europe, by the high post-war rates of economic growth and the scientific and technological triumphs of post-war reconstruction. The problem of development is, however, fundamentally different from the problem of reconstructing war-damaged advanced economies.

(2) Priority was given to industrialisation and infrastructure (power and transport) which came to be almost synonymous with development. Hence also the strong emphasis on capital accumulation as the strategic variable in development. It was found, however, that capital accounted for only a relatively small portion of growth, and that growth was not synonymous with development.

(3) Central government planning from the top down and the need for a 'big push' dominated thinking and policy-making, and the limitations of administrative capacity, of human and institutional constraints, and the need for participation, decentralisation and mobilisation of local labour were not recognised.

(4) Policies were dominated by the reaction to colonialism. The governments of many newly independent states wanted to do what the colonial powers had neglected to do. This reinforced the desire for planning, for industrialisation and for import substitution. It also fed the desire, after the achievement of political independence, for economic independence, which, however, was often equated (wrongly) with a high degree of economic self-sufficiency, mistaken for self-reliance. Latin American countries, which had been independent for a long time, felt that economic independence, which did not follow from political independence, was elusive.

(5) Thinking was deeply influenced by foreign trade pessimism, which led to the formulation of two-gap models. Pessimism about export prospects and the terms of trade reinforced policies of import-substituting industrialisation, which in turn created strongly-entrenched vested urban interests that resisted efforts to liberalise trade.

(6) There was a belief that high average growth rates of production would lead to reduced poverty either as a result of trickle-down or of government policies: that the best way to attack poverty was indirectly – by supporting growth poles ('if it moves, push it'); and that the spin-offs would, at any rate after a time-lag (during which inequality and poverty must be tolerated), benefit the poor.

(7) The rate of population growth and the problems generated by it were underestimated and diplomacy ruled out the topic for both bilateral and multilateral development agencies.

(8) The goals of development were defined narrowly in terms of GNP and its growth, and other goals, such as greater equality, eradication of poverty, meeting basic human needs, conservation of natural resources, abating pollution, and the enhancement of the environment, as well as non-material goals, were neglected or not emphasised sufficiently. When they were brought out into the open, 'trade-off pessimism' prevailed.

(9) The contribution by the developed countries was seen too narrowly in terms of capital aid and technical assistance, instead of as the impact of all policies pursued by the rich countries, whether or not they were pursued with the express purpose of assisting development efforts: these would include science policies, the thrust of research and development expenditure, policies towards transnational companies, migration policy, monetary policy, regional policy, trade and employment policies, agricultural policy, as well as foreign policy and military alliances generally.

(10) The 'Third World' was considered, rather monolithically, as an area with common problems, whereas it became increasingly clear that some of the differences within the group of developing countries were at least as great as those between them and the developed countries.

(11) Development was considered exclusively a problem of underdeveloped countries becoming less so. In contrast development is now beginning to be viewed as a problem common to the whole world: it gives rise to problems that are shared by the rich, over-developed, and by the poor, with some interests in common, others conflicting.

IV. THE NEW STRATEGY

The new development strategy may be summarised in the following way:

(1) We must start with meeting the basic needs of the majority of the people who are very poor. These are more and better food, safe water at hand, security of livelihood, health, sanitation, education, decent shelter, adequate transport; in addition there are 'non-material' needs like self-confidence, self-reliance, dignity, capacity to make one's own decisions, to participate in the decisions that affect one's life and work, and to develop fully one's talents, all of which interact in a variety of ways with 'material' needs.

(2) Meeting the basic needs of the billion poor people requires changes not only in the income distribution, but also in the structure of production (including distribution and foreign trade). It calls for increases in basic goods bought in the market, as well as in the purchasing power to buy them, and for an expansion in public services. To ensure that these actually reach the poor, restructuring public services will be necessary, as well as greater participation at the local level, better access to these services, and an appropriate delivery system.

(3) Since the majority of the poor live (and will continue to live for some time) by agriculture in the countryside, priority has to be given to growing food for domestic consumption. Agriculture has been the lagging sector; it has been

holding up development and its produce has been unevenly spread. Agriculture also forms an important potential mass market for industrial goods.

(4) In order to meet the needs of the rural population, credit, extension services, fertiliser, water, power, seeds must be made available so that these reach the small farmer. He must also be given security of tenure of secure ownership of his land and a guarantee that he gains from the improvements that he makes. He needs inputs, including information, appropriate institutions and incentives.

(5) The small farmer must also be provided with access to markets in market towns and regional cities through feeder roads and marketing facilities.

(6) A group of smallholdings should be serviced by modern centres of processing, marketing, financial services and extension services; but this must be done in a way which does not call excessively for scarce managerial resources.

(7) Efforts should be made to develop efficient labour-intensive technologies or, more accurately, technologies that economise in the use of capital and sophisticated skills and management, and are appropriate for the social, cultural and climatic conditions of developing countries, especially in farming, processing and agro-industries, as well as in exports and import-substitution. Construction with appropriate building materials also offers opportunities for creating efficient employment.

(8) The rural towns should provide middle-level social services, such as health and family clinics, secondary schools and technical colleges.

(9) The new structure will reduce the rush to the large cities, economise in the heavy costs of certain services, and will increase the scope for regional and local participation.

(10) The whole process should embrace human and social, as well as economic development. More particularly, hundreds of millions of people will not become more productive for some time. They need social help.

All policies, such as price controls, allocation of inputs, financial and fiscal measures, credit control, foreign exchange controls, etc. should be scrutinised with respect to their final impact on the specified goals. Although some increase in inequality may be inevitable in the early stages, as long as it does not impoverish the poor those measures whose incidence is to benefit the rich at the expense of the poor should be abandoned or redesigned.

V. THE DISTRESSING POLITICAL RECORD AND OTHER NEGLECTED OBSTACLES

Side by side with the new 'economic' focus on poverty, underemployment and inequality went certain political developments. In the international debates on the widening 'income gap' between rich and poor countries and in the domestic debates on growing inequality, inequality stood to some extent as a proxy for discontent with political (or tribal or ethnic) results. Both domestically and internationally the uneven process of development had important, and in some cases disastrous, side-effects. The development disasters of the Nigerian civil war and the war of the cessation of Bangladesh are extreme instances of the discontent and frustration generated by unequal access to the opportunities offered by development, and growing intolerance of this inequality.[8] The same forces encouraged a turn towards greater authoritiarianism and military dictatorships.[9] While the aggregate growth record therefore has been spectacular and the evidence on distribution and poverty alleviation ambiguous, the political record has been distressing.

Moreover, there are important areas for analysis which tend to be either neglected ('opportunistic ignorance') or treated, in separate compartments, as 'exogenous' variables, not integrated into development analysis and policy, or dismissed as biased partisan views. Yet any serious, objective analysis of development ought to incorporate them, because they are closely linked to the development process. Here they can only be enumerated.

(1) The unwillingness of governments to grasp firmly the political nettles: land reform, taxation, especially of large landowners, excessive protection, labour mobilisation.

(2) Linked with the first, nepotism and corruption.

(3) Behind these, again, various forms of oligopoly and monopoly power: the power of large landowners, of big industrialists and of the transnational enterprises.

(4) In a different field, but often equally disruptive to development efforts, the power of organised urban labour unions and the obstacles to an incomes and employment policy and to a wider spread of employment opportunities, particularly to the rural poor.

(5) Restricted access to educational opportunities and the resulting job certification that both reflect and reinforce the unequal structure of power and wealth. Similar restrictions in access to health, housing and other public services.

(6) Weak entrepreneurship and defective management and administration of public-sector enterprises, of the civil service and of private firms granted protection or other forms of monopoly power.

(7) Lack of co-ordination between central plans and executing ministries, central plans and regional, local and project plans, and between the activities of different ministries.

(8) The weakness of the structure, areas of competence, recruitment, training and administration of the UN specialised agencies charged with development,

[8]See Albert O. Hirschman 'Changing Tolerance for Inequality in Development', *World Development* (1974).
[9]It would be quite erroneous to equate this trend towards authoritarianism with a turn away from what Myrdal has called 'the soft state'. Violence is not hardness, though some of the regimes came to power with the pretence to eradicate 'softness', like corruption. See Gunnar Myrdal, *Asian Drama* (Penguin Books, 1968) vol. 2.

combined, too often, with a narrowly technocratic approach, encouraged by the historical origin and organisation of these agencies and their politically 'non-controversial' approach.

(9) There are also the terrible facts of mass slaughter, expulsion of ethnic minorities (often entrepreneurial and therefore hated) and political opponents, imprisonment without trial, torture, and other violations of basic human rights, and the $370 billion spent on armaments, compared with $17 billion on net concessional transfers (in 1975).

The list is not exhaustive but merely illustrative, to indicate some of the obstacles to an attempt to tackle human and social development in the full sense and to pinpoint some of the reasons for the disenchantment with what has turned out to be, by narrow economic criteria, unexpectedly and unprecedentedly high growth.

VI. GENERAL CONCLUSIONS

No doubt there were errors, false starts and dead ends in the development story of the last three decades. In accounting for these, there are Keynesians and Marxians. Keynes attributed (at least in a much-quoted passage in the *General Theory*) the errors of 'practical men, who believe themselves quite exempt from any intellectual influence' to 'some defunct economist'. He thought 'that the power of vested interests is vastly exaggerated compared with the gradual encroachment of ideas'. On this interpretation it was the mistaken doctrines of Nurkse, Singer and Rosenstein-Rodan that led governments to subsidise industrial capital equipment, support high urban wages, overvalue exchange rates, raise the costs of farm inputs by protecting domestic industry, lower the prices of farm outputs and generally neglect or, worse, exploit, agriculture and the rural poor.

Marxians believe that it is the power of class interests that is reflected in ideas. The above-mentioned doctrines, on this view, are merely an ideological superstructure, reflecting the powerful vested interests of the urban industrialists and their workers.

But there is a third way of looking at the succession of problems and difficulties: there is a Hydra-like aspect to development (and perhaps to all human endeavour). Many of the difficulties encountered in the path of development were neither the result of economic errors, nor attributable to vested interests, but were the offspring of the successful solution of previous problems. Scientific confidence asserts that there is a solution to every problem, but history (and not only the obstructionist official) teaches us that there is a problem to every solution.

The solution of one problem creates a series of new ones. Success in manufacturing industry has brought out the lag in agriculture. The need to expand the production of food for domestic consumption became so acute partly because of the remarkable growth of industrial output. The seed-fertiliser revolution has spawned a collection of new problems about plant diseases, inequality, unemployment and the other so-called second-generation problems. The need for population control arose from the successful attack on mortality through cheap and efficient methods of malaria eradication. Growing unemployment is (partly) the result of high productivity and the growth of manufacturing investment. Education raises excessive aspirations and contributes to the movement to the cities and the consequent unemployment of the educated. The success and the attractions of urban development have shown up the need to accelerate rural development, which, however, by the turmoil it creates, may further accelerate the migration to the cities.

This Hirschmanesque generalised doctrine of unbalanced growth cannot, of course, be used to justify and legitimise errors in development thinking and policy. Of these there were plenty. But, on the other hand, not all difficulties are the result of past mistakes, and some are the consequences of the successful solution of preceding problems.

'Hydra' is the wrong metaphor, for it suggests the hopelessness of all endeavours. 'Second-generation' problems, on the other hand, may be too optimistic a term. The question is whether, in spite of the subsequent emergence of new problems, the series converges to, or diverges from, a solution. While some solutions are worse than the problems, others represent progress. It is important to bear in mind that solutions are not readily transferable between places and periods.

Another lesson is what more sophisticated colleagues like to call 'the counter-intuitive character of systems analysis'. Things are not necessarily true because they are paradoxical, but in development studies, as in other fields, commonsense does not always lead to the correct answer. Job creation may cause more, rather than less unemployment; import restrictions and physical allocations, intended to reduce inequalities, may strengthen monopoly power; a strategy that sacrifices economic growth of consumption in order to create more jobs may require *faster*, not slower, growth; policies designed to help the poor may benefit the middle and upper classes, and so on. As these illustrations show, the implications of this view can be profoundly conservative or startlingly revolutionary. In a given power structure, attempts at piecemeal reform *may* be self-cancelling and the system will then tend to re-establish the initial wealth and power distribution. Only a deep, structural change *may* enable reform to take root.

On the other hand, piecemeal reform *may* trigger off pressures that lead to further reforms, whereas revolutionary change, as the many revolutions that failed show, may not achieve its objective.

A third lesson is that in many areas only a concerted, properly phased, attack on several fronts yields the desired result and the application of some measures without certain others may make things worse. 'Correct' prices in a society with a fairly equal distribution of assets and available appropriate technologies may raise efficiency and reduce inequality, but to use 'correct' prices in a society with very unequal ownership of assets will only change the manifestation of inequality.

Not only are there Myrdalian cumulative processes, but the processes require packages; the causation is cumulative and joint. The appropriate metaphor is the jigsaw puzzle, the fitting together of different parts, not the toothpaste or the sausage machine which respond to pressures with homogeneous outputs. To do something in a certain sequence, together with other things, brings success; to do it in isolation may be worse than doing nothing. A programme of education without employment opportunities will only accelerate the brain drain. What is needed is a range of interrelated, properly phased, measures. There are no simple remedies. The solution of underdevelopment is not to be found in making the soil more, and women less fertile, in a combination of fertiliser and pill (the technocratic solution); nor, for that matter, by staging a revolutionary solution; or implementing a radical land reform (the radical solution), nor by 'getting prices right' (the economist's solution) – though each, in conjunction with the others, may have something to contribute to a total solution.

A fourth lesson is that few problems are narrowly economic ones. The difficulties often lie with human attitudes, social institutions and political power structures, more than, or as well as, with scarcities of productive inputs and their correct allocation. Scarce inputs – capital and skills – will probably also be needed to attack social and political obstacles, but the link between resources and outcomes is a tenuous one: there are no fixed capital coefficients between resources spent and an effective land reform, or between money and a successful birth control campaign.

Finally, the response of the rich countries to the challenge of development is not to be found in development aid alone, whether it consists of capital or brains even if it were 2 per cent instead of 0.3 per cent of GNP, or in freer access to the markets of the rich countries. It is the *total* relationship, the impact of *all policies* of the rich countries, that is relevant, and that has to be our concern, if we are serious about international cooperation.

Appendix

TABLE 1

DEFENCE EXPENDITURE AS % OF BUDGET EXPENDITURE

	1955	56	57	58	59	1960	61	62	63	64
UK	24.9	24.6	20.3	18.6	18.0	17.3	16.7	16.7	16.2	15.6
USA[1]	58.7	–	–	53.7	50.1	49.8	48.4	47.8	46.9	45.2
France	25.4	25.7	25.9	24.8	24.6	25.0	24.6	23.3	18.8	20.0
Germany[1]	16.9	13.9	13.0	13.0	15.2	16.2	16.5	18.8	20.4	17.3

	1965	66	67	68	69	1970	71	72	73	74
UK	14.9	14.4	13.8	12.8	11.6	11.3	11.4	11.3	10.6	10.1
USA[1]	41.9	42.2	44.3	45.0	44.0	40.8	36.7	33.8	30.6	29.3
France	19.1	18.3	18.0	17.0	16.6	17.1	17.1	16.5	–	–
Germany[1]	17.2	16.4	16.0	14.0	14.1	13.4	13.8	12.8	12.5	–

SOURCES For France and Germany: U.N., *Statistical Yearbook*;
For USA: United States Bureau of the Census, *Statistical Abstract of the United States*;
For UK: Central Statistical Office, *National Income and Expenditure*.

NOTES [1] For the USA the budget expenditure refers to the Federal Government; for Germany it refers to the combined Federal Government and Länder.

Where estimates have been revised, the latest ones have been used.

TABLE 2

DEFENCE EXPENDITURE AS % OF GNP (FACTOR COST AND CURRENT PRICES)

	1949	1950	51	52	53	54	55	56	57	58
France	6.2	6.3	8.2	10.0	10.6	8.5	7.4	8.8	8.4	7.8
UK	7.0	7.3	8.9	11.2	11.2	9.9	9.2	8.8	8.0	7.8
USA	5.1	5.5	10.8	14.9	14.7	12.7	11.0	10.7	10.9	10.9
Germany	–	–	–	–	4.9	4.7	4.8	4.2	4.7	3.4

	1959	1960	61	62	63	64	65	66	67	68
France	7.7	7.4	7.3	7.1	6.5	6.3	6.1	5.9	5.9	5.5
UK	7.4	7.3	7.0	8.0	6.9	6.8	6.6	6.5	6.5	6.2
USA	10.3	9.9	10.0	10.2	9.7	8.9	8.3	9.2	10.3	10.2
Germany	5.0	4.6	4.6	5.5	6.0	5.4	5.0	4.7	5.0	4.1

	1969	70	71	72	73	74
France	4.9	4.6	4.5	4.3	4.2	4.1
UK	5.8	5.6	5.8	5.9	5.6	5.8
USA	9.6	8.7	7.7	7.3	6.6	6.6
Germany	4.1	3.7	3.8	3.9	3.9	4.1

SOURCE NATO, *Facts & Figures* (Brussels, Jan 1976) pp. 294–5.

TABLE 3

NET FLOW OF OFFICIAL DEVELOPMENT ASSISTANCE AS % OF GNP
(AT MARKET PRICES)

	1960	61	62	63	64	65	66	67
France	1.38	1.41	1.30	1.01	0.89	0.75	0.69	0.71
UK	0.56	0.59	0.52	0.48	0.53	0.47	0.46	0.44
USA	0.53	0.56	0.57	0.60	0.57	0.50	0.45	0.44
Germany	0.33	0.41	0.45	0.41	0.44	0.38	0.37	0.43

	1968	69	1970	71	72	73	74
France	0.69	0.69	0.66	0.66	0.67	0.58	0.59
UK	0.40	0.39	0.37	0.41	0.39	0.34	0.38
USA	0.38	0.33	0.31	0.32	0.29	0.23	0.25
Germany	0.41	0.39	0.32	0.34	0.31	0.32	0.37

SOURCE For 1960–69, OECD, *Development Assistance*, Dec 1970.
For 1970–74, OECD, *Development Cooperation*, Nov 1975.

Part II
International Policies

7 Development Theory and the New International Economic Order

Centre for Development of Planning, Erasmus University, Rotterdam, Netherlands

I. THE PROBLEMS

Development is generally defined as growth plus structural change. Therefore, a theory of development should explain both phenomena. However, it is widely recognised that any explanation of structural changes presents many unsolved problems. Moreover, it is even doubtful whether a credible deductive scheme that could explain the usual features which characterise the process of development will ever be formulated. Even less ambitious schemes dealing with the variations experienced by comparatively stable structures represented by the economies of developed societies run into difficulties which are not insignificant.

The purely growth part of the picture is certainly amenable to a more deductive treatment. But growth theory as it has so far developed has not proved especially illuminating even in regard to the purely quantitative side of the development process. While some part of this theory is of considerable interest in optimum analysis, the so-called descriptive theory of growth cannot throw much light on behaviour outside the 'steady states'.

What, then, do we mean by development theory in relationship to the New International Economic Order? Does development theory suggest any propositions that can help delineate the characteristics of the new economic order or throw light on transitional arrangements that can be considered by the international community? It is perhaps legitimate to say that, even in the absence of a complete theory, something useful can be said provided we have sufficient knowledge of regularities, even though of a somewhat empirical character, which suggest certain concomitant variations as more probable than others. Certain types of proposal may, then, be regarded as more relevant than others.

Few would deny that we do possess some knowledge of such regularities. Furthermore, even when we have limited knowledge we are still in a position to ask questions which growth theory has taught us should be asked. To begin with, our present state of knowledge would suggest that, irrespective of considerable variations in time and space, no cumulative process involving an upward movement in per capita income has worked successfully over a significant stretch of time unless socio-economic conditions have permitted a

steady increase in the stock of material and human capital, accompanied by
substantial increases in knowledge of the material environment and involving
the use of new combinations of existing resources for producing goods that
satisfy desires more efficiently or generating new desires.

Such a statement may be broken down into four major components, each of
which must be separately stressed: (i) sustained increases in capital stocks are
necessary; (ii) increases in capital stock have by and large been complementary
to growth in knowledge (although in strict theory this need not be so);
(iii) periodic transformations in production processes, in the widest sense of the
term, have been occurring – perhaps to sustain the demand for new capital;
and (iv) our economic environment requires the creation of new wants which
are beyond the scope of what is currently demanded.

While growth, or development, has often been treated as a process occurring
over time, it is historically true that there has been a spatial dimension as well,
since development has generally taken place within a network of interacting
spatial entities with different components growing at characteristically different
rates. This immediately suggests that we may have situations in which certain
component entities decay while others grow. At this point it becomes
interesting to know whether the growing parts are thriving at the expense of
those which are decaying.

The major intellectual reasons which make this subject worthy of serious
analysis include the following propositions: (i) the gap between the per capita
products of the developed and the less developed countries is increasing in
absolute and relative terms, however it is measured; (ii) growing
interdependence among various countries at different stages of development
has been accompanied by increasing pressures – these pressures presently
seem to be centred over such common assets of the globe as oceans,
environment, and non-renewable resources; (iii) some part of the widening gap
between nations must be explained in terms of exploitation, in one sense or
another.

What is basic to the argument for the New International Economic Order is
that (i) the idea of equity is universal and includes all existing persons;
(ii) intermediate levels of decision-making may be necessary so long as people
are organised into nation states; and (iii) interdependencies among nations are
sufficiently strong to rule out 'autarkic' solutions on the one hand, and a
laissez-faire system on the other. To phrase the point differently: discussions of
the New International Economic Order are best considered as attempts to
conceptualise the nature of purposive adaptation of the world economy that is
needed to ensure equitable and sustainable global development.

II. THE GAP BETWEEN RICH AND POOR

Evidence on the question of the 'gap' is on the whole very strong, even though
quantitative measures vary depending on the assumptions which one makes.
We shall cite two examples. One is a very detailed study by Kuznets on the

concept and measurement of the gap between the 'rich' and the 'poor' countries.[1] By defining developed countries as those with per capita products exceeding $1000 in 1965, plus Japan, and the less developed countries as those with per capita products not exceeding $120 in that year, he finds that the ratio of the average per capita product of the first group was in 1965 twenty times as high as that of the less developed countries. Kuznets uses data collected by Hagen and Hawrylshorn from various United Nations sources and uses official exchange rates for expressing gross domestic products of different countries in US dollars. He makes no adjustment for differences in production boundaries in different countries.

Using more recent data, Tinbergen also measures the 'gap'. He uses various adjustments that purport to reduce 'nominal' income differences to 'real' differences and finds a much smaller measure of the so-called gap,[2] using the Kuznets-type definition. However, he prefers to work on the basis of the ratio of topmost decile to lowest decile. Therefore, his measure of the gap turns out to be 13 to 1. Difference is admittedly a significant one no matter which system of measurement we use.

Is the gap growing over time? According to Kuznets,

> a reasonable conjecture is that, in comparison with the quintupling of the per capita product of developed countries over the last century, the per capita product of the 'poor' LDCs rose two-thirds at most; and that this solution would hold roughly even if we were to measure the century back from 1965 (rather than from the mid-1950s).

Kuznets guesses that, if the relative gap in 1965 was either 20:1 or 16:1 (depending on the definition of the poor), a century ago the ratio would have ranged from 7:1 to 5:1. Against this evidence of the widening gap between the rich and the poor nations collectively, it appears that regional income differentials within large-sized 'rich' countries has narrowed substantially.[3] Clearly we have sufficient evidence of 'unequal growth'. Since this growth has taken place within an international framework in which increasingly nations have co-operated in trade and factor movements, it becomes relevant to know whether some nations have exploited other nations in order to create unequal growth. We should also enquire whether continued growth at high levels in the developed world will prejudice the future opportunities of less developed countries.

---

[1]See S. Kuznets, 'The Gap: Concept, Measurement, Trends', in G. Ranis (ed.), *The Gap between Rich and Poor Nations* (Macmillan, 1972), pp. 3-43.
[2]See J. Tinbergen, *Reshaping the International Order* (E. P. Dutton, 1976).
[3]See J. Tinbergen, ibid.

III. THE CONCEPT OF EXPLOITATION

The word *exploitation* is generally regarded as a value-loaded term; it would also appear to suggest that world economic growth is in some sense a zero-sum game, so that an answer to unequal growth can only be found if the roles of the two groups are reversed. Those who object to the concept of exploitation usually operate on the basis of a conceptual apparatus which eliminates problems of unequal strength in terms of market power, cumulative advantages gained through learning over time, many forms of indivisibilities, and numerous external effects.

In so far as development is thought of as a process over time, conventional modes of analysis lack explanatory power. Hence, we are faced with a genuine problem that cannot be handled merely by classifying more and more variables as 'endogenous' and by introducing an arbitrary number of shifts in functions as distinguished from movements – logically reversible – along the same set of functions. Those who recognise that not much is gained through such procedures may react by adopting a competitive attitude or by turning completely empirical. Either approach has obvious dangers. In the first case we may wish away real problems altogether, while in the second one loses any clear sense of how things are connected – even if from the point of view of prediction an empirical approach could do as well. The first group will dismiss the question of exploitation as 'noise', since in a purely competitive world there is no scope for exploitation by definition, although there may be inequalities. Such inequalities are caused by accidents of resource endowments and taste. Technical change is also seen as an exogenous event that need not be incorporated as a part of the system. Such views will obviously affect the approach to the problem of the new economic order and will distinctively colour the attitudes upon which such persons base their actions.

The second group may look for evidence in 'terms of trade' data, to see whether these have secularly changed in a manner prejudicial to the less developed countries. More recently they have tried to assess the impact of transnational corporations in terms of their contributions to the host country's gross national product, balance of payments, internal distribution of income, choice of technology, and so forth. There is considerable likelihood that the second group will come up with recommendations and assessments only on a case-by-case basis. Lacking an overall reference point, they may find it difficult to integrate the proposals into one overall framework.

In sharp contrast we have the Marxist or Neo-Marxist authors. In their analytical framework exploitation is not a value-loaded term in the simple sense that exploitation is a bad thing. They would define exploitation in terms of such well-known Marxian categories as value and surplus value. While Marx's observations on foreign trade were essentially in the nature of critical comments on such issues as free trade, neither he nor Engels made any systematic attempt to extend the scheme of value analysis to the domain of international trade. While this is not the place to go into the reasons underlying

Marx's lack of interest in this respect, it is worth pointing out here that by adapting the Marxian scheme of transformation of values into 'prices', A. Emmanuel has done precisely what Marx has not done.[4]

Since Emmanuel's analysis suggests that developing countries are being exploited by developed countries through the mechanism of adverse changes in terms of trade, and since this analysis figures prominently in many recent discussions of international trade written from a radical perspective, we consider it useful to discuss in this context.[5] In short, what Emmanuel has done is to depart from Marx in assuming wages to be variable between different countries where the rates of profit on invested capital are assumed to be equalised by the free movement of capital. On these assumptions and the assumption of different compositions of capital, Emmanuel tries to demonstrate that 'prices of production' will differ from 'values', causing one unit of labour of developing countries to be exchanged for less than one unit of labour of the developed countries. In other words, developing countries are faced with unequal exchange, since they pay lower wages while capital earns the same rate of return everywhere.

We do not have the space to discuss here the Marxian transformations problem which is crucial to the argument. Under certain simplifying assumptions this problem has been shown to be a soluble one. However, not merely are these assumptions quite restrictive in nature; they do not even allow, in general, two separate normalisation conditions to be satisfied. That is, 'total prices' cannot equal 'total value' as long as 'total surplus value' also equals 'total profits'.

Moreover, given the critical nature of the assumption relating to wages, along with the specific use that Emmanuel makes of the transformation problem, it would appear that Emmanuel's analysis can at best be regarded as a suggestion for further work; and at worst it is completely unacceptable.[6]

This leads us to the question of whether we cannot find evidence of 'exploitation' in the sphere of international economic relationships, using tools and concepts that figure in the literature on imperfect competition. In a well-known article written nearly three decades ago, Singer[7] found strong support for the proposition that underdeveloped countries were being exploited because they concentrated almost exclusively on producing primary commodities with the help of foreign capital for the markets of developed countries.

Singer's analysis was strongly supported by the work that was being done at ECLA under the leadership of Prebisch. The Singer–Prebisch argument has

[4]See A. Emmanuel, 'Unequal Exchange', *Monthly Review Press*, 1972.
[5]See S. Amin, *Unequal Development* (London: Harvester Press, 1972).
[6]We may refer here to the work of neo-Ricardian trade theorists who generally employ a Sraffa-type model for analysing questions related to gain from trade.
[7]See H. W. Singer, 'The Distribution of Gains between Investing and Borrowing Countries', *American Economic Review*, May 1950. Reprinted in *Readings in International Trade*, edited by R. E. Caves and H. G. Johnson, pp. 306-17.

been decidely influential, if not highly controversial. The argument has two separate components: (i) that foreign investment has been foreign only in a geographical sense; and (ii) the pattern of specialisation and exchange has been decidedly adverse from the point of view of developing countries as they have specialised in commodities where the benefits of technical progress tend to be passed on to the consumers in advanced countries, because of differences in market structures. Singer attributes adverse movements in terms of trade to this latter factor.

From a formal point of view Singer's analysis is unclear. None the less, it is possible to give formal explanations that conform to Singer's 'law' relating to the terms of trade, based on the sluggish demand for primary products and the need to step up imports of capital goods, etc., from developed countries.[8] While it is possible to state conditions under which the 'terms of trade' will go against the developing countries, it has been a moot point whether data do in fact show such a movement. Although the terms of trade will continue to be the topic of much discussion, it cannot be denied that foreign investment and the production areas it opened up has had extremely limited spread-effects in most developing countries. Whatever may have been the beneficial effects of this type of trade to the investing countries, only a very small minority has benefited in the developing countries. As most of the backward and forward linkages of the export sector have been with the developed countries, the multiplier effect of such investment in the Leontief sense has hardly been felt within the developing countries. Furthermore, neither the choice of technology nor the composition of imports has borne any clear relationship to the needs of the economy in terms of its required transformation into a progressive state.

Within sectors such as agriculture, it is the production of commercial crops which generally benefited, whereas production of food-grains stagnated. Development of infrastructure has been usually outer-directed. Simple manufactures of traditional type were often allowed to die out while imports of mass-manufactured consumer goods swelled in volume. Above all, while the internal distribution of incomes became more skewed, there was not sufficient compensating benefit from facilitating a higher ratio of productive accumulation to national income.

Can these facts be cited as evidence of exploitation? It is difficult to give any clear reply, as such attempts would require the widespread acceptance of a reference case that may be regarded as embodying the 'no exploitation' situation.[9] It is also necessary to distinguish between a positive 'trade' situation with a situation without 'trade'. Even within the former, it is necessary to

[8]A model which deduces adverse movements in the terms of trade for the topics based on productivity of labour in producing food is to be found in Arthur Lewis's Wicksell lectures titled 'Aspects of Tropical Trade, 1883–1965' (Stockholm, 1969).
[9]The use of 'perfect competition' as a reference case was made in neo-classical economics until the early years of this century. However, subsequent critical analysis has taken away much from the optimality property of competitive markets. While

distinguish between the 'pure trade' case and the case of 'trade cum capital movement'.

However, if by assumptions this theory excludes certain typical features that characterise the behaviour of spatially interacting units, then it may be a little academic to debate the virtues of such a theory. It is recognised that features such as increasing returns to scale, indivisibilities, external effects, etc., are powerfully involved in regard to the generation of trade flows, as economists from Smith to Hicks have particularly observed. Could it be the case that these productivity-raising aspects of trade have had differential impacts on the welfare levels of developing and developed countries?

In certain cases, certain technological changes in the developed countries have had deleterious effects, as in the case of the development of synthetic substitutes, or in the case of displacement of local industries; a few cases have caused disturbances to the ecological system. There have also been cases where non-renewable resources have been depleted at faster rates and also helped at the same time in destroying the markets for specialised products of less developed countries. The petrochemicals industry is perhaps the most glaring example of this type.

Thus, it can be maintained that in certain situations trade has had certain adverse impacts on growth. However, it is also necessary to point out that, in general, it has been a question of *distribution of gains*. Furthermore, it is also necessary to point out that trade cannot be viewed in isolation from the overall socio-economic environment in which trade takes place. Much more could have been done by many aspects of trade while trying to mitigate its adverse effects. It would have required in many cases important institutional changes, along with substantial efforts at adapting technical knowhow and directing resources to a wider stratum of education, as well as efforts at diversifying the structure of production.

IV. THE PRIMARY ISSUES OF THE NIEO

What are the most important issues surrounding the question of the New International Economic Order? Putting aside the questions of outstanding external debt and the future of the international monetary system, the remaining issues can be classified into three *sets* of major issues: (i) restructuring the character of world trade in order to lead to greater diffusion of some of the dynamic benefits associated with trade, in addition to promoting better use of existing factor endowments; (ii) improving the capacity of the LDCs to import on a steady basis through devising commodity

---

Weizsäcker has proposed a new definition of 'exploitation' using the Marxian concept as a starting-point, its usefulness in the present context is yet to be demonstrated. See C. C. von Weizsäcker, *Modern Capital Theory and the Concept of Exploitation* Kyklos, 1973).

agreements of various sorts; (iii) creating conditions for maximising benefits from the operation of transnational corporations, judged by the interest of the developing world. As regards (iii), discussion has quite often tended to include all 'host' countries. However, for our purpose, it is the developing countries which are relevant.

The set of proposals under (i) is based on several facts: (*a*) the low share of developing countries' trade in the total amount of world trade; (*b*) the low proportion of intra-developing-country trade; (*c*) high concentration on slow-growing or stagnant items on the export lists of developing countries; (*d*) very uneven share of manufactures in the trade of different developing countries; and (*e*) the very large volume of intra-developed-country trade along with its (until recently) high rate of growth.

While the above observation would suggest the need for deeper analysis of trade flows and the necessity to evolve a more integrated theoretical frame for giving guidance on comparative advantage, it cannot be denied that greater market access would need to be given a high priority on the list of measures as a part of the new international order, especially if export-oriented industrialisation had to succeed in the less developed countries.

The question of generating larger flows of trade amongst the developing countries themselves is generally seen to fall within the area of customs union theory. But it is generally recognised that the conventional theory with its emphasis on 'trade creation v. trade diversion' cannot do adequate justice to the scope and complexity of the subject. It has been pointed out repeatedly that the subject at best is seen as a part of a theory of regional investment planning and not merely as a part of the subject of tariff unification.

We can now turn to a discussion of the so-called 'commodities' policy which has figured quite prominently in recent discussions. Here one has to distinguish between several distinct sets of questions. There is the obvious distinction between instability of export prices and that of export earnings. Secondly, there is the question of changing the relative price of the export commodity in real terms by resort to cartelised forms of action. Finally, there is the question, somewhat related to the preceding discussion, of greater processing of raw materials within the less developed countries themselves. So far as the first proposition is concerned, there has been a great deal of discussion bearing on the export instability question. Consensus would appear to favour the proposition that instability is significantly higher. Disputes have ranged as to whether export instability affects growth adversely. There is one group of opinion which would appear to suggest that there is little evidence pointing towards negative correlation between export instability and growth. This is strongly controverted by others.

The real points at issue are whether stability in prices can be achieved at reasonable cost; and secondly, whether such cost can be reduced through an 'integrated programme'. The last point would depend on 'complementarities' amongst different commodities. The UNCTAD studies would seem to indicate that there is evidence of such 'complementarity', which implies some possible savings in cost.

Stability in prices would appear to possess advantage from the point of view
of producing countries as well as from that of the consuming countries.
However, in certain situations this will not result in stabilising earnings. In that
case supplementary measures may be called for if the maintenance of earnings
is what is wanted.

Opinions differ very considerably regarding the widespread use of
commodity cartels, both as to the feasibility and the desirability of this
particular type of action.[10] It is perhaps more prudent to approach the problem
from the point of view of further processing of raw materials rather than from
the point of view of maximising short-term monopolistic earnings.

There is one general point that should be made about the commodities
problem: it is the possibility that overly strong preoccupation with the
commodity problems – however justified from the point of view of maximising
short-term earnings – may divert attention away from the much-needed long-
term structural adaptation of the countries concerned. The other side of the
argument is that these exports, especially exports of minerals, frequently
contain large rent elements; or to put it differently, domestic resource costs are
low. Hence, they appear to provide an easy way of increasing the capacity to
import in real terms, only if price-output decisions could be altered suitably
from the point of view of rent-receiving countries.

We may now address ourselves to the question of transnational
corporations. The literature on this question is by now quite substantial,
even though it is of a highly variable character. Most sharp differences of
opinion are to be found in this area, with strong advocates, on the one side,
who condemn it in most violent terms, and on the other with its proponents. A
large part of this discussion deals with political and sociological aspects.
Important as they are, we cannot deal with these issues here. From the strictly
economic point of view, it is first of all necessary to be clear as to the ways in
which transnational corporations operate in so far as they affect the interests of
host and source countries differently from the way that private investment did
in earlier days. Those who find evidence in transnational corporations of a
qualitative change in capitalism naturally tend to think that the differences are
rather profound. They perceive in this context profound changes in market
powers brought about by vast improvements in technology and significant
accumulation of capital in a few hands.

Transnational corporations do raise a few important questions relating to
the present topic. Firstly, what role, if any, can these corporations play in
transforming the productive structure of less developed countries? Secondly, if
they are found capable of exerting a significant growth-promoting effect, can
this be combined with policies aimed at better distribution of income? Evidence
such as exists today reflects the combined effects of the operation of these
corporations *and* the manner of operations of the governments existing in the
host countries. This has naturally led to diametrically opposed sets of

[10]See N. Kaldor, 'Inflation and Recession in the World Economy', *Economic
Journal*, December 1976.

conclusions. We cannot therefore answer this question on the basis of existing evidence alone. However, it would appear plausible that transnational corporations combine several different functions: an ownership function, a production and management function, and a marketing function combined in many cases with control of infrastructure in areas such as shipping, banking, insurance, etc. If these functions can be decomposed, then it can be argued that in certain areas related to production and marketing they may prove to be of help to less developed countries, provided the choice of products is appropriate and technology is in some appropriate sense more relevant to the resource endowment of these countries.

While the income distribution in many less developed countries is unfavourable from the point of view of encouraging production of basic necessities, it is not legitimate to regard income distribution as an *autonomously* given datum. Transnational corporations tend to increase on the margin dualism that would have characterised these economies otherwise. Furthermore, from the point of view of foreign exchange earnings of these countries, multinational corporations are said to involve loss of potential earnings through inclusion of export-restrictive clauses. In addition, losses inflicted through transfer pricing and so forth are frequently involved.[11] Finally, as regards choice of technology, evidence is unclear and it is difficult to be categorical as to whether the dimension of the loss is sizeable or not.[12]

Our discussion here has concentrated on the strictly economic side of the question and that too very briefly. But it is perfectly possible to maintain (although not so easy to substantiate) that the problem is essentially a political one. In that case the choice may lie between outright rejection, on the one hand, and improvisation of a suitable international organisational framework, on the other.

If it is the case that for many developing countries it is considered, for one reason or another, difficult to manage certain productive operations efficiently in the complete absence of such corporations, it may still be useful to divorce the 'ownership' function from the 'control' function. Even within the area of control, various types and degrees of control may be distinguished. Under such modified rules of the game these corporations may, from the economic point of view, play a useful role in areas of high technology and high capital-intensity, especially if they facilitate the transfer of knowhow, not to speak of adaptation of technology.

V. SOME CONCLUSIONS

We have discussed somewhat briefly some of the major issues figuring in the

[11]See C. Vaitsos, *Intercountry Income Distribution and Transnational Enterprises* (Oxford University Press, 1974).

[12]F. Stewart, 'Choice of Techniques in Developing Countries', *Journal of Development Studies*, 1972.

ecent debate on the new international economic order against the general
ackground provided by development theory. Our analysis would seem to
uggest that contrary to thinking in certain circles these issues cannot be
lismissed as peripheral in character. Those who do seem to ignore the fact that
,rowth takes place in *space* as well as in *time*. Furthermore, the purely
emporal aspects cannot be divorced entirely from the spatial aspects. Uneven
ncidence of growth in space tends to produce inhibiting influences which help
o perpetuate a state of relatively arrested development. The proposals outlined
arlier, if they are judiciously implemented, may help to mitigate some of the
olarising influences that *an international market economy, dominated
ubstantially by market imperfections, etc., tends to produce.* Furthermore,
inlike national economies, where countervailing forces have been developed
vhich take care at least in part of some of the inefficiencies and inequities of
instable and imperfect markets, no such institutions yet exist in the
nternational sphere of any meaningful dimension whatsoever.

While one presses for a greater measure of international equity, one has
qually clearly to pay attention to intranational equity. While the question of
rowth with equity is very much in the air, for many developing economies
vith limited resources and large and growing demographic pressures, the
roblem of devising an equitable growth strategy is exceedingly complex. The
roblem basically reduces itself to one of achieving a rate of capital formation
igh enough to achieve the desired rate of growth, if the gap between the rich
ind the poor nations is to be bridged. At the same time, if the distribution of
ncomes internally is not to suffer – let alone show an improvement – the ques-
ion of getting the well-to-do to pay for the costs of growth becomes essential.
That this implies many hard decisions which require profound socio-economic
idaptations can easily be imagined. According to a recent study by Leontief
ind his associates,[13] accelerated development in developing regions would
equire somewhere between 30 and 35 per cent of gross national product for
:apital investment, if the currently widening 'gap' between the rich and the
oor is to be narrowed.

While such a large quantum jump in investment cannot be achieved without
he utmost domestic austerity, what role can the proposals discussed earlier
lay in this context? It is possible to maintain that the direct impact of these
roposals would lie in improving the capacity to import of the developing
:ountries. In so far as accelerated investment is likely to create acute balance of
ayments problems for many developing countries, these proposals will help in
nitigating the so-called foreign exchange 'bottleneck'. This implies that the so-
:alled structural problem of converting savings into investment will be eased.
Secondly, by facilitating fuller use of a more abundant factor such as labour,
hey will help in maximising incomes. Thirdly, with the adoption of suitable
iscal policies, including the use of an appropriate regulatory framework

[13]See W. Leontief *et al.*, 'The Future of the World Economy', United Nations, 1976.

towards transnational corporations, savings, especially public savings, are likely to comprise a greater proportion of income than currently. Finally, these measures can lead to a wider diffusion of technological knowledge. While some of this knowledge is of doubtful utility from the point of view of developing countries, it is of undoubted significance in certain productive spheres.

It is quite clear, then, that the different measures discussed here that do not deal with concessional transfer of financial resources (since they raise a different class of issues)[14] are sufficiently important to merit careful attention to all concerned.

To sum up, the design of a New International Economic Order implies concurrent changes on the national and international fronts. Disabilities from which developing countries suffer have no single remedy, as they are the result of multiple factors. Any simple causal model is unlikely to prove adequate to the complexity of the job. The exercise is as yet in a beginning stage. While the nature and magnitude of the required changes is beginning to be somewhat better understood, the analysis of how to steer these changes has received very much less attention. While certain proposals have attracted great attention, they are often seen in isolation. What economics can do, in addition to providing comprehensive studies of alternative patterns of global development on a suitably disaggregated basis, is to suggest assignment of appropriate instruments of policy to different levels of the decision-making process, both nationally and internationally.[15]

[14]The case for concessional capital transfer formed the key proposal behind the strategy for the Second Development decade. While little progress has been made in reaching the target, objections usually cited do not include questions of principle.

[15]Mr J. G. Waardenburg of Erasmus University, Rotterdam, made helpful comments on a first draft of this paper, for which I wish to thank him.

3 Factors of Economic Development and the New International Economic Order

Jozef Pajestka

The Planning Commission, Warsaw, Poland

I. INTRODUCTION

Two basic features stand out predominantly among the world's recent and prospective developmental characteristics. These are (i) the great and still growing discrepancies in economic performance, in socio-economic efficiency, and in the general conditions of life among the nations and great regions of the world; and (ii) the ever-increasing clamour for a just and equitable relationship among the various peoples and nations of the world.

The dynamics of these two current tendencies, combined with our current better understanding of their underlying mechanisms, have resulted in a spate of political activities dedicated to the establishment of a New International Economic Order (NIEO), which it is hoped will be both more efficient and more humane than the present inequitable conditions.

The great economic discrepancies between rich and poor countries may be regarded as a historical phenomenon of transient character, most typical for the twentieth century. It may well be argued that the contemporary industrial–scientific civilisation is the product of the particularly favourable combination of cultural, societal and economic factors which appeared initially within one particular part of the world, i.e. the part which is now developed. It should not be forgotten that the evolution of the present order was, of course, greatly supported by the exploitation of other peoples and of the world's most valuable natural resources. In its dynamics, however, the growing self-perpetuation of industrial–scientific civilisation is evident. Industrial patterns were soon adopted by new nations and thus spread across the continents.

It is true that the benefits of such an expansion were limited by the fact that it followed primarily (though not exclusively) the channels opened by the 'white man's' influence. It may still be argued, however, that the visible proliferation of industrial civilisation is continuing at such a rapid pace that after a period of time – perhaps a half-century – most of the people of the world will be able to benefit from the fruits of science and technology and enjoy the standard of living now confined to limited areas.

While this may be a plausible perspective, it is clearly not a self-evident one. Not all of the presently dominant tendencies are leading towards such a pleasant outcome. It would be comforting indeed were we able to regard the present century as a 'wild age' of terrible discrepancies and inequalities, of domination of the rich over the poor – but nevertheless still a transient stage destined historically to be followed by a new age of justice, rationality, and common access to the benefits of the achievements of the human mind and of science and technology. Alas, such an optimistic perspective will not easily materialise: it has to be engineered, and in the face of strong opposing forces.

II. RESHAPING DOMINANT TRENDS IN WORLD DEVELOPMENT

Extrapolation of the strongest trends in global development patterns only emphasises the growing discrepancies between nations; that is, future projections that are based on current trends negate, rather than confirm, any optimistic predictions regarding the future global outlook, particularly for the last quarter of the twentieth century. Furthermore, extrapolation is unacceptable as the basis of future projections simply because it improperly presupposes the continuation into the future of the powerful, effective forces and mechanisms of the present moment.

However, in studying developmental interrelationships we have extremely relevant feedback that should receive careful analysis, although in fact it is largely neglected. Ultimately, economic development depends upon the qualitative improvement of human factors, such as the capabilities of individuals and societies to master technology and organisation, to innovate creatively in all fields of socio-economic activities. These qualitative capabilities depend, in turn, on progress in societal and economic development. Therefore, growing economic discrepancies affect and deepen existing differences in human qualities. This may be easily observed throughout the world; and, moreover, its effect is to revivify and petrify existing discrepancies.

Since such a vision of the world's future is unacceptable, it then argues in favour of the early reversal of current dominant trends: it is easier to reverse them today than it will be in some distant future. Such a judgement of unacceptability is not based on moral argumentation alone but also on realistic appraisal of socio-political factors and forces which are, of course subject to discussion.

Extrapolation reveals how much has to be changed, reshaped, reoriented, in order to halt the dominating tendencies. Such considerations provide the proper scope for the New International Economic Order. Though we may not be bold enough to formulate the scale of the desirable change in quantitative terms, there seems to be no doubt that it should be great; and therefore the task of the new economic order is tremendous.

The socio-political drive towards equity now obvious on the world scene constitutes the basic propelling force for the construction of the new economic order. This is a crucial hypothesis implicit throughout the forthcoming discussion. Moreover, it seems to be substantiated by recent developments in the international community. This hypothesis permits us to formulate certain observations and conclusions, as follows:

(1) The drive towards equity is a function of time; it is going to grow, to intensify in the coming future. Two factors seem relevant:

    (*a*) the economic tendencies perpetuating the growing discrepancies and thereby stimulating the socio-political reaction against them; and

    (*b*) the role of education and the mass media in awakening a wide social stratum to new needs and aspirations.

(2) The NIEO then should be conceived as a process and not as a single reform of world patterns. Factors lying behind this process are growing in intensity, and so will the process itself. There is before the world community a whole era in which the NIEO will be shaped, an era which has hardly started. If the initial actions heralding the new era do not bring full-fledged results, one must not turn to disappointment.

(3) The driving forces of this new order are socio-political in nature; the mechanism for shaping these forces and for running the new order must be politico–economic. The feedback between political factors and forces on the one hand, and economic patterns on the other, plays a particular role in this situation. Ignoring this aspect of the problem will lead to an unnecessarily erroneous conceptual foundation.

(4) Economics is not always best equipped to deal with such problems. Its subject-matter is not susceptible to mono-disciplinary, homogeneous theories. But we are certainly not helpless in applying reason to the analysis and solution of problems faced by humanity, and in this endeavour economics has much to contribute.

III. EXTERNALLY INDUCED VERSUS INTERNALLY GENERATED DEVELOPMENT

It is not my intention in this paper to present any survey of views and theories relating to the factors and mechanisms of developmental processes; neither would it be possible to do so in a short paper. Still, arguments cannot be presented without reference to certain concepts. My interest, however, is not in the history of theoretical deliberations but rather in the concepts themselves, which, explicitly formulated or not, are behind the actual patterns of behaviour of the world. Conceptual constructs which govern political behaviour and influence actual policies should be carefully scrutinised even though they are not accessible in the form of clearly formulated theories. Therefore, it seems useful to distinguish two conceptual models of development, with a proviso allowing necessary simplifications. There is on the one hand development induced by external factors, and on the other development which is internally generated. Of course it is difficult and even impossible to describe such developmental concepts in simple terms, as developmental patterns have more than one salient feature. Thus, the formulated phrases are intended to emphasise one feature that is foremost in helping us to understand the context under discussion. Other pertinent and related aspects will be dealt with in the somewhat wider description which follows.

IV. MODEL I: EXTERNALLY INDUCED DEVELOPMENT

Development induced by external factors may not be very widely and actively supported by theoretical arguments nowadays. Still, it is a powerful working concept in quite a number of developing countries as well as in goals formulated internationally. It has been argued that this concept also lies behind the main ideas of the international development strategy for the Second Development Decade of the United Nations. Although one could quarrel with that statement, it is not completely without reason.

One can easily recognise that a few notions in current circulation are simply applications of externally induced development theories. Only a few years ago it was quite popular to consider the various 'gaps' in the economies of the world as the chief obstacles or bottlenecks in the developmental process of developing countries. Most often cited as 'gaps' were the discrepancies between balances of payment, savings and technology of the various countries. To associate the aforementioned gaps with external factors seems obvious; moreover, extremely influential world development projections were based on this kind of 'gap' philosophy. However, the concept of international 'transfers' presented as the best mechanism for overcoming gaps in the developmental process has been, and still is, even more influential. The concept of 'transfers', with its underlying categories, corresponds to that of gaps (financial transfers, transfer of technology).

It is not of course the mere notion of transfers which is challenged, nor the purposefulness of the transfers, but the claim that they are the main mechanism for determining the course of developmental processes in the developing countries. It is just because of this emphasis on the transfers mechanism that the Second Development Decade of the United Nations is criticised. Although this policy did indicate the need for internal change and for the mobilisation of internal resources, some still feel that its main concepts and implications relied principally on the validity of the transfer mechanism.

Recent thinking, and particularly that which has developed with respect to the NIEO, has revealed certain important features and linkages of the externally induced development model. In a simplified manner, these may be presented as follows: (i) the fundamental nature of the model relates to its provisions for imported life-styles and consumption patterns; (ii) this leads to the import of the goods necessary for the imported life styles, and/or to industrialisation; (iii) industrialisation requires imported capital goods, raw materials, etc.; and (iv) the deployment of the capital goods and raw materials leads to the import of foreign technologies, skills and management. Clearly, all the links between phases of the externally induced development process pinpoint external factors, which then appear to be the main determining elements and the main bottlenecks of development. The model and its linkages are obviously not of a purely theoretical type – the linkages are deeply anchored in realities and policies.

A conceptual model of international development strategy corresponds to the above model. Its basic premise relies on the 'transmission' of economic development from the developed to the developing countries, through such mechanisms as trade, development finance, technology and skills transfer. The operation of this mechanism, it is implied, should lead to economic expansion in the developed countries, which in turn leads to their increased demand for the export products of the developing countries, which will lead to an increased importing capacity of the developing countries. Moreover, this expansion should lead to increased flows of financial resources; and all this should strengthen the external linkages, and thus produce steady progress in the developing countries.

This kind of strategic diagnosis provides grounds for policy recommendations which concentrate on strengthening the mechanisms through which impulses to growth can be transmitted from the developed to the developing countries. These recommendations aim at removing barriers to the free flow of trade, investment and technology; at achieving a substantial expansion in the flow of development finance; and at promoting the transfer of technology, etc. Policy recommendations of this sort can be found in many international documents.

However, this described development model requires the deep and fundamental reappraisal which is now going on. Of the arguments against such a model, three merit particular attention is this context. First, the impetus to growth in developing countries – which has arisen because of the economic growth of already developed countries – has been declining since 1973, and its future prospects are not at this time very bright. Grave structural problems in the developed capitalist countries cause us to think that the growth rate in those countries will be well below that of past trend indications. In the long run, according to persuasive arguments, the socially acceptable goal which aims at high growth rate in material output will become increasingly eroded and unacceptable. When the slowing down of the growth rate in developed countries becomes confirmed, it will reduce in importance, if not undermine completely, the concept of growth transmission. While this reasoning is valid for the Third World as an aggregate, one must take into account that for the majority of developing countries external linkages play a relatively minor role. Though they are of some importance, to rely on their growth-transmission power as a main mechanism for ensuring development would be quite unrealistic. While for future forecasts one can anticipate that a group of presently developing countries – particularly the resource-rich countries – will intensively increase their linkages with the developed countries, the majority in terms of population cannot reckon on development propelled by external forces.

The second argument against this model is connected with the attitudes of the developed countries towards application of generous transfers for the sake of development of the poor and underprivileged nations. Experience in this field is not encouraging, and such prospective conditions as outlined above may even worsen the situation.

The third argument is concerned with the changing character of the international market. A major problem here is the dominant role of transnational corporations which control a substantial part of the foreign trade of developing countries and have a growing power to manipulate the international markets, including pricing. By their operations the transnational corporations capture a large share of the profits from trade between developing and developed countries and – what is every bit as important – they impose inappropriate patterns of development upon the developing countries. They have become a powerful factor drastically altering the operation of external development linkages.

V. MODEL II: INTERNALLY GENERATED DEVELOPMENT

The second conceptual model is based on an internally generated development. I use these terms deliberately preferring them to the term *self-reliance*, which in recent times has become most popular. Because *self-reliance* is a new term it might be thought that it describes a new invention in the development strategy. This is not at all bad, for certain reasons, although it may also lead to a disregard for historical experience. It may also imply emphasis on autarky. It is worth noting that most of the known cases of successful development in modern history (though the argument could be extended over much wider historical experience) have been cases of internally generated development. This does not imply that external linkages did not play an important role in quite a number of such successful cases. There are also no strong reasons why a developmental strategy should renounce external linkages, providing that they do not paralyse or misdirect the internally generated development; but this is something rather different from autarky. With these qualifications the term *self-reliance* could be accepted (as well as the term *endogenous development*, which is also used).

I would now like to put forward the proposition that the development of Western Europe, North America, Japan, the Soviet Union, the Eastern European socialist countries, the People's Republic of China, etc., was in every case according to the model of internally generated development. This proposition does not ignore the appearance of great differences in the socio-political and economic patterns characteristic of these cases. Granting the existence of sometimes profound differences, they all have one thing in common: *their development was initiated, engineered, and steadily supported by basically internal forces of a political, social, and economic nature, and accompanied by endogenously shaped socio-cultural patterns.* Only in the historical conditions of domination did the dependence relationships of an externally induced development model appear.

Another historical observation is tempting. It is that the later the take-off period for modern industrialisation, the stronger is the tendency to apply protective measures against the external forces that could impede internally generated development. Socialist countries present a most notable case in this respect, although the experience is wider. The indicated tendency can be explained by an argument based on the growing political-economic forces operative on the world scene. In this environment reliance on internal generated development calls for protective measures. I do not refer here to the traditional measures of market protection alone, but to a wide range of unconventional measures which defend a country against undesirable external influence. The above argument contains its own dynamics, from which conclusions have to be drawn. These conclusions reflect the pattern of development strategy that necessarily takes into account the power and the character of external forces.

VI. THE GOALS OF INTERNALLY GENERATED DEVELOPMENT

On the basis of the historical experience of the socialist countries one could indicate certain features of the internally-generated development model as it was applied in those countries. In a simplified manner, these features may be formulated as follows:

(1) The basic premise concerns the understanding of development: The development of a country is tantamount to the development of a people – of their qualitative features, individual and societal. People are the purpose and the measure of development.
(2) Development of human capabilities is strongly linked with the development of material factors, particularly of improved technical equipment; and this requires capital accumulation. Capital accumulation should be based principally on national efforts.
(3) The benefits from development should go to everyone in the nation; social justice in the distribution of developmental benefits is not only a praiseworthy moral principle, but it can also favour the development of human capabilities; and thus of overall development.
(4) At the low level of economic development, the sharing of benefits is tantamount to ensuring a policy aimed at satisfaction of the basic needs of a wide stratum of the population. This policy can, as indicated, lead to general development.
(5) The above policy leads to full utilisation of manpower resources and has a positive impact on the development of skills and on income distribution; it also contributes to capital formation.
(6) Structural development patterns and the choice of technology should as far as possible conform to the above premises.
(7) External linkages should be efficiently controlled in order not to impede the implementation of the above premises. If this principle is adhered to, utilisation of financial transfers and particularly of technological transfer can favour development.
(8) Implementation of all of the above premises requires adequate socio-political changes and institutional instrumentation. Social ownership of the means of production, which allows for integration and observation of broad social interests, has a crucial role to play in this process.

VII. THE ROLE OF THE NIEO IN FOSTERING DEVELOPMENT

With the possible exception of a few specific cases, internally generated development seems to be the only alternative open to the developing countries. And this is not the second-best solution but the best one. Internally-generated development is not only the way to economic progress – it also integrates the nation and gives the people pride in their own achievements, the satisfaction of creativity, and the feeling of self-confidence and dignity. Internally generated development is a basic concept for understanding and devising the main factors of socio-economic development policy. It is a conceptual approach, not a uniform recipe.

But one must go still further. Most of the developing countries face terrible economic obstacles. For the sizeable number which constitute the hard core of underdevelopment, it is difficult even to visualise realistically how they could begin an accelerated economic programme, and sustain it, based on their own efforts and their own resources alone. The vicious circle of poverty is aggravated particularly by extremely unfavourable relations between population and natural resource endowment in developing countries. Their grave problems require international measures.

Another crucial factor is the external environmental condition of the developing process. The world market system and the forces which operate in international relations work considerably against the poor developing nations, as indicated earlier. Reshaping these negative forces is the proper goal of the NIEO. Only political measures can achieve this, and the growing drive towards equity is the main force behind these measures.

The New International Economic Order, then, both could and should be perceived as a set-up for engineering external factors favourable to the growth of developing countries. As a new, emerging international system, the NIEO should design new patterns for development of the external environment. Would this imply a changed pattern of internally generated development in regard to external protection? This is not an easy question to answer. One might venture a proposition that the NIEO could at least partially replace the drastic protective measures taken by certain countries by relying strongly on internally generated development aimed at protecting it from undesirable external linkages. It is my opinion, however, that this can be accomplished only to a certain extent. But to this extent, the NIEO would imply wider utilisation of external linkages and therefore faster progress. This would mean a breakdown in the trend towards intensifying defensive measures. In the light of historical experience this is a bold forecast, although not an implausible one. The capacity of the developing countries for collective action and joint economic co-operation will certainly be a most important factor affecting the realisation of the new international economic order.

The NIEO programme is an international programme that concentrates on reshaping the international economic order. Its final aims will not be achieved unless the developing countries fully embrace the internally-generated development strategy. And with that task completed, the reshaping of international relations will be much easier, since a basic feedback process will have been established: the more efficient and internally integrated a country or group of countries is, the better can it utilise international linkages for the sake of its own progress. At this point, both national and international economic patterns will work together to achieve the new order, based on internationally and internally generated development for the purpose of creating a more harmonious world and the greater global rationality of mankind.

9 The North–South Relationship and Economic Development

Rikard Lang

Zagreb, Yugoslavia

I. THE PROBLEM

Economic relations between countries on very different levels of economic development – referred to as north–south relations – lie at the centre of proposed changes in the institutional structure of international economic relations and the world economy. New patterns of specialisation and co-operation are now being envisioned for the purpose of guiding and accelerating economic development within developing countries, with emphasis on the urgent need to restructure the world's economy and the institutional framework of international economic relations.

In this paper, north–south relationships are viewed in the context of the very urgent needs of the great majority of the countries of the world, inhabited by the bulk of mankind, to accelerate their economic development. At present north–south relationships are so constituted that they generate huge obstacles to the achievement of this aim. Solutions to the problem are now being devised within the setting of a new international economic order that is nevertheless to a very high degree still influenced by events that occurred during the process of decolonisation and affected both the responsibilities and the functions of the participants in the relationship. Moreover, the north–south relationship deeply affects the functioning of the world's economy; its impact is not confined to the development problems of developing countries. Therefore, any discussion of the linkages between developed and developing countries – their ensuing dependencies, interdependencies, and interactions – involves south–north, north–north, and south–south relationships as well as the north–south relationship. Viewed in this light, the true nature of the problem becomes more apparent.

The structural features of the world economy are of basic importance for understanding its present functional difficulties and for devising solutions to its problems. North–south relationships are symptoms of structural deficiencies in the world economy; they have a high explanatory value for the differences between the development trends and development potential of countries on different economic levels. Structural change is therefore an issue that cannot be bypassed when discussing the negative impact of the north–south relationship upon developing countries.

II. THE SITUATION OF DEVELOPING COUNTRIES

Developing countries are not homogeneous but they do share among themselves structural characteristics that adversely affect their developmental potential. The fact that the bulk of mankind lives in countries on a low level of economic development, experiencing great hardships and difficulties, is a fact that fundamentally affects international relations: it cannot be separated from issues regarding the structure of the larger world economy. Moreover, the broadening of the spectrum of international economic relations, a consequence of the progressive internationalisation of production, increases the possibilities for polarisation.

The very deep differences between the economic development of various nations are often measured and analysed. According to the *1975 World Bank Atlas* (Volume I, p. 8), at the one pole are those countries with an average GNP per capita (at market prices of US$120; at the other pole are those with an average of $5970 per capita. In other words, out of a total population of 3836 million, at one pole there is a group of countries with a total population of 316 million and an average GNP of $5970, while at the other end there are two groups, one comprising 1151 million with an average per capita GNP of $120 and another comprising 1184 million with an average of $280 GNP per capita.

It is estimated that the group of least developed countries[1] (with a total population of 239 million) had in 1974 an average per capita GNP, in 1973 prices, of US$104 – $217 below the average of the developing countries as a whole of $321.

The data for the mid-1970s[2] proves that the differences between the richest and the poorest countries have not basically changed, nor has the distance between them been reduced. Changes have occurred only within the so-called southern group and affected the ranking of a small number of developing countries.

The *UN World Economic Survey for 1975*[3] presents data on the distribution of the developing countries according to the rates of economic growth during the 1970–75 period. Of 105 countries with a population of 215 million (12 per cent of the 1805 million of the population of developing countries included), only 14 had an average annual per capita increase in production (gross domestic product in 1970 US dollars) of 9 and more per cent. Developing countries with a total population of 805 million experienced during the same time a rate of growth of less than 3 per cent.

[1]'Least Developed Among Developing Countries, Developing Island Countries, and Developing Land-Locked Countries', Table 1, UNCTAD IV, Nairobi, 1976, Document TD/191/Suppl. 1.
[2]'Basic Data on the Least Developed Countries' (UNCTAD, 1977, Document TD/B/AC.21/3) Table 1.
[3]*United Nations World Economic Survey 1975*. (New York: United Nations Department of Economic and Social Affairs, 1976) p. 87.

The levels and rates of economic growth explain the estimated outstanding differences in the annual average increments in real product per head in the period 1960–75 between countries on different economic levels.[4] The projections[5] to 1980 of the per capita growth of GNP for the developing countries are based on three assumptions: (i) a continuation of the growth rate of the per capita real product achieved during the period 1960–70; (ii) a continuation of this growth rate into the 1970–80 period; and (iii) a growth rate of 3.5 per cent of the per capita gross product. Such projections certainly do not anticipate a narrowing of the gap between the north and the south. Within the present setting one could even expect such tendencies to lead to increased tensions.

Economic development is of primary importance to the majority of mankind and ranks as a policy goal of the highest priority. A higher rate of economic growth is a necessary condition for the solution of the huge and very urgent human, social, economic, and political problems of developing countries. It is a question of survival for vast numbers of people. The low level of economic development in these countries is explained by their structure of production, which is closely related to the north–south relationship, to its historical roots in the colonial era, and to the economic, political, and social structure of this period.

III. NORTH–SOUTH RELATIONS HISTORICALLY AND CURRENTLY

Of special significance is the creation of a network of permanent links which tie the developing countries to the developed and result in dependencies on the foreign trade, technology, financing, and other unilateral links tying developing to developed nations. An economically powerful nation thus becomes the nucleus of linkages with other less developed countries. The southern pole of nations are in such a process dependent upon the centre. In such a situation a key issue becomes the manner in which economic power is applied as a combination of the economic potential and the economic strategy of the dominant country. Using different combinations of strategies,[6] such conditions permit the introduction of specific relations of dependence and dominance which are in fact, or potentially, the foundations for different types of exploitation by developed, industrialised countries.

[4]'Review and Appraisal of the Implementation of the International Development Strategy, the Declaration and the Programme of Action on the Establishment of a New International Economic Order, the Charter of Economic Rights and Duties of States, and General Assembly Resolution S-VII on Development and International Economic Cooperation', UNCTAD Document TD/B/642 (Geneva, 1975) p. 8.

[5]'Basic Data on the Least Developed Countries', op. cit.

[6]'Declaration and Programme of Action on the Establishment of a New International Economic Order', op. cit.

For instance, the dominant country can decisively influence the formation of the structure of production of the dominated one in such a manner that it serves the aims of the economically more powerful country. Its socio-economic development is subordinated to the goals and criteria of the dominant country, which is thus able to realise its own economic and other goals. Mechanisms of domination in international economic relations serve this purpose.

The inadequacies of the institutional structure of international economic relations and the deficiencies in the structure of the world economy became more evident after the Second World War, due to the impact of several factors. One of the most important events following the end of the war was the achievement of political independence by a significant number of countries which had previously, under colonial rule or quasi-colonial dependence, not been in a position to decide independently on their own development strategies. In the currently changed environment they have asserted this right.

While the present north–south relationship evolved over a long period, requests for change are comparatively recent. Proposals for solutions to the problems created by this relationship were initially prompted after the Second World War, but the intensity of the discussions increased and then later shifted under the impact of more experience and deeper insights. In the mid-1970s efforts directed towards change entered an important new phase. Proposals for global solutions which demand deep structural change have been advanced recently on the initiative of developing countries and have received broad international support.

The breakdown of the post-war monetary system, the failures of the world market, the difficulties arising out of the developing countries' exports of primary products, the absence of countervailing powers to the emergence of new power relations continuing the states of economic dependence of the developing countries in general, the increasing role of transnational companies, and other aspects of the present conditions of the world economy – all these have affected the economic development of developing countries for the worse and helped to widen the gap separating one country from another. The fact that the rate of economic growth of developing countries is falling behind those rates required to achieve a higher level of economic development, capable of satisfying even the basic needs of their populations, gives a specific importance to this phenomenon.

IV. PRESSURES FOR CHANGE IN NORTH–SOUTH RELATIONS

It is a characteristic feature of the international situation that the developing countries no longer confront passively the consequences of the north–south relationship. They insist that fundamental changes in these relations ought to assume the highest priority and stress that it is not possible to resolve the problems generated by them without fundamental changes in the existing international division of labour, a main feature of the north–south relationship.

The developing countries maintain that the urgent need to change the present framework of international economic relations is not merely a consequence of the increasing evidence of inadequacy in the present relationship. A more fundamental argument is raised. Even when according to the criteria of its architects it worked satisfactorily, the present structure did not respond to the needs of the countries of the south; nor were international development policies successful. Any changes must therefore be fundamental structural changes, not simply revisions of the old structure.

It cannot be expected that reorganisation of the presently unbalanced and inequitable north–south relationship will spontaneously conform to the requirements and priorities of developing countries, given the impact of the forces which govern trade and other economic relations between countries. On the other hand, a better understanding of the sources of underdevelopment may contribute to the identification of changeable variables of a policy of economic development within an appropriate national as well as international setting.

Economic independence will require a reversal of the sequence of development policies so that economic relations become a function of the developing countries' development strategies and not vice versa. The present system of international economic relations rests on the concepts of neo-classical theory, which assumes that the free circulation of goods, services, capital and knowledge is automatically conducive to a rational allocation of resources, to a more equitable distribution of wealth, and to a more efficient structure of production. However, a number of factors caused a failure in this mechanism: the assumptions of neo-classical theory have not been confirmed. Market distortion, for one thing, renders this mechanism imperfect; prices in international trade fall under the impact of protection and discrimination; money is turned into a manipulative transfer mechanism of the developed countries; inflation is transferred mostly from countries on a higher level of economic development to those on a lower level. In addition there are other factors that impair the market mechanism and affect its efficiency, thus leading to polarisation of countries with different levels of economic development.

The control of strategic resources, capital markets, patents, and licences is more conducive to a trade pattern intended to continue unilateral economic dependencies than it is to rational and efficient interdependence. The possibilities at the disposal of developed countries – economies of scale, the introduction and diffusion of technical progress, monopolistic advantages, etc. – contribute to differences in the rate and level of economic development and to inequalities in development opportunity, particularly under the impact of the market mechanism. Consequently developing countries generally are experiencing growing difficulties in their efforts to reach economic, financial, technological, research, organisational, and other thresholds of economic development.

Under these conditions technical progress has also become an important factor, resulting in the redistribution of wealth in favour of developed countries. The impact of technical progress has been enhanced because it is connected

with the process of monopolisation and the activities of transnational
companies.

The proposals for an alternative system of international economic relations
that were advanced in the mid-70s were a result of the present crisis of
development, past experience with the system, and the perspective which such
experience opened to developing countries in the light of the failure of
development policies to create possibilities for sustained growth in developing
countries. According to new proposals, the new economic relations would be
based on 'equity, sovereign equality, interdependence, common interest, and
co-operation'.[7] The co-ordinated efforts of developing countries comprise in
themselves an important new phenomenon. They have asserted their
sovereignty over their own natural resources and development strategies; they
demand greater participation in the growing world production and distribution
of goods and services. Their new approach emphasises structural changes in
the economy, and particularly changes in the structure of world production. To
merely increase trade or economic aid within the boundaries of the present
system is unacceptable and inadequate to developing countries.

The envisaged institutional restructuring includes the major areas of
economic relations between countries, most especially international trade.
Restructuring is aimed at bringing about improvements in the terms of trade,
the ensuring of fair and remunerative prices for primary exports (in real terms),
price indexation, and the conclusion and implementation of an integrated
programme regarding international trade in commodities.

One condition for successful development efforts is the allocation of an
appropriate share of world trade to the developing countries. The present
unsatisfactory situation requires an expansion of processing, diversification,
and opportunities for access to the markets of the developed countries –
including full participation in the transporting, marketing and distribution of
their products. The developmental needs of developing countries demand a
general expansion of trade in the common interest of all countries, whatever the
level of economic development or type of socio-economic system.

An important element in the new institutional structure will be changes in the
international monetary system, including the areas of reserve creation,
adjustment mechanisms, the right of developing countries to participate in
decision-making, and especially the establishment of a proper link between the
creation of liquidity and developmental finance.

Changes in the common interest demand an adequate transfer of resources
from the developed to the developing countries. Experience has proved the
importance of supporting criteria of independence of the recipient country in
such a transfer. The heavy burden of the developing countries' debts is

---

[7]See, for example, Ivo Fabinc's analysis of the north–south relationship in his
recent book, *Strategija medjunarodnih ekonomskih odnosa* ('Strategy of International
Economic Relations') (Belgrade: BIGZ, 1976).

becoming a very serious obstacle to their economic development and urgently requires measures of alleviation.

V. DEVELOPMENT AND THE NORTH–SOUTH RELATIONS

A characteristic feature of the new approach to the north–south relationship is the integration of different aspects of economic development. Economic development is a global process; the separation of development issues has not in the past borne fruitful results. The emphasis on trade alone or on economic aid alone did not solve the problems of the north–south relationship. The underlining of the need for changes in the area of production is an important characteristic of the approach to the north–south relationship within the new international economic order. Particular emphasis will be placed on the need for industrialisation of the developing countries and its interdependence and interaction with other aspects of economic development.

A three-pronged strategy promoting economic development is an essential part of the developing countries' approach to the solution of the north–south problem. This approach recognises as basic an interaction between internal development strategies of developing countries, the strategies promoting economic development in the north–south relationship, and development strategies affecting relations between developing countries.

The imbalance in world industrial production and consumption is an essential consequence of the asymmetry of the world's economy and is characteristic of the north–south relationship. The share in world production of the developing countries is extremely low, and it has not changed significantly for this group as a whole during the past two decades. Acceleration of economic and social development within developing countries has under such conditions no better chance than in the past.

While alternative development strategies can be envisaged for different developing countries, industrialisation is a common, key element for all countries. Industrialisation introduces new elements into the structure of production, answering the specific needs of developing countries; it is of critical importance for long-term economic development. Experience has amply proven that industrialisation is a dynamic force affecting decisively the developing countries' economic and social progress, and it is therefore an integral part of the optimal course to be followed by developing countries.

To gain an increased share in world industrial production is therefore prominent in the global development strategy. In the UNIDO Lima Declaration and Plan of Action, developing countries announced their goal of achieving 25 per cent of the world's industrial production by the end of this millenium. None the less, even after this target is attained, the per capita manufacturing output in the developing countries would still be very low in comparison with developed countries. But even this minimal target cannot be reached without a significant acceleration of the overall rate of growth in developing countries, based on concerted action of countries on different levels of economic development. Of course the developing countries themselves will have to exert a concerted developmental effort.

Industrial production is not an isolated phenomenon; there are numerous prerequisites for industrialisation. This deep structural change cannot be successful without an acceleration of the rates of growth and without structural changes in such other sectors as agriculture, the services, and mining and forestry if appropriate.

Investment by developing countries constitutes an important factor in any effort to increase the developing countries' share of world production. Such a change also has an impact on domestic consumption, the share of investment goods in the structure of production, and resource requirements.

A country in the process of industrialisation has requirements for capital equipment and intermediate inputs that can be satisfied through an expansion and diversification of that country's foreign trade. Their imports as well as their exports are involved, since they will need markets for their increased manufacturing output. The international community must support the accelerated industrialisation and technological development of these countries, in particular by introducing adequate industrial and trade policies in developed countries. Thus, industrialisation depends on a changed international division of labour. A dynamic division of labour, especially in the field of industrial production, is a means and a consequence of international economic relations promoting economic development of the developing countries.

Trade patterns between north and south reflect the structures of their economies, and especially the function of industry in overall production. The structure of imports and exports undergoes changes in the process of industrialisation. The sectoral export and import propensities will not remain the same in a number of branches. In a dynamic international division of labour there are aspects of changes which are conducive to the furtherance of the economic development of the developing countries.

VI. CONSEQUENCES FOR DEVELOPED COUNTRIES

An argument against changes in the international division of labour is that imports of manufactures from the developing countries are more damaging to the economies of the developed countries than are imports from countries on the same level of economic development. The bulk of world trade in manufactures is now conducted among the industrialised countries. A number of analyses stress the fact that specialisation of the developed countries is increasingly of the intra-branch type, whereas trade with the developing countries is characterised by inter-branch specialisation. Because of these differences in types of specialisation (a feature of the north–south relationship), there appear to be much greater possibilities for compensatory trade flows within the north–north sector than within the north–south sector. The argument against a dynamic division of labour can therefore be reversed. As a consequence of the higher level of industrial development of developing countries – accompanied by structural changes in their economies – their markets will expand and offer new possibilities for the exports from developed countries. There exist numerous possibilities to multiply the channels through which north–south trade can expand and diversify, thus coming closer to reaching its potential volume and composition.

In the process of beginning and accelerating industrialisation the developing countries will become very dynamic markets for the exports of manufactures from the developed countries, exerting a positive impact on world trade in the common interest. Until the present, intra-trade in manufactures among developed countries has increased considerably faster than have their exports to developing countries.

According to foreign trade projections, the exports of developing countries will have to increase – assuming that the Lima target for growth in industrial production is implemented – at such a rate that expansion of trade among developing countries themselves will become an important aspect of the new international division of labour. This development would lead to a more efficient mobilisation and allocation of those resources that are important for the economic development of developing countries. For example, the intra-trade in manufactures among developing countries is presently far below its potential.

VII. CO-OPERATION AND TRADE AMONG DEVELOPING COUNTRIES

The links which exist between developing countries have assumed a prominent place in the efforts of these countries to reshape international economic relations. If successful, the progress of developing countries will be such as to permit them to increase and diversify their economic relations with countries on a higher level of economic development. This move towards the establishment of a comprehensive programme of economic co-operation, based on collective self-reliance, is an essential element in a global policy aimed towards the promotion of their economic development. It contributes to the reduction of excessive economic dependence on developed countries and increases their possibilities for participating in the international environment affecting their economic development.

Formerly developing countries had almost no possibility of directly establishing trade or other economic relations among themselves, since their economies could be interlinked only through metropolitan countries. Consequently there is a very low percentage of trade among the developing countries in comparison with total trade. Moreover, over the long term the potential for mutual trading relationships is considerably expanded. Now, because of the variety of resources and stages of economic development among developing countries, new complementary roles are opening great opportunities to expand the areas of economic co-operation. Economic co-operation between developing countries is a means to better utilising resources and thereby activating developmental potential. Concerted actions are contemplated in such key areas of international economic relations as raw materials, foreign trade generally, financial co-operation, industrialisation, infrastructure, services, science, technology, and other fields in which developing countries may work toward closer economic co-operation.

Concepts and ideas for this co-operation have passed through a marked evolution. First, the emphasis shifted from trade toward joint endeavours in the field of production as the importance of co-operative efforts within the new global strategy became apparent. The concept was primarily applicable in schemes of regional and sub-regional economic co-operation in the beginning; currently, however, the idea refers to collective self-reliance and economic co-operation beyond territorial contiguity; it relates to sub-regional, regional, and interregional co-operation. Wider possibilities are now envisaged.

The aim of collective self-reliance is not the autarky of developing countries. It is the mobilisation and more rational use and allocation of national resources in order to accelerate economic development among countries of the southern sector. The ensuing restructuring of the world's economic relations will in the long run be in the common interest of all. Such restructuring will open new areas for economic analysis and introduce new criteria for the relevance of economic theory, as well as correct the current imbalance between the economic development of countries of the world.

10 Exports and Economic Development of Less Developed Countries

Hla Myint

London School of Economics, United Kingdom

INTRODUCTION

The question of how far exports, particularly primary exports, are capable of providing the underdeveloped countries with a satisfactory basis of economic development has been extensively discussed during the last two decades and may still be regarded as something of an open question. *Prima facie*, the broad facts relating to the export and development experiences of these countries during the period seem to support those who advocated policies of freer trade and export expansion rather than those who advocated policies of protection and import-substitution. Thus, despite the 'export pessimism' of the latter, which persisted well into the 1960s, the period 1950–70 has turned out to be a period of very rapid expansion in world trade and those underdeveloped countries which responded to the buoyant world market conditions have been able to expand their exports rapidly, typically above 5 per cent per annum. This export expansion included not only the primary exports produced by the large mining and plantation enterprises, but also those produced by the small peasant farmers. In addition, a smaller group of countries have expanded their exports of manufactured and semi-processed products. Furthermore, the countries which expanded their exports have also tended to enjoy rapid economic development and significant correlations have been found between the growth of export and the growth of national income among the underdeveloped countries by cross-section studies; by time-series studies; or by a combination of both methods (Emery, 1967, Maizels, 1968, Kravis, 1970a and 1970b and Chenery, 1971). Conversely it has been found that the countries which concentrated on import-substitution tend to have lower rates of growth than those which expanded their exports (Balassa, 1971).

In this paper, we shall be concerned both with the causal analysis and with the policy implications of the relationship between the exports and the economic development of the underdeveloped countries. In Section I, we shall consider this relationship, not as a simple one-way causation running from exports to economic development, but as a mutual interrelationship involving other important elements of the economic system. In Section II, we shall argue that it is necessary to take into account not only the 'direct gains' from trade in terms of the allocative efficiency of resources, but also the 'indirect effects' of trade on the productive efficiency of resources in a broader sense in order to have a better understanding of why the export-oriented underdeveloped countries tend to enjoy a more rapid rate of economic growth than those which have pursued import-substitution policies. In Section III, we shall argue that the expansion of peasant exports from the 'traditional sector' of the underdeveloped countries tends to promote economic development, directly by a fuller and more effective utilisation of their under-utilised resources in the 'subsistence sector', and indirectly, by extending and improving their domestic economic organisation which is incompletely developed. In Section IV, we conclude that the outcome of our analysis is to support the *prima facie* view that freer trade and export expansion policies tend to promote the economic development of the underdeveloped countries.

I. POSSIBLE CAUSAL RELATIONSHIPS

A positive statistical association between the expansion of exports and the growth of national incomes among the underdeveloped countries does not tell us much about causal relationships. It may mean (*a*) that export expansion is the cause of economic development; or (*b*) that economic development is the cause of export expansion; or (*c*) that both are caused by some third factor. Further, the causal link running in each direction can be interpreted in a variety of ways. Without attempting to be exhaustive, we may review some of these potential elements in the mutual interrelationships between export and economic development.

(*a*) The hypothesis that the expansion of exports is the cause of economic development may be interpreted in three ways. (*a*.1) The first is the conventional free trade argument that the expansion of exports according to comparative costs will increase the direct gains from trade and thus help to promote economic development. (*a*.2) Next, we have the widely-held belief that exports contribute to economic development mainly by providing the underdeveloped countries with the foreign exchange necessary for the purchase of capital goods and inputs from abroad. (*a*.3) Third, we may think of the 'indirect effects' of freer trade and export expansion on domestic productive efficiency, such as the 'educative effect' of an open economy, facilitating the spread of new wants and activities and new technology and new economic organisation; or the gains in the productivity and the economies of scale from specialisation for the export market.

It is fair to say that (*a*.1), viz, the direct gains from trade through a more efficient allocation of resources, provided the theoretical basis on which freer trade policies were advocated for the underdeveloped countries during the last two decades. Yet the causal link running from the direct gains from trade to economic development appears to be rather weak. During the decades 1950–70, the growth rates of the underdeveloped countries with rapid export expansion have been typically between 5.5 per cent and 7 per cent while those with slow or stagnant exports have been about 3 to 4 per cent; and the difference in the growth rates between the two types of countries became more pronounced during the decade 1960–70 (cf. Chenery, 1971, Balassa, 1971 and also Meier, 1970). On the other hand, it seems to be widely held that the static gains from the removal of the distortions created by protection tend to come out as a rather 'small' percentage of the aggregate national product (Harberger 1959 and Corden, 1975). Even if the whole of this gain is reinvested, this would seem to be too small and short-lived to explain the difference in growth rates between the successful and the unsuccessful countries. Later, we shall see that the picture may be modified by extending the concept of the 'direct' gains and losses to include those arising from the allocation of the investible funds. But even so, we shall find it necessary to go beyond the 'direct gains' to the 'indirect effects' of the type listed under (*a*.3).

Leaving (*a*.2) and (*a*.3) for later consideration, let us now go on to the second hypothesis (*b*); viz, that economic development is the cause of export expansion. This may be interpreted in two ways. (*b*.1) Economic development may lead to an expansion of exports via increasing the supply of exportable goods. This is most easily seen when we assume exports as a constant proportion of a growing national output, but this proposition will hold so long as the share of exports does not decrease sufficiently to counteract the effects of the growth in total output. (*b*.2) Economic development may act via the increase in demand and the widening of the domestic market, having beneficial effects both upon the domestic industries and upon the export industries. Both these propositions are unexceptionable and may be included in the process of interaction between exports and economic development. The crucial question here is not whether a given increase in national output and income will tend to increase exports but what is to be regarded as the main cause of this increase in output and income.

This leads up to the third hypothesis: (*c*) viz., that both the expansion of exports and economic development are caused by a third factor. Here we approach the central battle-ground of the debates on trade and aid policies during the post-war decades; for it turns out that the choice of the 'third factor' is nothing short of the choice of a theory of economic development which shapes our views about the relationship between exports and economic development. There are two main theories here.

(*c*.1) The first is deeply rooted in the thinking of the 1950s when the supply of resources available for capital investment was regarded as the central problem of economic development. On this view, the level of investment (financed out of domestic savings and aid) is regarded as the 'third factor' which will increase the total national product according to some assumed capital-output ratio and thus increase the supply of the exportable commodities. Combined with the 'export pessimism' and the jaundiced attitude towards international trade which prevailed well into the 1960s, this has led to the familiar 'inward-looking' policies.

(i) It was held that an underdeveloped country seeking a rapid rate of economic growth should step up the rate of capital investment oriented towards its internal investment opportunities independently of its external economic opportunities which were assumed to be unfavourable.

(ii) Earlier on, these internal investment opportunities were supposed to be generated by a 'balanced-growth' between the domestic manufacturing and the domestic agricultural sector. But given the prevailing faith in the power of modern manufacturing industry based on capital-intensive advanced technology to promote economic development, both domestic agriculture and primary exports came to be increasingly neglected in favour of the import-substituting manufacturing industry.

(iii) The expansion of the modern manufacturing industries however required imports of capital goods and other inputs and materials. Thus, the importance of foreign exchange as the means of acquiring the imported capital goods came to be emphasised. However, since it was assumed that the world market demand for primary exports would be extremely inelastic, it did not lead to export expansion policies (suggested by *a*.2 above), but to the restrictions on the imports of consumers' goods to save foreign exchange for the imports of capital goods and to the renewed pleas for greater international aid to fill the 'foreign exchange gap'.

(*c*.2) The alternative view regards both the expansion of export and economic development as being caused, not so much by the level of domestic investment *per se*, as by the appropriate domestic economic policies which enable a country to allocate its resources more efficiently, taking into account both its internal and external economic opportunities. This is the position adopted by most economists who advocated policies of freer trade during the last two decades. They emphasised that an underdeveloped country would not be able to reap fully the direct gains from international trade unless it also pursued appropriate domestic policies: viz. (1) appropriate pricing policies in both factor and product markets which remove discriminatory treatment of different lines of economic activities, both within the domestic economy and between the domestic and the foreign trade sectors; (2) appropriate macro-economic policies which prevent over-valuation of the foreign exchange rate and avoid the need for *ad hoc* import restrictions and quantitative controls resulting in an unplanned protection arising from a chronic foreign exchange shortage; and (3) appropriate investment policies which reflect the country's comparative costs by valuing both the inputs and the outputs of investment projects at world market prices (cf. Johnson, 1976, Little, Scitovsky and Scott, 1970, and Little and Mirrlees, 1974).

It is fair to say that there are considerable empirical and theoretical grounds for supporting (*c*.2) against (*c*.1).

First, most economists would agree nowadays that the earlier approach to economic development in terms of increasing the *supply* of resources available for capital investment has turned out to be seriously inadequate, and that in a fundamental sense economic development involves the raising of the productive efficiency in the use of resources. Despite the low ratios of domestic savings to their GDPs in the early 1950s, the overall rate of growth of the underdeveloped countries during the 1950–60 decade was about 4.5 per cent per annum – much higher than was generally expected. This growth rate in GDP was maintained between 4.5 to 5 per cent during the 1960–70 decade. During this time, the ratio of their domestic savings also increased to some 15 per cent of the GDPs. A comparison of the savings ratio and the growth rates serves to bring out the modest contribution of capital to economic development. Thus if we follow Cairncross (1962) and assume the average rate of return on capital investment in the underdeveloped countries to be 10 per cent, then the 15 per cent saving ratio would have contributed no more than 1.5 per cent of the total growth rate between 4.5 and 5 per cent. If the level of domestic investment cannot explain the average growth rate of the underdeveloped countries as a whole, it is also not able to explain the difference in the growth rates between the successful and the unsuccessful countries. There does not seem to be any striking difference in the level of domestic investment between the successful countries which pursued export expansion policies and the less successful countries which pursued import-substitution policies (Bruton, 1967).

Second, in the perspective of the 1950–70 decades during which world trade expanded at an unprecedented rate, it is now difficult to maintain the extreme type of export pessimism which dominated discussions on trade and development well into the 1960s. Of course, it is anyone's guess whether world trade will resume its previous rate of expansion after the current recession. But even so, a more reasonable hypothesis would be that 'under normal conditions' most underdeveloped countries could expand their exports, provided they pursued appropriate domestic economic policies. Kravis (1970a and 1970b) has taken considerable pains to dispel the fatalistic view that the underdeveloped countries' exports depend solely on the world market factors over which they have no control. He has shown that successful export performance among the underdeveloped countries during the post-war decades is determined mainly by the domestic supply factors and the 'competitiveness'. Thus the successful countries expanded their primary exports mainly by increasing their shares of the world market for their traditional exports and, to some extent, by diversifying into new exports. De Vries (1967) has also shown that some underdeveloped countries have succeeded in expanding their 'minor' exports substantially by controlling their domestic rate of inflation with given exchange rates.

Third, the limitations of the concept of the 'foreign exchange gap', popularised by UNCTAD economists during the 1960s have been extensively discussed (e.g. Findlay, 1971) and here we need only touch upon one aspect of the subject. We have seen above that the once-for-all gains obtainable from the removal of the static distortions are likely to be a small percentage of the GDP and that therefore the reinvestment of these once-for-all gains would have a very small effect on economic development. But this is not to deny that losses can be great and economic development can be seriously retarded when the *annual* flow of investible funds, including the supply of foreign exchange, is directed into unproductive channels by the import-substitution policies. This suggests an important qualification of the role of foreign exchange in economic development.

In the standard case in which a country acquires imports as final consumption goods, the 'direct' gains from trade can be readily identified with the cheaper imports leading to a greater consumers' welfare. In the case of an underdeveloped country wishing to acquire the imports, not for final consumption but as capital goods and inputs for further production, the concept of 'direct' gains from trade has to be defined more carefully. Following Hicks (1960), we may picture the country as being faced with a problem of choice in two stages. In the first stage, the country has the choice of converting its given savings into capital goods either by producing them at home or by converting the savings into exports which can be exchanged for the imported capital goods from abroad. Having acquired the capital goods in one way or another, the country has the further choice of either using them to produce the final consumers' goods at home or using them to produce exports which can be exchanged for the imported consumers' goods from abroad. Comparative advantage enters into both stages of choice and the country will not maximise its final consumers' gains unless the correct choices have been made at both stages.

We can now see why we need to qualify the popular argument that foreign exchange plays a crucial role in economic development by enabling an underdeveloped country to purchase the much needed capital goods and technical inputs which it could not produce at home except at a prohibitive cost. This is true enough as far as it goes, but the gain from the opportunity to import the capital goods is only a potential gain; it can be turned into an actual welfare gain only if the imported capital goods are *economically* suitable, that is to say, only if the technology they represent fits in with the factor proportions of the country and the final products they produce are in accordance with the country's comparative costs. If the 'wrong' type of capital goods is imported because of the protection of the domestic manufacturing industry and if, moreover, the importation of the wrong type of capital goods is actively encouraged by the provision of cheap capital funds and foreign exchange by government policies, it is not difficult to see that the potential gain from the availability of foreign exchange may be reduced or even turned into an actual loss (cf. Johnson, 1967 and Myint, 1969). Bruton's study (1967) of import substitution of five Latin American countries vividly illustrates this point. According to him, during the war period 1940–45 when these countries could not obtain their supplies of capital equipment and materials from abroad, the productivity of domestic resources rose through a process of improvisation and adaptation of the existing capital equipment to fit the local market size and the product to fit the local market demand, resulting in a fuller utilisation of the productive capacity. In contrast, in the post-1955 period when import-substitution policies were actively pursued with overvalued exchange rates and subsidies on the import of capital goods and technically necessary inputs, there was virtually no increase in the 'pure' productivity of resources. On the contrary, with a growing inappropriateness of input mix of production due to the overvaluation of currency and distortions in the factor markets, and with a growing inappropriateness of the composition of output due to protection and to a decline in competition, 'an industrial structure has tended to emerge that is so alien to factor endowments that full utilisation of existing capacity came to depend more, not less, on a constant flow of imports' (Bruton, loc. cit., pp. 1112–13).

In this section we have been considering the mutual interrelationship between export and economic development in terms of its constituent elements: (*a*) the effects of export expansion on economic development; (*b*) the effects of economic development on export expansion, both through an increase in total supply and an increase in total demand; and (*c*) the effects on both export expansion and economic development of a 'third factor', notably the appropriate domestic economic policies. We have found that the causal link running from the direct gains from trade to economic development (*a*.1) is rather weak, but that the static theory of comparative costs can be effectively extended to explain the *negative* proposition why the countries which pursued import-substitution policies tended to enjoy a lower growth rate through a misdirection of the investible resources. This has also suggested an important qualification to the proposition (*a*.2), viz. exports can contribute to economic development through the foreign exchange earnings only if these are correctly reinvested, according to comparative costs. We now turn to (*a*.3) the 'indirect effects' of exports on economic development through its effects on the productive efficiency of the domestic economic system.

II. INDIRECT EFFECTS OF TRADE ON PRODUCTIVE EFFICIENCY

If we adhere strictly to the assumption of the static comparative costs theory and the 'perfect competition' model on which it is based, then there would be little scope for the indirect effects of trade to operate on the domestic economic system. In such a model, the country's maximum production possibility frontier is supposed to be determined in an unambiguous manner by the autonomously given resources and technology. The country is assumed to be already on the production possibility curve before trade takes place and it responds to the opportunity to trade by reversible movements along this curve. Since the country's production possibility curve cannot be shifted except by autonomous changes in the supply of resources and technology, all that trade can do is to change the allocation of resources. The possibility that the country's productive efficiency in a broader sense might be affected, either favourably or unfavourably, by the process of adapting its capacity to the requirements of international trade is ruled out by assumption.

(1) The possible increase in productive efficiency through the 'educative

effect' of an open economy in facilitating the spread of new skills and technology is ruled out if we adhere strictly to the assumption of 'perfect knowledge' which implies a zero cost of search for information and transmission of knowledge. Thus 'given' the technology in the outside world, the producers within a country would be supposed to be able to adopt this technology in an instantaneous and costless manner.

(2) The possible increase in productive efficiency through the response of the domestic entrepreneurs to the pressure of foreign competition is similarly ruled out. Each producer is already supposed to be operating on his production function representing the minimum combinations of inputs required to produce a given output. With the given technology, these production functions are assumed to be determinate and can be changed only through an autonomous technological change.

(3) The possible increase in productive efficiency through the process of specialisation for a wider export market in a genuine sense, involving the adaptation in the quality of resources and investment in durable productive capacity and human capital to meet a specific international demand, is ruled out by the static assumptions. Movements along the production possibility curve are reversible and resources of each type are assumed to be homogeneous and divisible. There are no differential rents arising out of the differences in the quality of the resources and their suitability to international demand; all that adjustments to trade can bring about are the changes in the relative scarcities of different types of resources or their scarcity rents. The assumption of perfect divisibility of resources rules out the economies of scale. If there are no gains in productivity from specialisation for the export market, there are also no risks or commitments in specialisation. The economic system is assumed to be able to allocate resources either to expand or to contract exports in a smooth and flexible manner.

(4) Finally, it is assumed that with a given physical endowment of resources and given technology, the production possibility curve of a country cannot move upwards through a fuller utilisation of these given resources. Resources are assumed to be fully employed, given the assumptions of their perfect mobility and the flexibility of their prices. This is reinforced by the assumption of 'perfect knowledge' according to which the producers are supposed to know about the availabilities of the resources within the country in the same way as they are supposed to know about the available technology in the outside world. Further the 'perfect competition' model has an implicit assumption which is of considerable importance to our later analysis: viz., that the domestic economic organisation of a trading country including its market system and network of transport and communication is sufficiently well developed to bring the physically available resources into full utilisation. This excludes the possibility that the process of international trade might introduce improvements of the organisational framework of the domestic economic system resulting in a fuller utilisation of its existing resources.

Let us now consider how far we can combine these indirect effects of trade on the broader productive efficiency of the domestic economic system with the direct static gains from trade.

(1) The 'educative effect' of an open economy arises not only from free commodity trade, but also from the auxiliary functions of trade in facilitating the spread of new wants and activities, and new methods of production and economic organisation through a greater degree of international mobility of resources and human contacts. The conditions favourable for the 'educative effect' are thus not identical with the static optimum conditions of free trade. A moderate degree of tariff or indirect controls on trade (as distinct from detailed quantitative controls) need not reduce the 'educative effect', provided other aspects of international economic contacts are relatively free. Similarly, some of the concepts of static welfare analysis, e.g. 'the tariff equivalent' of quantitative controls may be inappropriate for the analysis of the 'educative effect'. But on the whole there does not seem to be any inherent logical difficulty in combining it with the static gains from trade.

(2) It is not clear how far the possible increase in productive efficiency or X-efficiency arising from the response of domestic entrepreneurs to the 'pressure of foreign competition' can be grafted on to the static framework of analysis. A protectionist can argue that while the sheltering from foreign competition may lead to entrepreneurial inefficiency, exposure to the pressure of competition, particularly from the producers in the advanced countries, may present the domestic producers of the underdeveloped countries with an excessive challenge which outclasses them; and that they are likely to succumb rather than respond to such a challenge. In spite of this indeterminacy, there can be no disagreement about the proposition that under the typical conditions in which import substitution policies are pursued by means of a network of controls the domestic entrepreneurs of the underdeveloped countries would find it more profitable to direct their energies to the task of procuring the government licences or exploiting the loopholes in the regulations rather than to the task of raising productivity. Thus a removal of such controls and a redirection of entrepreneurial incentives would tend to raise productive efficiency in addition to the purely static gains from the correction of the distortions.

(3) We shall definitely have broken out of the static framework of the comparative costs theory when we try to broaden the argument for export expansion by incorporating the gains from 'specialisation' for a wider export market involving the adaptation of the quality of resources and the building up of special skills and productive capacity to meet the specific requirements of the export market. These gains represent a non-reversible outward shift of the production possibility curve of a country in the direction of export production. In order to obtain them, a country would usually have to commit its resources to export production on a large enough scale to overcome the indivisibilities in the production process or in the auxiliary facilities such as transport and communications. This is likely to take the country beyond the static optimum point indicated by the given comparative advantage before the process

of specialisation takes place and is therefore likely to impose some initial sacrifice of static gains from trade and also the risks of specialisation. On the other hand, there is a general presumption, dating back to Adam Smith, that a country is likely to increase its productive efficiency by taking advantage of the opportunity to exploit the economies of scale and specialisation in certain selected lines of export production for a wider world market instead of matching its resource allocation to the pattern of domestic demand inside the narrow home market.

There is some empirical evidence to suggest that indirect effects of this nature are more relevant for the understanding of the higher growth rates of the export-oriented underdeveloped countries than the conventional approach in terms of the removal of the static distortions. Bhagwati and Krueger (1973) have found that some of the export-oriented countries, such as South Korea, appear 'to have intervened virtually as much and as 'chaotically' on the side of promoting new exports as others have on the side of import substitution' and that their success cannot be attributed to 'the presence of a neo-classically efficient allocating mechanism *in toto* in the system'. Similarly, one may deduce that the need for the 'free trade zones' in other export-oriented countries such as Taiwan and Mexico implies that the rest of the economy, outside these zones, is not so free. Bhagwati and Krueger suggest that the success of the export-oriented countries may be attributed to the factors emphasised by the older writers on international trade, viz. the built-in budgetary constraints preventing excessive export subsidisation; the relatively greater use of indirect, rather than direct interventions in export promotion; the pressure of international competition on the producers of the subsidised exports; and the economies of scale.

The protectionist case against primary exports is entirely based on the alleged unfavourable indirect effects of such exports on the long-run productive efficiency of the domestic system contrasted with the external economies and 'linkages' from the manufacturing industry. Since the whole argument is based on the presumption that it is normally worth while for an underdeveloped country to sacrifice some of the direct gains from trade to secure these longer-run indirect benefits, the issues of the debate are not properly joined so long as the free trade argument is limited to the direct gains from trade. We have to go on to consider the adverse indirect effects attributed to the expansion of primary export production.

The belief that primary exports tend to create the colonial-type 'export enclaves' and tend to 'fossilise' the economic structure of the underdeveloped countries still exerts a powerful influence and requires a critical examination. Basically, the argument envisages the primary exports as being produced by the larger mining and plantation enterprises operated by direct private foreign investment. The objections usually advanced against such exports may be summarised as follows: (1) There may be 'unfair' distribution of the gains from trade because the foreign investors have been able to obtain cheap concessions to exploit the country's natural resources, paying less than the 'economic rent' for the use of these resources. (2) An 'export bias' may be created because too large a portion of government revenues from the exports and the external supply of capital has been devoted to the type of social ove.head capital, e.g. transport and communications and research, which benefits the larger enterprises in the export sector rather than the small peasants in the domestic sector. (3) This tends to 'fossilise' the production structure, trapping resources in special lines of primary export production in the face of a long-run decline for the world market demand for primary products. (4) Primary export production tends to result in 'enclaves' with few 'linkages' with the rest of the economy, in contrast to the manufacturing industry's capacity to create such linkages and external economies.

(1) Leaving aside the complications introduced by the exhaustible natural resources, the possibility of 'unfair' distribution of the gains from trade is an argument for the government of an underdeveloped country to charge the full economic rent on its natural resources rather than an argument against allowing either the foreign or the domestic investors to use these resources for the production of primary exports (see Myint, 1972, for a fuller discussion of the issues). It does, however, serve to bring out a weakness in the standard Heckscher–Ohlin type of trade theory, based on the assumption of homogeneous resources and concerned with the effects of trade on the relative scarcities or the scarcity rents of the different types of homogeneous resources. Typically the 'economic rents' on the natural resources required for primary exports largely consist of 'differential rents' arising from the qualitative differences in a country's natural resources, including their location. This means that the direct gains from trade from primary exports are likely to be much larger than the conventional gains in terms of allocative efficiency based on the assumption of homogeneous resources. If withdrawn from export production, the earnings of special types of natural resources, such as land bearing mineral deposits or suitable for particular types of tropical product, would drop sharply in their alternative uses in domestic production. Thus so long as the governments of the underdeveloped countries are able to extract the full economic rent from the investors (and they have increasingly proven their ability to do so) this argument strengthens the case for primary export production.

(2) There are two different versions of the 'export bias' argument. The first is directed against the flow of external capital into the underdeveloped countries for the construction of social overhead capital to facilitate the primary exports from the mines and plantations. But since this type of capital investment is 'induced' by the specific purpose of expanding these exports and would not have been available to the country for other purposes, the country does not suffer from forgone opportunities of investment elsewhere. It is true, for example, that a railway line running straight from the seaport to the mines without the 'feeder' lines to develop the surrounding countryside may give little stimulus to domestic economic development. But it would not have come into existence without the mines and it does not hinder domestic development in

ny way. It may be easier subsequently to build the feeder lines because of the existence of the trunk routes than if they had not existed. Further, the mines should provide the government with the revenues for domestic economic development. This brings us to the second version of the 'export bias' arguments, viz. that in the past the colonial governments have devoted too much of the country's revenue for the benefit of the larger mining and plantation enterprises in the export sector rather than for the benefit of the small peasants in domestic agriculture. Whatever the truth of this allegation, it would now be entirely within the control of the independent governments of the underdeveloped countries to correct this bias against the 'domestic sector'. Unfortunately, however, in many underdeveloped countries the 'domestic sector' has come to be identified with the modern manufacturing industry in the urban centres rather than with the small peasant producers in traditional agriculture. Thus the small peasant producers in the traditional sector may have suffered doubly – under the old 'dualism' because of the colonial governments' encouragement of the larger-scale mining and plantation enterprises, and under the new 'dualism' because of the independent governments' encouragement of the modern manufacturing industry.

(3) The argument that the underdeveloped countries would tend to 'fossilise' their domestic economic structure by specialisation in primary exports has two aspects. The first stems from pessimistic views of the long-term patterns of world market demand for primary exports. These have proved unfounded in the light of the experiences of the post-war decades and the present concern with raw-materials shortage and exhaustible resources. In particular, Porter (1970) has shown that while the demand for primary products may be typically very price-inelastic or very income-inelastic, they are not both price- and income-inelastic and that the advanced countries of North America and Western Europe have managed to become dominant producers of the income-elastic primary products at least partly through an ability to cut costs. The second strand of the 'fossilisation' argument stems from the view that it is more difficult to shift resources out of primary production than out of manufacturing industry. Here, as we have seen, any genuine process of specialisation in an export production, involving specific investment in durable productive capacity and infrastructure, is bound to give rise to heavy costs of readjustment in output, not taken into account in the conventional trade model with reversible movements along the production possibility curve. The question is whether it is significantly more difficult to shift out of specialisation in primary production than from specialisation in manufacturing industry. Although this is widely supposed to be so, it is difficult to find cogent theoretical or historical reasons for it. Historically, it is not difficult to find instances of successful switches from one line of primary exports to another. Thus Malaysia switched from coffee production to her highly successful rubber industry and is in the process of switching at least some of her land to palm oil. Brazil is in the process of shifting from coffee to soya beans. Conversely, the British textile industry has for long been a well known example of 'fossilisation'

in manufacturing industry following an early leadership in the export market (cf. Allen and Donnithorne, 1962 and Kindleberger, 1961). (See however Chenery, 1976, who argues that few governments would have sufficient foresight to switch out of primary exports in time as though this 'foresight' in an operational sense could be obtained from broad cross-section average relationships between the level of per capita incomes and the share of manufacturing industry in GNP.)

(4) Finally, we come to the widely held opinion that primary exports are inherently less capable of creating 'linkages' with the rest of the economy than manufacturing industry. On the face of it, there are as many technical possibilities for primary export production to create 'forward linkages' – say, by increasing the supply of locally produced raw materials for processing industries – as for manufacturing industry to create 'backward linkages' by setting up demand for locally produced inputs. How far these technical possibilities in either case can be economically realisable depends on the relativ costs and prices of inputs and outputs; in other words, on the comparative costs principle which operates on the pattern of vertical international specialisation between different intermediate stages of production in the same way as it operates on the pattern of horizontal international specialisation between different final products. Advantages in location and the saving of transport costs may help with the creation of linkages. Here, as we shall see, the expansion of primary exports by peasant producers located in the traditional sector of the underdeveloped countries may be more favourable for the generation of some kinds of linkages than manufacturing industry located in the urban centres.

III. PEASANT EXPORTS AND ECONOMIC DEVELOPMENT

So far we have been concerned with the exports from the 'modern sector' of the underdeveloped countries. We may now turn to the peasant exports from the 'traditional sector' and their effect on economic development. At this point, it is necessary to re-examine the two related assumptions of the conventional trade theory: viz. that the domestic economic organisation of the trading country, including its market system and its internal network of transport and communications, is fully developed before trade takes place; and that its resources are fully employed, given that they are internally mobile and that their prices are flexible. These two assumptions effectively rule out the possibility that the process of 'opening up' an underdeveloped country to international trade will extend and improve its domestic economic framework and thereby enable it to utilise its 'given' resources more fully and effectively.

There is, however, considerable historical evidence to show that in the early stages of development, peasant exports from the underdeveloped countries expanded, typically, not by a contraction of domestic outputs as implied by the full employment assumption of the comparative costs theory, but by bringing in the hitherto underutilised resources of the 'subsistence sector' as suggested

y the 'vent-for-surplus' theory (Myint, 1958). On the demand side, there were
he foreign merchants and entrepreneurs who actively searched for the sources
of the exportable peasant products from the underdeveloped countries and
ubsequently built up the channels of trade consisting of the chains of transport
nd communications and retail–wholesale links which connected the
raditional sectors of these countries to the world market. On the supply side,
here were the peasant producers who responded vigorously to the stimulus of
ew or cheaper imported consumer goods, by clearing more land and by
evoting the labour they did not require for subsistence production to export
roduction. This historical process started in the late nineteenth century, but its
otentialities were by no means exhausted in the post-war decades, particularly
or the peasant export economies of Africa and South East Asia (Lewis, 1966
nd Myint, 1972). Thus the rapid rate of economic growth of some of the
xport-oriented countries, such as the Ivory Coast and Thailand during the
ecade 1960–70, may be largely accounted for in terms of the vent-for-surplus
heory. The direct gains from trade obtainable by bringing in the under-utilised
esources from the subsistence sector into export production offer a more
onvincing explanation of their growth than the conventional gains in terms of
n increase in the static allocative efficiency of the 'given' and fully employed
esources.

The protectionist reaction to this type of export expansion policy would be
o say that since the extension of peasant production takes place on the basis of
nchanged agricultural techniques, it would sooner or later be stopped by the
mits of the cultivable hinterland and that in order to forestall this and obtain a
elf-sustained basis for economic growth, the proceeds from peasant exports
hould be used to finance domestic industrialisation. There has been no
hortage of underdeveloped countries which have followed this protectionist
omestic industrialisation policy, in spite of the fact that their resource
ndowments and stage of development would seem to indicate that they could
till greatly benefit from the expansion of peasant exports. Thus Ghana and
Burma have used the device of State Agricultural Marketing Boards with
onsiderable ruthlessness to extract the revenue from their peasant exports of
ocoa and rice for the purposes of domestic industrialisation. Their poor
erformance both in export and economic growth contrasts sharply with those
of their respective neighbours, the Ivory Coast and Thailand.

The idea that, unlike manufacturing industry, peasant export production is
ncapable of generating the 'linkages', and should therefore be treated merely as
he milch-cow for the domestic industrialisation programmes, is very
widespread. It arises from a failure to appreciate the strategic position which
easant exports occupy in the incompletely developed domestic economic
rganisation of the underdeveloped countries.

First, there is the familiar 'dualism' in their economic organisation
haracterised by the co-existence of a 'modern sector', consisting of the larger-
cale economic units engaged in mining, plantation or manufacturing industry,
nd a 'traditional sector', consisting of small economic units engaged in

peasant agriculture and handicraft industries. The larger economic units in the modern sector are well provided with the auxiliary facilities such as transport, communications, power, etc., and have access to a modern banking system and organised capital market. Even with a neutral government policy, the small economic units would have been handicapped by the incomplete development of the domestic economic organisation, by the higher transport and transactions costs in retail trade, by the higher risks and costs of organising a credit-supply for small borrowers and by the higher administrative costs of providing transport and communications and other public services to the widely dispersed small economic units in the rural areas. These natural handicaps are greatly aggravated when the government pursues a deliberate policy of encouraging domestic industrialisation by discriminating in favour of the larger economic units engaged in import-substituting manufacturing industry.

Second, although all types of peasant agriculture are handicapped compared with the economic activities in the modern sector, peasant export production is relatively favoured under free market conditions compared with subsistence production and with cash production of food crops for the local or the domestic market. Thus peasant export crops are better served with marketing, transport and credit facilities than cash crops for the local market. Few other types of peasant products would enjoy a nation-wide marketing network normally associated with the export products. Now the vent-for-surplus theory is concerned with the process whereby the surplus land and labour not required for 'subsistence production' is attracted into export production in the early stages of the development of the traditional sector. At a later stage of development, it becomes necessary to consider also the relationship between the staple export crops and the development of cash crops for the domestic market and of the new subsidiary export crops. It is in this context that the full employment assumption of the conventional trade theory has to be modified.

An underdeveloped country which has apparently exhausted the more obvious possibilities of extending cultivation into the unused hinterland may nevertheless possess considerable 'pockets' of under-utilised resources which can be brought into fuller use, by improvements in transport and communications and by widening of the local markets which extend the marketing facilities to cover some of the 'gaps' in the existing network. In this setting of an incompletely developed domestic economic organisation there would be possibilities for *complementary* relationships between the expansion of peasant exports and the development of cash production for the domestic market and the new peasant exports. The full employment assumption stresses the *competitive* relationship in allocating the 'given' resources between one use and another. But if there were considerable 'slacks' arising from the gaps in the organisational framework, the complementary relationships may be more important than the competitive relationships. Thus it has been observed that in some of the West African countries, the trade credit advanced by the export–import firms to the middlemen for the purchase of cocoa is frequently turned over two or three times to finance the local food crops before it is used for its original purpose of purchasing the export crop (Jones, 1972, p. 251). Similarly, the 'slacks' in other trading and transport facilities in the staple export crop can be used in the marketing of local food crops and subsidiary exports. Thus the effect of introducing State Agriculture Marketing Boards into the export economies of West Africa and South East Asia has been not only to retard the growth of peasant exports by fixing buying prices well below the world market prices, but also to repress the growth of the credit and marketing institutions in the traditional sector by replacing the private middlemen with state purchasing agencies at the local level.

Third, it is true that in the past peasant exports have expanded on the basis of more or less unchanged methods of production, mainly relying on the possibility of extending cultivation into unused land. But this is not to say that peasant exports are inherently incapable of technical improvement. They may also indirectly contribute to the productive efficiency of the resources in the traditional sector in a number of ways. (i) First, there are the gains in productive efficiency from the division of labour and specialisation through the widening of the local markets. In the initial stages, peasant producers entered into export production on a spare-time basis while continuing to produce all their subsistence requirements. At a later stage, some of them would 'specialise' or devote all their resources to export production, so setting up a cash demand for locally produced foodstuffs. The consequent development of 'specialised' food producers for the local markets tends to stimulate the growth of a marketable food surplus for the country as a whole, so enabling a labour-abundant underdeveloped country to take up its potential comparative advantage in labour-intensive exports of manufactured and semi-processed products. (ii) The growth of cash crops both for the export and the domestic markets should in turn facilitate the adoption of the improved cash-intensive methods of production based on purchased inputs, such as high-yielding seeds, fertiliser and more efficient farm equipment. So far, these improved agricultural methods introduced by the 'Green Revolution' have been mainly taken up by the food-deficit countries for the purpose of attaining 'national self-sufficiency' in food, based on a considerable amount of agricultural protection. Freer trade and export expansion policies have an important role of counteracting this tendency towards import-substitution in agriculture and in bringing out the potential export possibilities of peasant agriculture after the introduction of these new methods. (iii) Finally, the development of both the product and the factor market within the traditional sector, which is perhaps the most important indirect effect of the expansion of peasant exports, should serve to improve the information network linking up the technology available in the outside world with the local availability of resources within the traditional sector. Since agricultural technology is 'location-specific', this should facilitate the adaptation of new technology to local requirements.

To sum up: the expansion of peasant exports would tend to promote the economic development of the underdeveloped countries, both directly, through the 'vent-for-surplus' mechanism, and indirectly, through the extension and improvement of their domestic economic organisation, particularly in relation to the traditional sector of their economy. These indirect effects will continue to be important as long as these countries are characterised by a pronounced 'dualism' between the modern and the traditional sectors and so long as a considerable proportion of resources in the traditional sector still remains in 'subsistence production'.

IV. EXPORT POLICY AND ECONOMIC DEVELOPMENT

The result of our analysis is to support the *prima facie* impression that the economic development of the underdeveloped countries is likely to be promoted by freer trade and export-expansion policies rather than by protection and import-substitution policies. This result has been arrived at both in terms of the 'direct gains' from trade within the conventional framework of the comparative costs theory and in terms of the broader 'indirect effects' which take us beyond the confines of the conventional theory.

(1) The conventional approach yields the negative proposition that the countries which pursue import-substitution policies tend to suffer from a lower rate of growth. Thus, although the re-investment of the once-for-all gains obtainable from the removal of static distortions may only have a small effect in increasing the growth rate, the misallocation of the *annual* flow of investible funds into inappropriate channels dictated by the import-substitution policies is likely to lead to serious losses and a significant retardation of economic growth.

(2) In order to put forward the positive proposition that freer trade and export expansion policies are likely to lead to a higher growth rate, it is necessary to bring in the 'indirect effects' of trade. These include the 'educative effect' of the open economy, the pressure of foreign competition in stimulating productive efficiency and the economies of scale and increasing returns from specialising for a wider export market. The last type of gain involves a commitment of resources on a large enough scale to overcome indivisibilities and may require a pro-export policy instead of a strict neutrality between exports and domestic production implied by the static comparative costs theory. It also involves changes in the production structure which can be reversed only at considerable cost. But, on the other hand, genuine 'specialisation' in any line of economic activity, whether in manufacturing or primary products, would entail the commitment of resources and the risk of wrong or excessive investment. Specialisation for the export market at least exposes the country to the discipline of international competition. The existence of these 'indirect effects' are not theoretically demonstrable in the same way as the 'direct' static gains from trade and are not susceptible of accurate measurement. But they are based on widely acceptable general presumptions which are, at least in principle, capable of empirical verification.

Our analysis of the relationship between the expansion of peasant exports and economic development gives an additional support to our general conclusion. The expansion of peasant exports tends to promote economic development, both directly through the 'vent-for-surplus' mechanism and indirectly by improving the domestic economic organisation of an underdeveloped country.

REFERENCES

Allen, G. C., and A. Donnithorne, *Western Enterprise in Indonesia and Malaya* (Allen & Unwin, London, 1954).

Balassa, B., 'Trade Policies in Developing Countries', *American Economic Review*, May 1971.

Bhagwati, J., and A. Krueger., 'Exchange Control, Liberalisation and Economic Development', *American Economic Review*, May 1973.

Bruton, H. J., 'Productivity Growth in Latin America', *American Economic Review*, December 1967.

Cairncross, A. K., *Factors in Economic Development* (Allen & Unwin, London, 1962) ch. 4.

Chenery, H. B., 'Growth and Structural Change', *Finance and Development Quarterly*, vol. 8, no. 3, 1971.

Chenery, H. B., 'Transitional Growth and World Industrialisation', Nobel Symposium on the International Allocation of Economic Activity, Stockholm, 1976

Corden, W. M., 'The Costs and Consequences of Protection. A Survey of Empirical Work', in Peter B. Kenen, ed., *International Trade and Finance: Frontiers for Research* (Cambridge University Press, 1975).

De Vries, B. A., *The Export Experience of Developing Countries*, World Bank Staff Occasional Papers, No. 3 (Washington, 1976).

Emery, R. F., 'The Relation of Exports to Economic Growth', *Kyklos*, vol. 20, fasc. 2 (1967).

Findlay, R., *International Trade and Development Theory* (Columbia University Press, 1973) ch. 10.

Harberger, A. C., 'Using the Resources at Hand More Effectively', *American Economic Review, Proceedings*, May 1959.

Hicks, J. R., *Essays in World Economics* (Oxford University Press, 1960) ch. 8.

Johnson, H. G., 'The Possibility of Income Losses from Increased Efficiency or Factor Accumulation in the Presence of Tariffs', *Economic Journal*, March 1967.

Jones, W. O., *Marketing Staple Food Crops in Tropical Africa* (Cornell University Press, 1972) ch. 9.

Kindleberger, C. P., 'Foreign Trade and Economic Growth: Lessons from Britain and France, 1850–1913', *The Economic History Review*, Vol. XIV, no. 2, 1961.

Kravis, I. B., 'Trade as a Handmaiden of Growth: Similarities between the Nineteenth and Twentieth Centuries', *Economic Journal*, December 1970.

Kravis, I. B., 'External Demand and Internal Supply Factors in LDC Export Performance', *Banca Nazionale del Lavoro Quarterly Review*, June 1970.

Lewis, W. A., 'Aspects of Tropical Trade, 1883–1965', Wicksell lectures 1969, Stockholm.

Little, I., T. Scitovsky and M. Scott, *Industry and Trade in Some Developing Countries, A Comparative Study* (Oxford University Press, 1970).

Little, I., and J. Mirrlees, *Project Appraisal and Planning for Developing Countries* (Heinemann, London, 1974).

Maizels, A., *Exports and Economic Growth of Developing Countries* (Cambridge University Press, 1968).

Meier, G. M., *Leading Issues in Economic Development*, second edition, (Oxford University Press, 1970) p. 37.

Myint, H., 'The "Classical" Theory of International Trade and the Underdeveloped Countries', *Economic Journal*, June 1958.

Myint, H., 'International Trade and The Developing Countries' in P. A. Samuelson (ed.), *International Economic Relations* (Macmillan, London, 1969).

Myint, H., *South East Asia's Economy: Development Policies in the 1970s*, (Penguin Books, Harmondsworth, 1972).

Porter, R., 'Some Implications of Post-war Primary Product Trends', *Journal of Political Economy*, May–June 1970.

11 A 'Stages Approach' to Comparative Advantage

Bela Balassa*

INTRODUCTION

The purpose of the paper is to analyse the changing pattern of comparative advantage in the process of economic development. The investigation will be limited to exports, since the commodity pattern of imports is greatly influenced by the system of protection in the importing countries. And as trade in natural resource products depends to a considerable extent on the country's resource endowment, we will deal with comparative advantage in manufactured goods alone.

Section I of the paper considers the relevance for the developing countries of explanations of international specialisation based on factor proportions and technological variables. Section II describes the product classification schemes and country characteristics used to evaluate comparative advantage. The empirical results on the changing pattern of comparative advantage are presented in Section III; they are further analysed in Section IV. Section V examines the policy implications of the results.

I. EXPLANATIONS OF COMPARATIVE ADVANTAGE

Hufbauer (1970) was the first to introduce the distinction between the neo-factor proportions and the neo-technological explanations of comparative advantage. The former combines human capital with physical capital and relates the sum of the two to (unskilled) labour. In turn, the latter emphasises the role of technological change, the product cycle, and economies of scale in determining the pattern of international specialisation.

According to Hufbauer, if technological factors 'were somehow combined into a single characteristic, that characteristic might prove as powerful as

* The author is Professor of Political Economy at the Johns Hopkins University and Consultant to the World Bank. The paper presented at the Congress was prepared in the framework of a consultant arrangement with the World Bank but it should not be interpreted to reflect the Bank's views. The author is indebted to Dominique de Crayencour, Jonathan Levy and especially to Kishore Nadkarni for research assistance. He has benefited from comments on an earlier version of the paper by T. N. Srinivasan and other participants in a seminar held at the World Bank.

122   *Economic Growth and Resources*

Lary's single measure (value added per man) of human and physical capital in explaining trade flows' (1970, p. 196). While such a single characteristic has not been established, it has been suggested that 'there appears to be a new consensus emerging concerning the power of the neo-technology theory over the neo-factor proportions theory' (Goodman–Ceyhun, 1976, p. 511).

The results of several recent studies on US trade tend to support this conclusion. Goodman and Ceyhun have found that 'the variables describing different facets of the technology phenomena are singularly the most important variables, which suggest the importance of the neo-technology hypothesis in the explanation of international trade in manufactures' (op. cit., p. 547). Similar results have been reached by Baldwin (1971) and by Branson and Junz (1972).

These authors have shown that net US exports are negatively correlated with physical intensity. Baldwin also finds that general measures of human capital, such as the average cost of education, average years of education, and average earnings, are not statistically significant[1] in explaining US trade. And, while the human capital variable is positively correlated with net exports in the Branson–Junz study, its level of statistical significance is greatly reduced once technological variables are introduced in the equation.

Among technological variables, R & D expenditure performs the best in the Branson–Junz study, whereas Baldwin finds the number of engineers and scientists to be the most important explanatory factor, adding further that 'probably of even more importance is the fact that a significant part of this labor group is engaged in research and development activities' (1971, p. 142). Finally, Morall concludes that 'the United States' comparative advantage in skill-intensive products must be due to mechanisms such as the product cycle model, the government subsidy of R & D explanation, the economies of scale in R & D arguments, or the dynamic shortage theory' (1972, p. 120).[2]

The results obtained for the United States, however, have limited relevance for our inquiry into the changing pattern of comparative advantage for the developing countries. These countries are at the other end of the spectrum from the United States and engage in research and development to a very small degree, if at all.[3] Accordingly, we will next consider the determinants of trade

[1]This conclusion applies also in US trade with Canada, Western Europe, the developing countries, and the rest of the world other than Japan, although statistically significant results were obtained for US trade with Japan (1971, p. 140).

[2]A dissenting voice is that of Harkness and Kyle (1975). However, the results of these authors were obtained by replacing a continuous variable (net exports or export–import ratios) with a binary variable, classifying industries into two groups according to whether exports exceed, or fall short of, imports. This choice brings into question the validity of the results, in part because of the error possibilities involved in a binary classification and in part because large and small export–import balances are given equal weight.

[3]This conclusion also applies to Leamer's findings as to 'the clear superiority of the research and development variable' (1974, p. 369) in determining export–import ratios for two-digit SITC categories in a group of twelve developed countries, including the United States, who carry out much of their trade with each other.

between developed and developing countries.

Postulating that light manufactures are relatively labour-intensive and heavy manufactures capital-intensive, Kojima (1970) has concluded that the factor proportions explanation is valid for trade between developed and developing countries. Defining capital-intensity in terms of value added per man, taken to reflect the use of physical as well as human capital, Lary has also found that developing countries tend to export labour-intensive manufactures (1968, ch. 4). This conclusion has been reinforced as regards US imports from developing countries by Mahfuzur Rahman (1973), who defined capital in physical terms, and for German imports from developing countries by Fels (1972), who defined capital as the sum of the value of the (physical) capital stock and the discounted value of the difference between average wages and unskilled wages in particular industries, taken as a proxy for human capital.

In examining trade between developed and developing countries, however, these authors have divided a continuum more or less arbitrarily into two segments, hence their estimates cannot be used to indicate changes in the pattern of comparative advantage in the process of economic development. Continuous variables as regards country characteristics have been used by Hufbauer in attempting to explain inter-country differences in the average values of particular product characteristics.[4] But, in his sample of twenty-four countries. Hufbauer has included only nine which may be considered developing, and most of these belong to the semi-industrial group (1970, p. 157).[5]

In turn, Hirsch (1974) has classified eighteen industry groups in three categories, according to whether the correlation between export performance and value added per worker in the non-agricultural sector, estimated in an inter-country framework, was positive, zero, or negative. Hirsch has also made estimates for individual countries by regressing export–output ratios in the eighteen-industry breakdown on the skill, physical capital, scale, and natural resource characteristics of these industries, and has grouped the results obtained for the twenty-nine countries studied into four categories according to their per capita incomes (high income, medium-high income, medium-low income and low income groups). No attempt has been made, however, to establish a relationship between the two sets of estimates. Considering further the low level of significance of the estimated regression coefficients in the country equations, the crudeness of the fourfold country classification scheme, and the high degree of commodity aggregation,[6] the results have remained rather impressionistic.

[4] E.g. the average physical capital intensity of exports was related to intercountry differences in physical capital per man.

[5] On the definition used, see Section III below.

[6] An even greater level of aggregation (1-digit Standard International Trade Classification categories) is used by Banerji, who distinguishes among four commodity categories and has not been successful in introducing variables directly expressing comparative advantage in the regression equations (1975, Ch. III).

Finally, Herman and Tinbergen (1970) and, subsequently, Herman (1975) have classified countries into eleven categories on the basis of their physical and human capital endowments. However, the sources cited provide no information that would permit estimating physical capital endowments and the proxy used for human capital (the cost of educating professional, technical, and related workers classified in Group 0/1 in the International Standard Classification of Occupations used by the ILO) includes personnel in liberal occupations, such as jurists, preachers, artists, and athletes while excluding production supervisors, foremen, and skilled workers that are of considerable importance in the developing countries. Also, the results derived regarding comparative advantage have not been subjected to statistical testing.

II. CLASSIFICATION SCHEMES FOR EVALUATION OF COMPARATIVE ADVANTAGE

We have briefly reviewed recent efforts made to examine the pattern of comparative advantage,[7] with emphasis on the relevance of the results for the developing countries. It has been shown that applications of the neo-technological theory largely pertain to US trade, particularly with the developed countries. In turn, in statistical investigations that have included developing countries, these countries have been considered as a group or, alternatively, they have been classified on the basis of a single criterion, such as per capita incomes or average value added per employee in the non-agricultural sector.

In the latter case, inter-country regressions have been estimated by relating average product characteristics for all manufactured exports or for aggregate industry-groups to a particular country characteristic. A considerable degree of commodity aggregation has been employed also in examining the relationship between product characteristics and the export structure of the individual countries in an inter-industry framework. At the same time, no linkage has been established between the inter-country and inter-industry estimates.

A different approach has been followed in the present study. Thirty-six countries have been chosen for the investigation, of which eighteen are developed and eighteen developing. For each country, regression equations have been estimated relating their 'revealed' comparative advantage in 184 product categories to various product characteristics. The regression coefficients thus obtained have in turn been correlated with particular country characteristics in inter-country regressions. In this way, the results obtained in 'commodity space' have been transposed into 'country space', so as to indicate the effects of these country characteristics on international specialisation.

The first question concerns the choice of product characteristics for the investigation. Harry Johnson has suggested extending the concept of capital to

[7]For an excellent review of earlier contributions the reader is referred to Stern (1975).

include human capital as well as intellectual capital in the form of production knowledge, noting that 'such an extension is fully consistent with Irving Fisher's approach to the relation between capital and income' (1970, p. 17). However, as Branson observes, the aggregation of various forms of capital assumes that they are perfect complements or perfect substitutes in production 1973, p. 11).[8]

In the present study, we have experimented with an aggregate measure of capital as well as with separate variables for physical and human capital.[9] Investment in research and development has been subsumed under the two as this is in part embodied in physical capital (e.g. laboratories) and in part in human capital (scientists and engineers engaged in R & D). This procedure appears appropriate in an investigation of the changing pattern of comparative advantage in the process of development since, as noted above, developing countries engage in research and development to a limited extent, if at all. Thus, little is lost in combining intellectual capital in the form of production knowledge with physical and human capital.

Capital intensity may be defined in terms of flows (Lary's measure of value added per worker) or stocks (the value of the capital stock plus the discounted value of the difference between average wages and the unskilled wage, divided by the number of workers). The latter approach was used by Kenen (1965) and, recently, by Fels (1972) and by Branson (1973).

The stock measure of capital intensity (k^s) is expressed in (1)

$$k_i^s = p_i^s + h_i^s = p_i^s + \frac{\overline{w}_i - w_i^u}{r^h} \tag{1}$$

for industry i, where p_i and h_i respectively, refer to physical and human capital per man, $\overline{w}_i$ is the average wage rate, w_i^u the wage of unskilled labour, and r^h the discount rate used in calculating the stock of human capital. This approach implicitly assumes that the rental price of physical capital, i.e. the risk-free rate of return and the rate of depreciation, is the same in all industries. This assumption is made explicit in expressing the flow equivalent (FE) of the stock

[8]On the complementarity of physical and human capital, see Fallon and Layard 1975).

[9]Physical and human capital have also been separated in a recent article by Hirsch, which has come to the author's attention since this paper was completed. Hirsch makes a distinction between high-skill and low-skill industries, further separating physical) capital and (unskilled) labour-intensive industries within each. For each group, export performance is related to incomes per head, taken as a proxy for physical *and* human capital (Hirsch, 1975). Thus, in contradistinction with the present study, an aggregated commodity classification scheme is used and capital endowment variables are not introduced in the analysis. Also, the human capital-intensity of the different product categories is defined in terms of skill-intensity, which was criticised in connection with the Herman–Tinbergen study above.

measure of capital intensity as in (2), where r^p is the

$$(FE) \quad k_i^s = p_i^s(r^p + d) + (\overline{w}_i - w_i^u) \qquad\qquad (2)$$

discount rate for physical capital and d is the rate of depreciation.

In turn, the flow measure of capital intensity (k^f) can be expressed as in (3) where va refers to value added per man. Now, non-wage value added per man ($va_i - \bar{w}_i$) is taken to represent physical capital-intensity and wage value added per man ($\bar{w}_i$) human-capital intensity.

$$k_i^f = va_i = p_i^f + h_i^f = (va_i - \overline{w}_i) + \overline{w}_i = (va_i - \overline{w}_i) + [(\overline{w}_i - w_i^u) + w_i^u] \qquad (3$$

As far as physical capital intensity is concerned, the two measures will give the same result in risk-free equilibrium, provided that product, capital, and labour markets are perfect and non-wage value added does not include any items other than capital remuneration. However, production is subject to risks that vary among industries, and, assuming risk aversion, profit rates will include a risk premium that will differ from industry to industry. Also, the situation in a particular year will not represent an equilibrium position and this fact, as well as imperfections in product, capital, and labour markets, will further contribute to inter-industry variations in profits. Moreover, non-wage value added may include items other than capital's remuneration, such as advertising.

Finally, while the stock measure imputes differences between average wages and the unskilled wage to human capital, the flow measure includes the entire wage value added under this heading, thus overestimating human capital-intensity by the amount of the unskilled wage. This would not give rise to problems if the unskilled wages were the same in every industry. However, unskilled wages may differ among industries due to factors such as the disutility of work and the power of labour unions.

The existence of inter-industry differences in risk, market imperfections, the inclusion of items other than capital's remuneration in non-wage value added, and the inclusion of unskilled wages in wage value added represent deficiencies of the flow measures of capital-intensity. In turn, the lack of consideration given to inter-industry differences in depreciation rates and in the extent of obsolesence of existing equipment, as well as the use of historical rather than replacement values for physical capital, represent disadvantages of the stock measure.

The implications of the described shortcomings of the two measures of capital-intensity for the results will depend on the particular circumstances of the situation. The usefulness of the stock measure would be greatly impaired in an inflationary situation where historical and replacement values differ and the magnitude of their differences varies with the age of equipment. This is not the case in the present study since the benchmark years used for estimating capital-intensity (1969 and 1970) are part of a long non-inflationary period. By contrast, the usefulness of the flow measure is limited by reason of the fact that profit rates show considerable variation over time and inter-industry differences in profit rates cannot be fully explained by reference to risk factors.[10]

These considerations tend to favour the use of the stock measure of capital-intensity. Nevertheless, given the error possibilities involved, interest attaches to making estimates by the use of both measures,[11] which also permits us to examine the stability of the results derived under alternative assumptions. This has been done in the present study, with emphasis given to the estimates obtained by the use of the stock measure in evaluating the results.

For the purposes of the calculations, we have attempted to obtain data on the capital-intensity of the production process for Japan, the factor intensities of which may be presumed to lie in between the relevant magnitudes for highly-developed and less-developed countries. However, for lack of information on physical capital and on unskilled wages in a sufficiently detailed breakdown, this attempt had to be abandoned and we have had to have recourse to US data.

The use of US data in the investigation will be appropriate if factor substitution elasticities are zero or they are identical for every product category. While this assumption is not fulfilled in practice, Lary has shown variations in capital-intensity to be small in US–UK, US–Japan, and US–India comparisons as regards his value added measure (1968, Appendix D). For lack of data, similar comparisons could not be made for the stock measure and the further investigation of this question had to be left for future research.

In defining the manufacturing sector for the purposes of the present investigation, we have taken the concept used in the US Standard Industrial Classification (SIC) as our point of departure. We have excluded from this category (SIC 19 to 39) foods and beverages (SIC 20) and tobacco (SIC 21), where the high cost of transportation and the perishability of the basic material give an advantage to primary-producing countries. We have further excluded primary non-ferrous metals (SIC 333) where transportation costs account for a high proportion of the delivered price of the basic material, and ordnance (SIC 19), for which comparable trade data are not available. In turn, given the prevalence of production for exports based on imported materials, we have retained petroleum products and wood products in the manufactured product category. We have also retained non-metallic mineral products by reason of the ubiquity of the basic materials.

Defining the manufacturing sector as SIC industry groups 22 to 39 less 333, the product classification scheme used in this study has been established on the

[10]Reference is made here to US data which were used in the calculations as noted below.

[11]Fels has employed both measures in correlating net German exports with capital-intensity in a nineteen-industry sample (1972, Table 3). In turn, Lary has used Hufbauer's data to calculate the rank correlation coefficient between country averages of value added per employee in exports and per capita incomes (1970).

basis of the 4-digit SIC categories. Particular 4-digit categories have been merged in cases when the economic characteristics of the products in question were judged to be very similar and when comparable data did not exist according to the UN Standard International Trade Classification, which has been used to collect trade figures. Appendix Table 1 provides information on the capital-intensity of the 184 product categories chosen, using the stock as well as the flow measure of capital, and further separating physical and human capital. In turn, Appendix Table 2 shows the SIC and SITC categories corresponding to these product categories.

Data on the capital stock, employment, value added, and wages used in calculating capital-intensity originate from the US Census of Manufacturing. In turn, the data for unskilled wages have been taken from the *Monthly Labor Review*, published by the US Bureau of Labor Statistics; they relate to 2-digit industries, thus involving the assumption that unskilled wages are equalised at this level.

In order to reduce the effects of variations due to the business cycle and non-recurring events, we have used simple averages of data for the two latest years (1969 and 1970) for which information was available. Finally, we have estimated the value of human capital under the stock measure by discounting differences between the average wage and the unskilled wage for the individual product categories at a rate of 10 per cent.[12]

As noted earlier, the study covers altogether 36 countries. The sample is evenly divided between developed and developing countries; the countries in the first group had per capita incomes exceeding $1800 in 1972; incomes per head did not exceed $1400 (more exactly, $1407) in the second group. The variability of per capita incomes is 1:3 in the developed country sub-sample, 1:13 in the developing country sub-sample, and 1:56 in the entire sample. Thus the sample, and, in particular the developing country sub-sample, exhibits considerable variability, which permits indicating the changing pattern of comparative advantage in the process of economic development.

The distinction between developed and developing countries has been introduced in the econometric analysis through the use of a dummy variable for developed countries. At the same time, we have used continuous variables to denote country characteristics, including physical and human capital endowment. These are shown in Table 11.1 together with per capita incomes.[13]

In the absence of data on the physical capital stock in the individual countries, we have taken the sum of gross fixed investment over the period 1955–71, estimated in constant prices and converted into US dollars at 1963 exchange rates, as a proxy for physical capital endowment. The data have been

[12]This is in between the discount rates of 9.0 and 12.7 per cent used by Kenen (1965); the same discount rate was used by Fels (1972) and by Branson (1973).

[13]On the use of per capita incomes as one of the explanatory variables, see Section IV below.

derived from the *World Tables, 1976*, published by the World Bank; they have been expressed in per capita terms.

A similar procedure has been employed by Hufbauer, except that he used data for the period 1953–64 and included manufacturing investment only (1970, p. 157). The choice of a longer period in the present study reflects the fact that capital equipment is used beyond eleven years; also, we have considered all capital, and not only that used in the manufacturing sector.[14] In turn, in using value added per worker (1974, p. 542) as a proxy for capital endowment, Hirsch does not separate physical and human capital and neglects inter-country differences in profit rates and in unskilled wages.

Hufbauer has taken the ratio of professional, technical and related workers to the labour force in manufacturing as a proxy for human capital endowment (1970, p. 158). As noted earlier, the use of this measure is objectionable, because it includes various liberal occupations while excluding production supervisors, foremen and skilled workers that are of considerable importance in the developing countries.

A more appropriate procedure appears to be to make use of the Harbison–Myers index of human resource development.[15] While this index is a flow measure,[16] the use of estimates pertaining to 1965 (Harbison, Maruhnic, and Resnick, 1970, pp. 175–6) permits us to provide an indication of a country's general educational level, and thus its human capital base, in 1972, the year for which trade data have been obtained. Nevertheless, we have also experimented with the skill ratio employed by Hufbauer, utilising the data reported in the ILO *Yearbook of Labor Statistics*.

III. SOME EMPIRICAL RESULTS

As noted in the introduction, the investigation is limited to exports since the commodity pattern of imports is greatly influenced by the system of protection. Following earlier work by the author (1975), a country's relative export performance in the individual product categories has been taken as an indication of its 'revealed' comparative advantage.

For this purpose, we have calculated the ratio of country's share in the world exports of a particular commodity to its share in the world exports of all manufactured goods. Thus, a ratio of 1.10 (0.90) means that the country's

[14]This choice can be rationalised on the grounds that, *ex ante*, capital can be allocated to manufacturing as well as to other sectors. And while adjustments would need to be made if there was complementarity between capital and natural resources, in certain uses, such as mining, information on the sectoral composition of investment was not available for a number of the countries under study.

[15]This index has also been used in a study of world trade flows by Gruber and Vernon (1970).

[16]It is derived as the secondary school enrolment rate plus five times the university enrolment rate in the respective age cohorts.

TABLE 11.1

COUNTRY CHARACTERISTICS AND REGRESSION COEFFICIENTS OBTAINED IN ESTIMATES FOR INDIVIDUAL COUNTRIES

	Country Characteristics					Regression Coefficients					
	DUMMY	GNPCAP	GDICAP	HMIND	SKILLS	β_j^s	β_j^f	β_j^{sp}	β_j^{sh}	β_j^{fp}	β_j^{fh}
Argentina	0	1139.65	2013.68	122.0	8.76	.32	.19	.25	−.04	.60	−1.49
Australia	1	3271.69	6675.24	183.3	10.93	.34**	.78*	.23	.12	.50*	.09
Austria	1	2741.26	5129.79	112.9	10.08	−.31*	−.93*	−.33*	.04	−.64*	.03
Belgium	1	3701.15	5441.70	140.5	11.62	.11	.04	.24*	−.11	.51*	−1.30*
Brazil	0	511.27	1016.00	29.3	8.57	−.69*	−1.48*	−.35	−.42	−.74	−.80
Canada	1	4691.51	7970.65	179.9	14.92	.75*	.87*	.46*	.25	−.22	2.25*
Colombia	0	357.08	751.59	32.3	7.41	−1.31*	−2.48*	−.06	−1.31*	−.33	−3.82*
Denmark	1	4187.67	6259.56	139.2	13.63	−.40	−.12	−.44	−.05	−.15	.08
Finland	1	2877.73	6999.27	109.9	14.89	−.26	−.62	.08	−.37**	−.32	−.34
France	1	3841.68	7211.24	138.8	13.46	−.07	−.08	−.06	−.002	.11	−.50**
Germany	1	4218.84	7102.15	114.3	10.71	.20*	.43*	−.05	.26*	.05	.69*
Greece	0	1407.20	2196.43	93.7	9.60	−.27	−1.05*	.11	−.49	−.08	−1.90*
Hong Kong	0	1048.88	1370.61	60.7	5.09	−2.30*	−2.84	−1.83*	−.52*	−.94*	−3.15*
India	0	102.03	214.25	50.2	9.64	−1.10*	−2.30*	−.93*	−.09	−.19	−4.58*
Ireland	1	1840.20	2701.89	110.7	12.53	−.48*	−.80*	−.44*	−.04	−.39**	−.66
Israel	1	2416.28	4280.96	148.9	19.19	−.37**	−.70*	−.02	−.41**	.27	−2.02*
Italy	1	2176.52	3366.47	91.3	7.05	−.33*	−.46*	−.20**	−.12	−.29**	−.06
Japan	1	2740.95	4765.11	146.2	8.26	−.31**	−.52*	−.42*	.11	−.70*	.86**
Korea	0	301.03	402.89	66.7	6.15	−1.67	−3.02*	−.46	−1.24*	−.69**	−3.91*
Malaysia	0	408.62	494.56	34.5	9.53	−.88*	−2.32*	−.26	−.63**	−.56	−3.65*
Mexico	0	745.41	1067.02	41.1	9.22	−.91*	−1.48*	−.17	−.80*	−.40	−2.38*

Country	DUMMY	GNPCAP	GDICAP	HMIND	SKILLS					
Morocco	0	279.13	293.08	27.9	8.23	-1.18*	-.18	-1.06*	-.23	-6.10*
Netherlands	1	3466.90	5375.15	158.6	11.62	.28*	.22*	.07	.55*	-.67*
Norway	1	3786.91	7806.11	107.4	13.91	.22	.44*	-.25	-.05	.18
Pakistan	0	104.11	197.76	33.1	4.63	-1.56*	-.93*	-.63	-.51	-5.78*
Philippines	0	223.50	448.72	134.2	10.98	-1.34*	-.07	-1.39*	-.53	-3.03*
Portugal	0	1084.26	1154.43	68.1	5.09	-.81*	-.01	-.90*	-.82*	-1.80*
Singapore	0	1354.41	1189.84	97.6	8.00	-1.47*	-1.11*	-.38	-1.03*	-2.01*
Spain	0	1333.76	2049.09	63.4	7.28	-.43*	-.03	-.42*	-.12	-.82**
Sweden	1	5141.10	9452.90	129.6	20.87	.21	-.16	.39*	-.44*	1.50*
Switzerland	1	4810.02	8852.63	112.6	13.13	.04	-.44*	.50*	.08	-.23
Taiwan	0	481.94	629.88	103.5	7.06	-1.56*	-.68*	-.87*	-.98*	-2.45*
Turkey	0	431.16	581.22	37.5	10.32	-.42	-.06	-.42	-.36	-2.01*
UK	1	2765.25	4844.68	136.2	11.44	.13	-.18**	.34*	.19	.31
USA	1	5679.47	7616.20	325.0	14.21	.84*	.24**	.62*	.23	2.22*
Yugoslavia	0	798.30	1162.06	110.0	13.73	-.47**	-.29	-.20	-.81*	-.60

Country Characteristics:

DUMMY − 1 for developed, 0 for developing countries; GNPCAP = GNP per capita in 1972, $US;

GDICAP = Cumulated gross fixed investment per capita, 1955−71, $US;

HMIND = Harbison−Myers index;

SKILLS = share of professional, technical and related workers in the total non-agricultural labour force.

Regression Coefficients have been obtained by regressing for each country the ratio of 'revealed' comparative advantage, estimated for 184 product categories, on measures of capital-intensity. The coefficient β^s has been estimated by regressing the comparative advantage ratio on the stock measure of total capital intensity as in (4), while β_j^{sp} and β_j^{sh} have been obtained by regressing this ratio on physical and human capital intensity, introduced simultaneously in the estimating equation as in (5), again using the stock measure of capital. β_j^f, β_j^{fp}, and β_j^{fh} are the corresponding regression coefficients estimated by substituting the flow measure of capital in the place of the stock measure in (4) and (5).

Regression coefficients that are significant at the 5 per cent level have been denoted by * and those significant at the 10 per cent level by **.

share in a particular product category is 10 per cent higher (lower) than its share in all manufactured exports.[17] These ratios can be considered to express a country's comparative advantage in manufactured goods that are characterised by product differentiation and are hence exported by a variety of countries.

For each of the 36 countries, the ratio of 'revealed' comparative advantage, calculated for the individual product categories, has been regressed on variables representing the capital-intensity of the individual product categories. Separate equations have been estimated using the stock and the flow measures of (total) capital intensity, as well as by simultaneously introducing physical and human capital under the two definitions of capital intensity.

The estimating equation is shown in (4) for total capital-intensity

$$\log x_{ij} = \log \alpha_j + \beta_j^s \log k_i^s \qquad (4)$$

and in (5) for physical and human capital-intensity. The equations have been estimated in a double-logarithmic form,

$$\log x_{ij} = \log \alpha_j + \beta_j^p \log p_i + \beta_j^h \log h_i \qquad (5)$$

so that the value of the β coefficient for country j indicates the percentage change in the country's comparative advantage ratio (x_{ij}) associated with one per cent change in capital intensity.[18] A positive (negative) β coefficient thus shows that a country has a comparative advantage in capital/labour-intensive products while the numerical magnitude of the β coefficient indicates the extent of the country's comparative advantage in capital/labour-intensive commodities.[19] The estimated β coefficients are reported in Table 11.1.

In the regression equations utilising the stock measure of (total) capital-intensity, the β coefficient is statistically significant at the 5 per cent level for 22 countries and at the 10 per cent level for 26 countries. In turn, in regression

[17]An alternative measure would involve relating exports to output in each country. In the absence of output figures, however, this measure could not be utilised in the present study. At any rate, it would require adjusting for country size (Balassa, 1968) while the measure used here does not require such an adjustment.

[18]Since the logarithm of zero is undefined, in the estimating equations, an export ratio of 0.001 has been used to represent cases when the exports of a country in a particular product category were nil. We have also experimented with the use of a 0.01 ratio and have obtained practically the same results. Nor are the results materially affected if we drop the zero observations from the regressions. This and other estimates not reported in the paper are available from the author on request.

[19]Alternatively, use may be made of non-parametric tests involving the calculation of the Spearman rank correlation coefficient between the 'revealed' comparative advantage ratio and the individual factor-intensity measures. This test has the disadvantage, however, that it cannot handle more than one explanatory variable and that it does not permit indicating the implications of the inter-country results for a country's future comparative advantage (on the last point, see the concluding section).

equations utilising the flow measure, the coefficient is significant at the 5 per cent level for 29 countries, with no additional countries included at the 10 per cent level. Note further that the β coefficients that have values near to zero have an economic interpretation even if they are not significantly different from zero; they indicate that a country is at the dividing line as far as comparative advantage in capital- and labour-intensive products is concerned.

The β coefficients estimated by using the stock and the flow measures of capital intensity are highly correlated, with a Spearman rank correlation coefficient of 0.956. In turn, in estimates obtained by disaggregating capital into its physical and human capital components, a high degree of correspondence has been obtained in regard to the β coefficients pertaining to human capital-intensity (Spearman rank correlation coefficient of 0.841) but not for physical capital-intensity (Spearman rank correlation coefficient of 0.650). These differences are explained if we consider that human capital-intensity was defined in a similar way under the stock and the flow measure of capital while this was not the case for physical capital intensity.

The level of statistical significance of the coefficients, too, is lower if we disaggregate capital into its physical and human capital components. The β coefficients are significant at the 5 (10) per cent confidence level in 14 (17) cases for the physical capital-intensity variable and in 13 (17) cases for the human capital-intensity variable if we use a stock measure of capital. The corresponding figures are 11 (15) for the physical capital-intensity variable and 21 (24) for the human capital-intensity variable under the flow measure.[20]

Next, we have tested the hypothesis that inter-country differences in the β coefficients can be explained by differences in country characteristics that determine the pattern of comparative advantage. This test has been carried out by regressing the β coefficients estimated for the individual countries on variables representing their physical and human capital endowments in an intercountry framework. (6) shows the estimating equation for the case when

$$\beta_j = f(GDICAP_j, HMIND_j) \tag{6}$$

per capita physical capital endowments (GDICAP) and human capital

---

[20]The results contrast with those obtained by Helleiner, who found total (physical and human) capital-intensity to have lower explanatory power than skill-intensity alone. But Helleiner's results pertain to the trade of the LDCs taken as a whole; he did not employ a stock measure of capital; and he used the average wage as a measure of skill intensity (1976).

Helleiner also used some additional variables, of which scale economies were statistically significant in trade between developing and developed countries (1976, p. 512). However, comparative advantage in products subject to scale economies is related to the size of the domestic market (Balassa, 1968) and, with developing countries having smaller markets, Helleiner's results raise problems of identification.

endowments (HMIND) are introduced simultaneously in the equation.[21]

In estimating equation (6) statistically significant results have been obtained for the physical as well as for the human capital endowment variables, regardless of whether the dependent variable originated in country regressions utilising the stock or the flow measure of capital intensity. In both regressions, the physical as well as the human capital endowment variables are significant at the 5 per cent confidence level, while the coefficient of determination is 0.65 using the stock measure and 0.78 using the flow measure of capital intensity (equations 1.3 and 2.3 Table 11.2).[22]

The level of statistical significance of the regression coefficients for the physical and human capital-endowment variables is hardly affected if we introduce a dummy variable (DUMMY) representing the level of economic development. In turn, the dummy variable is not statistically significant if used in combination with either or both capital-endowment variables, and its introduction does not increase the coefficient of determination.

We have also experimented with the ratio of professional, technical, and related workers to the total in the place of, and together with, the Harbison–Myers index. This variable (SKILLS) is not statistically significant at even the 10 per cent level. Nor does it appreciably affect the statistical significance of the other variables in the regression equation or raise the coefficient of determination. It can thus be rejected as an unsuitable substitute (complement) to the Harbison–Myers index.

It will be recalled that the level of statistical significance of the β coefficients for the physical capital intensity variable in the country regressions has been generally low. Statistically poor results have been obtained also in regressing these coefficients on variables representing physical and human capital endowment in an inter-country framework as in equation (6). The explanatory power of the regressions is low, as is the level of statistical significance of the coefficients in cases when the physical and the human capital-endowment variables are introduced simultaneously in the estimating equations. However, the coefficients are statistically significant when these variables are introduced separately (Table 11.3).

The explanatory power of the regressions is relatively high in cases when the β coefficients obtained in regard to the flow measure of human capital intensity are used as the dependent variable in equation (6). Also, both the physical and

---

[21]Note that, with variations in the standard errors of the β coefficients derived in equations (3) and (4), the regression results obtained in equation (5) will be subject to heteroscedasticity which increases the standard error of the coefficients. However, the estimates are little affected if we weight the data for the individual countries by the inversion of the standard error of the β coefficients to reduce heteroscedasticity.

[22]Regressing the rank correlation coefficients calculated as between the 'revealed' comparative advantage ratio and the factor-intensity measures on factor endowment variables has generally confirmed the reported results, although the level of statistical significance of the coefficients was somewhat lower.

TABLE 11.2
INTER-COUNTRY REGRESSION EQUATIONS FOR THE TOTAL CAPITAL-INTENSITY MEASURE

Dependent variable	Equation number	Coefficient of determination	Explanatory variables				
			GDICAP	HMIND	DUMMY	SKILLS	CONSTANT
β_j^s	1.1	0.61	1.90 (7.28)				−1.17 (−9.60)
	1.2	0.46		0.85 (5.35)			−1.38 (−7.25)
	1.3	0.65	1.46 (4.24)	0.34 (1.92)			−1.37 (−8.78)
	1.4	0.61	1.66 (2.87)		0.16 (0.48)		−1.16 (−9.38)
	1.5	0.59		0.45 (2.37)	0.69 (3.19)		−1.30 (−7.64)
	1.6	0.65	1.39 (2.40)	1.34 (1.83)	0.05 (0.15)		−1.36 (−8.44)
	1.7	0.62	1.63 (4.42)			0.03 (1.06)	−1.41 (−5.51)
	1.8	0.62	1.40 (2.23)		0.15 (0.45)	0.03 (1.04)	−1.40 (−5.39)
	1.9	0.66	1.27 (3.09)	0.32 (1.78)		0.02 (0.85)	−1.54 (−5.96)
	1.10	0.66	1.20 (1.93)	0.31 (1.70)	0.05 (0.15)	0.02 (0.84)	−1.54 (−5.80)
β_j^f	2.1	0.71	3.59 (9.12)				−2.27 (−12.43)
	2.2	0.58		1.67 (6.84)			−2.74 (−9.39)
	2.3	0.78	2.57 (5.37)	0.77 (3.12)			−2.72 (−12.54)
	2.4	0.72	2.72 (3.19)		0.57 (1.14)		−2.25 (−12.29)
	2.5	0.73		0.91 (3.42)	1.30 (4.30)		−2.60 (−10.83)
	2.6	0.78	2.11 (2.66)	0.74 (2.91)	0.33 (0.71)		−2.69 (−12.05)
	2.7	0.71	3.45 (6.14)			0.02 (0.34)	−2.39 (−6.13)
	2.8	0.72	2.60 (2.76)		0.57 (1.12)	0.01 (0.32)	−2.36 (−6.05)
	2.9	0.78	2.50 (4.46)	0.77 (3.05)		−.001(−0.03)	−2.71 (−7.44)
	2.10	0.78	2.12 (2.45)	0.74 (2.84)	0.32 (0.70)	−.001(−0.03)	−2.68 (−7.24)

NOTE For explanation of symbols, see Table 11.1. In the estimating equations, GDICAP has been expressed in units of 10,000 dollars and HMIND in units of 100.

TABLE 11.3
REGRESSION EQUATIONS FOR PHYSICAL AND HUMAN CAPITAL INTENSITY MEASURES

Dependent variable	Equation number	Coefficient of determination	Explanatory variables			
			GDICAP	HMIND	DUMMY	CONSTANT
β_j^{sp}	3.1	0.17	0.67 (2.86)	0.32 (2.64)		−0.56 (−3.81)
	3.2	0.19	0.45 (1.42)	0.16 (1.00)		−0.46 (−4.22)
	3.3	0.22	0.55 (1.03)	0.17 (1.01)		−0.55 (−3.83)
	3.4	0.22			−0.07 (−0.23)	−0.56 (−3.75)
β_j^{fp}	4.1	0.23	0.75 (3.39)	0.37 (3.16)		−0.65 (−4.66)
	4.2	0.25	0.50 (1.67)	0.19 (1.24)		−0.53 (−5.17)
	4.3	0.29	0.21 (0.43)	0.17 (1.08)		−0.64 (−4.74)
	4.4	0.30			0.21 (0.72)	−0.62 (−4.46)
β_j^{sh}	5.1	0.40	1.30 (6.99)	0.55 (4.74)		−0.87 (−6.23)
	5.2	0.59	1.07 (4.27)	0.17 (1.36)		−0.75 (−8.73)
	5.3	0.61	0.81 (1.95)	0.16 (1.18)		−0.86 (−7.55)
	5.4	0.62			0.19 (0.78)	−0.84 (−7.19)
β_j^{fh}	6.1	0.50	5.36 (7.77)	2.45 (5.87)		−3.91 (−7.81)
	6.2	0.64	3.96 (4.96)	1.07 (2.33)		−3.25 (−10.13)
	6.3	0.69	3.83 (2.58)	1.06 (2.24)		−3.87 (−9.65)
	6.4	0.69			0.09 (0.10)	−3.86 (−9.29)

NOTE For explanation of symbols, see Tables 11.1 and 11.2.

the human capital endowment variables are highly significant when introduced simultaneously in the equations. The level of significance is lower in cases when the stock measure of capital-intensity is employed instead of the flow measure.

IV. ANALYSIS OF THE RESULTS

We have further examined deviations from the relationships estimated in an inter-country context. Upward deviations from the regression line are shown with respect to the physical capital endowment, but not with regard to the human capital endowment, of Argentina and the United States. The results indicate that the actual capital-intensity of the exports of these countries much exceeded expected values based on their physical and human capital endowments.

The results for Argentina are explained if we consider that, during the period under study, this country represented an extreme case among the developing countries as far as distortions due to the application of protective measures are concerned. These distortions, in turn, have affected the pattern of exports and imports; in particular, with the implicit subsidy to capital goods through the overvaluation of the exchange rate associated with high protection, exports have been biased in a capital-intensive direction.

The results for the United States are somewhat of a puzzle as the findings of other authors would have led us to expect that actual US exports are less, rather than more, physical-capital-intensive than the hypothetical exports derived from inter-country relationships. And while the solution to the puzzle may well be that the ratio of physical to human, capital-intensity is even higher for the imports than for the exports of the United States, our results conflict with those of Hufbauer which show the US to be below the regression line (1970, p. 169). Note, however, that Hufbauer's results pertain to an earlier year and he provides evidence that US exports have become increasingly physical-capital-intensive over time. Finally, our calculations using direct input coefficients are preferable to earlier estimates derived by the use of direct plus indirect coefficients once we admit international trade in intermediate products.

In turn, the exports of Hong Kong are less capital-intensive than expected on the basis of its physical capital endowment. It would appear that Hong Kong's export structure does not yet fully reflect the large investments in physical capital carried out during the period under consideration. Finally, deviations from the regression line are relatively small in regard to human capital endowment.

Next we have estimated a matrix of Spearman rank correlaton coefficients for pairs of country characteristics in the 36-country sample. From Table 11.4 it is apparent that the extent of the correlation is the weakest in regard to the skill ratio, reinforcing our conclusion as to the inappropriateness of this variable.

In turn, the correlations between per capita GDI and the Harbison–Myers index, on the one hand, and per capita GDP on the other indicate the effects of investment in physical and in human capital on incomes per head. The existence of this correlation also explains that the inclusion of all three variables in the regression equation raises the standard error of the coefficients

TABLE 11.4

SPEARMAN RANK CORRELATION COEFFICIENTS FOR COUNTRY
CHARACTERISTICS IN THE 36-COUNTRY SAMPLE

	GNPCAP	GDICAP	HMIND	SKILLS
GNPCAP	1.000	0.984	0.754	0.674
GDICAP	0.984	1.000	0.730	0.697
HMIND	0.754	0.730	1.000	0.660
SKILLS	0.674	0.697	0.660	1.000

NOTE For explanation of symbols, see Table 11.1. All coefficients are
      statistically significant at the 1 per cent level.

to a considerable extent.[23] Nevertheless, the fact that the level of statistical
significance of the physical and human capital endowment variables much
exceeds that for incomes per head may be taken as an indication of the
'primacy' of the former.

We have seen that the inter-country regressions provide the same general
results, irrespective of whether we use a stock or a flow measure of capital-
intensity. This finding may be explained by the relatively high degree of
correspondence in the ranking of the product categories by the two measures
of capital intensity that is shown by the estimated Spearman rank correlation
coefficient of 0.782 (Table 11.5).[24]

The rankings of the 18 2-digit industry groups, too, are rather similar under
the two measures of capital intensity. Among the individual industry groups,
Apparel and other textile products, Leather and leather products, and Stone,
clay and glass products are relatively labour-intensive while Petroleum and
coal products, Chemicals, and Paper and paper products are relatively capital-
intensive (Table 11.6). In turn, considerable differences are shown between the
two sets of industry groups, with capital per worker under the stock measure
ranging between \$13,991 and \$23,142 in the three labour-intensive, and
between \$74,448 and \$191,739 in the three capital-intensive industry groups,
with the overall average being \$48,796.

[23]The relevant regression results with t-values in parentheses are

$$\beta_j^s = -1.36 + 0.14 \text{ GNPCAP} + 1.39 \text{ GDICAP} + 0.33 \text{ HMIND} \qquad R^2 = 0.65$$
$$\qquad (8.46)\ (0.06) \qquad\qquad (1.20) \qquad\qquad (1.52)$$

$$\beta_j^f = -2.70 + 1.66 \text{ GNPCAP} + 1.79 \text{ GDICAP} + 0.68 \text{ HMIND} \qquad R^2 = 0.78$$
$$\qquad (12.06)\ (0.51) \qquad\qquad (1.11) \qquad\qquad (2.25)$$

[24]Some major exceptions are various textile fabrics, reclaimed rubber, aluminium
castings, ball-bearings, and railroad cars, where a considerably higher degree of
capital-intensity is shown by the stock measure, and toilet articles, paints, electric
housewares, electric lamps, and motor vehicles, where this is shown by the flow
measure.

TABLE 11.5

SPEARMAN RANK CORRELATION COEFFICIENTS FOR ALTERNATIVE
MEASURES OF CAPITAL-INTENSITY

	(PC + HC)/L	VA/L	PC/L	HC/L	(VA − W)/L	W/L
(PC + HC)/L	1.000	0.782	0.758	0.907	0.680	0.835
VA/L	0.782	1.000	0.636	0.685	0.951	0.809
PC/L	0.758	0.636	1.000	0.488	0.604	0.562
HC/L	0.907	0.685	0.488	1.000	0.565	0.839
(VA − W)/L	0.680	0.951	0.604	0.565	1.000	0.631
W/L	0.835	0.809	0.562	0.839	0.631	1.000

NOTE   For explanation of symbols see Table 11.1. All coefficients are
statistically significant at the 1 per cent level.

At the same time, the results vary to a considerable extent within each
industry group. For example, fur goods are very capital-intensive although they
belong to the highly labour-intensive apparel and other textile products
industry group. In turn, explosives are relatively labour-intensive although they
belong to the capital-intensive chemicals industry group.

Moreover, substantial differences are observed among individual product
categories in terms of their factor intensity. At one extreme, we find woollen
yarn and thread with (total) capital per worker of $3215, followed by
earthenware food utensils ($3520), footwear ($3757), leather bags and gloves
($5483), vitreous china food utensils ($7221), costume jewellery ($8589), and
games and toys ($8654), which are the most labour-intensive among the 184
product categories. At the other end of the spectrum, petroleum products
($191,739), wood pulp ($135,474), organic chemicals ($124,198), synthetic
rubber ($120,631), carbon black ($101,161), inorganic chemicals ($92,762),
and paper ($89,089) are the most capital-intensive (Appendix Table 1).[25]

There is less of a correspondence in the rankings of product categories by
their physical and their human capital-intensity. The Spearman rank
correlation coefficient between these indicators is 0.488 under the stock
measure of capital and 0.631 under the flow measure. In turn, the correlation
coefficient is 0.604 between the two measures of physical capital intensity and
0.839 between the two measures of human capital-intensity. These differences
are explained by the fact that the flow measure of capital-intensity is sensitive
to inter-industry differences in profits that do not affect the stock measure
whereas both measures of human capital-intensity are affected by average
wages in the various product categories.

Among the individual product categories, organic chemicals, cellulosic man-
made fibres, dyeing and tanning extracts, fertilisers, carbon black, and

---

[25]The results obtained by the use of the flow measure of capital-intensity are broadly
comparable, although they differ in regard to particular commodities.

TABLE 11.6

AVERAGE FACTOR INTENSITIES FOR 18 AGGREGATED PRODUCT CATEGORIES (DOLLARS)

Slr NO.	NO.	PRODUCT CATEGORY	WEIGHT	p_i^s	h_i^s	k_i^s	p_i^f	h_i^f	k_i^f	p_i^s/h_i^s	p_i^f/h_i^f	w_i^u
1.	22.	TEXTILE MILL PRODUCTS	75.38	9404.	17814.	27219.	3885.	5919.	9804.	.528	.656	4222.
2.	23.	APPAREL + OTHER TEXTILE PRODUCTS	22.98	2024.	11967.	13991.	3583.	5165.	8748.	.169	.694	3968.
3.	24.	LUMBER + ODD PRODUCTS	31.75	11266.	12184.	23449.	4452.	6431.	10883.	.925	.692	5213.
4.	25.	FURNITURE + FIXTURES	9.80	4520.	21678.	26198.	4431.	6669.	11100.	.209	.664	4505.
5.	26.	PAPER + ALLIED PRODUCTS	43.30	57609.	40126.	97735.	11467.	10397.	21864.	1.436	1.103	6302.
6.	27.	PRINTING + PUBLISHING	13.54	8417.	36191.	44607.	8962.	8941.	17903.	.233	1.002	5323.
7.	28.	CHEMICAL + ALLIED PRODUCTS	117.73	41417.	33031.	74448.	19485.	9882.	29367.	1.254	1.972	6580.
8.	29.	PETROLEUM + COAL PRODUCTS	24.45	126110.	65629.	191739.	31310.	11910.	43220.	1.922	2.629	5342.
9.	30.	RUBBER + PLASTIC PRODUCTS	24.11	10188.	18579.	28766.	6406.	7784.	14190.	.549	.823	5922.
10.	31.	LEATHER + LEATHER PRODUCTS	7.75	5860.	17281.	23142.	4420.	6824.	11244.	.339	.648	5096.
11.	32.	STONE, CLAY + GLASS PRODUCTS	13.96	11843.	10003.	21846.	5571.	6742.	12313.	1.184	.826	6082.
12.	33.	PRIMARY METAL + ALLIED PRODUCTS	99.91	32937.	30130.	63066.	6774.	10385.	17159.	1.093	.652	7373.
13.	34.	FABRICATED METAL PRODUCTS	16.99	9073.	27860.	36933.	7330.	8715.	16045.	.326	.841	5927.
14.	35.	NONELECTRICAL MACHINERY	148.36	10045.	29011.	39056.	7326.	9704.	17030.	.346	.755	6831.
15.	36.	ELECTRICAL EQUIPMENT + SUPPLIES	96.98	7122.	30836.	37958.	5808.	8916.	14724.	.231	.651	5834.
16.	37.	TRANSPORTATION EQUIPMENT	190.14	11602.	27067.	38669.	11090.	10824.	21914.	.429	1.024	8114.
17.	38.	INSTRUMENTS + RELATED PRODUCTS	28.34	11147.	41230.	52376.	13530.	9619.	23150.	.270	1.407	5495.
18.	39.	MISC. MANUFACTURED PRODUCTS	24.71	5667.	17761.	23428.	6228.	9319.	15547.	.319	.668	5436.
		ALL CATEGORIES	1000.00	20518.	28278.	48796.	9645.	9308.	18953.	.701	1.036	5831.

NOTE The table shows average capital-labour ratios in a two-digit industry breakdown. The average capital-labour ratios for the individual product categories have been derived by weighting by the share of exports of the product category concerned in the total exports for all the 184 categories aggregated over the 36 countries. For explanation of the definitions and symbols used, see equations (1) to (3) in the text.

petroleum refining and products have relatively high physical as against human capital-intensity, regardless of whether we use the stock or the flow measure of capital. The opposite result has been obtained for canvas products, radio and TV equipment, aircraft, ships and boats, and scientific instruments and control equipment. The first group includes product categories where the ratio of physical to human capital was between 1.5 and 5 using the stock measure of capital intensity and exceeded 1.2 using the flow measure. In turn, product categories in the second group had a ratio of physical to human capital of between 0.1 and 0.2 under the stock measure of capital and less than 0.6 under the flow measure (Appendix Table 1).

V. POLICY IMPLICATIONS

This paper has investigated the changing pattern of comparative advantage in the process of economic development. Comparative advantage has been defined in terms of relative export performance, thus neglecting the composition of imports which is greatly affected by the structure of protection.

For each country, export performance has been related to the capital-intensity of the individual product categories, using a stock as well as a flow measure of capital, with further distinction made between physical and human capital. Next, the inter-country differences in the regression coefficients thus obtained have been correlated with country characteristics, such as physical and human capital endowment and the level of economic development.

The empirical estimates show that inter-country differences in the structure of exports are in a large part explained by differences in physical and human capital endowments. The results lend support to the 'stages' approach to comparative advantage, according to which the structure of exports changes with the accumulation of physical and human capital.[26] This approach is also supported by intertemporal comparisons for Japan, which indicate that Japanese exports have become increasingly physical capital and human capital intensive over time (Heller, 1976).

These findings have important policy implications for the developing countries. To begin with, they warn against distorting the system of incentives in favour of products in which the country has a comparative disadvantage. The large differences shown among product categories in terms of their capital-intensity point to the fact that there is a substantial penalty for such distortions in the form of the misallocation of productive factors.

Possible magnitudes of the economic cost of distortions are indicated in Table 11.7. This provides comparisons between production costs in the United States, assuming that pre-tax returns and depreciation amount to 30 per cent of

---

[26]The expression 'stages' is used here to denote changes over time that occur more or less continuously rather than to discrete, stepwise changes. It is thus unrelated to economic stages described by Marx, the exponents of the German historical school, and Rostow.

TABLE 11.7
HYPOTHETICAL PRODUCTION COSTS CALCULATED UNDER ALTERNATIVE ASSUMPTIONS (US DOLLARS)

Product Category	United States				Developing Country				Ratio of Total Costs
	Physical Capital	Human Capital	Unskilled Labour	Total Costs	Physical Capital	Human Capital	Unskilled Labour	Total Costs	
Capital-intensive									
1. Petroleum refining and products	37,833	6563	5342	49,738	54,215	9405	1781	65,401	1.315
2. Wood pulp	26,400	4747	6382	37,529	37,831	6802	2127	46,760	1.246
3. Organic chemicals	22,635	4875	6632	34,142	32,436	6986	2211	41,633	1.219
4. Synthetic rubber	20,826	5121	6632	32,579	29,844	7338	2211	39,393	1.209
5. Carbon black	18,669	3893	6632	29,194	26,753	5579	2211	34,543	1.183
6. Inorganic chemicals	16,044	3928	6632	26,604	22,991	5629	2211	30,831	1.159
7. Paper	14,778	3983	6382	25,143	21,177	5707	2127	29,011	1.154
Labour-intensive									
8. Games and toys	1521	359	5436	7316	2180	514	1812	4506	0.616
9. Vitreous china food utensils	1608	186	6082	7876	2304	267	2027	4598	0.584
10. Costume jewellery	978	533	5436	6947	1401	764	1812	3977	0.572
11. Leather bags and purses	711	311	5096	6118	1019	446	1699	3164	0.517
12. Earthenware food utensils	1056	0	6082	7138	1513	0	2027	3540	0.496
13. Woollen yarn and thread	486	160	4228	4874	696	229	1409	2334	0.479
14. Footwear	660	156	5450	6266	946	224	1817	2987	0.477
All Categories	6155	2828	5831	14,815	8818	4052	1944	14,815	1.000

NOTE US production costs have been calculated by adding 30 per cent of the gross value of physical capital, assumed to reflect pre-tax earnings and depreciation, to observed labour costs. In turn, for the hypothetical developing country it has been assumed that unskilled wages are one-third of US wages and the cost of capital is correspondingly higher. The latter has been estimated to exceed US costs by 43.3 per cent under the assumption that value added in the entire manufacturing sector is the same in the two cases. All data are expressed per worker.

the gross value of physical capital, and production costs in a hypothetical developing country where unskilled wages are one-third of US wages[27] and the cost of capital is commensurately higher.[28] In the latter country, the estimated cost of capital-intensive products is 15 to 32 per cent higher, and that of labour-intensive products 38 to 52 per cent lower, than in the United States, so that differences in relative costs between capital- and labour-intensive products range from 1.87 to 2.76.[29]

The economic cost of policy distortions may be especially high in countries that bias the system of incentives in favour of import substitution in capital-intensive industries and against exports in labour-intensive industries. Costs will also be incurred if capital-intensive exports are artificially promoted.

The results can further be utilised to gauge the direction in which a country's comparative advantage is moving. For this purpose, use may be made of the regression estimates obtained as regards total capital-intensity. As a first step, we substitute projected future values of a country's physical and human capital endowments in the inter-country regressions, so as to estimate the prospective values of the β coefficients.[30] Next, we derive the hypothetical structure of exports corresponding to the estimated β coefficients, which are taken to reflect the country's future physical and human capital endowments. Comparing the projected export structure with the actual structure of exports, one can then indicate prospective changes in export flows.[31]

The regression estimates obtained in regard to physical and human capital-intensity can also be used in the manner described above so as to indicate the relative importance of physical and human capital-intensive products in a country's future export structure. Given the poor statistical results of the regressions for physical capital intensity, however, one should utilise directly the data reported in Appendix 1, which show the physical and the human capital-intensity of individual product categories.

[27]In 1974, average wages in manufacturing in Korea were 9 per cent, and in the Philippines 6 per cent, of US wages (ILO, *Yearbook of Labor Statistics*).

[28]The difference in the cost of capital has been estimated at 43.3 per cent under the assumption that value added in the manufacturing sector was the same in the two cases. It has further been assumed that the absolute difference between skilled and unskilled wages remained the same.

[29]As elsewhere in the paper, the calculations do not allow for factor substitution in response to inter-country differences in factor prices.

[30]In line with the stages approach to comparative advantage, this is done on the assumption that new countries exporting manufactured goods will enter at the lower end of the spectrum. It is further assumed that the relative importance of capital-intensive goods in world exports will continue to increase over time.

[31]These projections further need to be adjusted in cases when observed values of the β-coefficients differ from values estimated from the inter-country regression. The results are also subject to the usual projection error and may be biased to the extent that high protection in countries with poor capital endowment affects the slope of the inter-country regression.

The stages approach to comparative advantage also permits one to dispel certain misapprehensions as regards the foreign demand constraint under which developing countries are said to operate. With countries progressing on the comparative advantage scale, their exports can supplant the exports of countries that graduate to a higher level. Now, to the extent that one developing country replaces another in the imports of particular commodities by the developed countries, the problem of adjustment in the latter group of countries does not arise. Rather, the brunt of adjustment will be borne in industries where the products of newly graduating developing countries compete with the products of the developed countries.

A case in point is Japan, whose comparative advantage has shifted towards highly capital-intensive exports. In turn, developing countries with a relatively high human capital endowment, such as Korea and Taiwan, can take Japan's place in exporting relatively human capital-intensive products, and countries with a relatively high physical capital endowment, such as Brazil and Mexico, can take Japan's place in exporting relatively physical capital-intensive products. Finally, countries at lower levels of development can supplant the middle-level countries in exporting unskilled-labour-intensive commodities.

The prospects of economic growth through exports thus appear much brighter once we understand the character of the changing pattern of comparative advantage. Further work on the experience of individual countries over time would be necessary, however, in order to study this process in more depth.

REFERENCES

Balassa, B., 1965, 'Trade Liberalization and Revealed Comparative Advantage', *Manchester School*, May, vol. 33.

———, 1969, 'Country Size and Trade Patterns: Comment', *American Economic Review*, March, vol. 59.

Baldwin, R. E., 1971, 'Determinants of the Commodity Structure of U.S. Trade', *American Economic Review Papers and Proceedings*, March, vol. 61.

Banerji, R., 1975, *Exports of Manufactures from India* (Kieler Studien, Institut für Weltwirtschaft an der Universität Kiel, JCB Mohr (Paul Siebeck), Tübingen).

Branson, W. H., 1973, 'Factor Inputs, U.S. Trade, and the Heckscher–Ohlin Model', Seminar Paper No. 27, Institute for International Economic Studies, University of Stockholm.

Branson, W. H., and H. Junz, 1971, 'Trends in U.S. Comparative Advantage', *Brookings Papers on Economic Activity*, vol. 2.

Cornwall, A. B., 1972, 'Influence of the Natural Resource Factor on the Comparative Advantage of Less-Developed Countries', *Inter-mountain Economic Review*, Fall, vol. 3.

Fallon, P. R., and P. R. G. Layard, 1975, 'Capital-Skill Complementarity, Income Distribution, and Output Accounting', *Journal of Political Economy*, April, vol. 83.

Fels, G., 1972, 'The Choice of Industry Mix in the Division of Labor between Developed and Developing Countries', *Weltwirtschaftliches Archiv*, Band 108, Heft 1.

Goodman, B., and R. Ceyhun, 1976, 'U.S. Export Performance in Manufacturing Industries: An Empirical Investigation', *Weltwirtschaftliches Archiv*, Band 112, Heft 3.

Gruber, W. H., and R. Vernon, 1970, 'The Technology Factor in a World Trade

Matrix', in *The Technology Factor in International Trade*, ed. R. Vernon (National Bureau of Economic Research, Columbia University Press).

Harbison, F. H., J. Maruhnic and J. R. Resnick, 1970, *Quantitative Analyses of Modernization and Development* (Industrial Relations Section, Dept. of Economics, Princeton University, Princeton).

Harkness, J., and J. F. Kyle, 1975, 'Factors Influencing United States Comparative Advantage', *Journal of International Economics*, May, vol. 5.

Helleiner, G. K., 1976, 'Industry Characteristics and the Competitiveness of Manufactures from Less-Developed Countries', *Weltwirtschaftliches Archiv*, Band 112, Heft 3.

Heller, P. S., 1976, 'Factor Endowment Change and Comparative Advantage', *Review of Economics and Statistics*, August, vol. 58.

Herman, B., 1975, *The Optimal International Division of Labor* (International Labor Office, Geneva).

Herman, B., and J. Tinbergen, 1970, 'Planning of International Development', *Proceedings of the International Conference on Industrial Economics, Budapest, April 15–17*.

Hirsch, S., 1974, 'Capital or Technology? Confronting the Neo-Factor Proportions and the Neo-Technology Accounts of International Trade', *Weltwirtschaftliches Archiv*, Band 110, Heft 1.

——, 1975, 'The Product Cycle Model of International Trade – A Multi-Country Cross Section Analysis', *Oxford Bulletin of Economics and Statistics* November, vol. 27.

Hufbauer, G. C., 1970, 'The Impact of National Characteristics and Technology on the Commodity Composition of Trade in Manufactured Goods', in *The Technology Factor in International Trade*, ed., R. Vernon (National Bureau of Economic Research, Columbia University Press).

Johnson, H. G., 1970, 'The State of Theory in Relation to Empirical Analysis' in *The Technology Factor in International Trade*, op. cit.

Kenen, P. B., 1965, 'Nature, Capital and Trade', *Journal of Political Economy*, October, vol. 73.

Kojima, K., 1970, 'Structure of Comparative Advantage in Industrial Countries: A Verification of the Factor-Proportions Theorem', *Hitotsubashi Journal of Economics*, June, vol. 11.

Krueger, A. O., 1974, *Foreign Trade Regimes and Economic Development: Turkey*, National Bureau of Economic Research, Columbia University Press.

Lary, H. B., 1968, *Imports of Manufactures from Less-Developed Countries*, National Bureau of Economic Research, Columbia University Press.

——, 1970, 'Comments on The Technology Factor in a World Trade Matrix' in *The Technology Factor in International Trade*, op. cit.

Leamer, E., 1974, 'The Commodity Composition of International Trade in Manufactures: An Empirical Analysis', *Oxford Economic Papers*, November, vol. 26.

Mahfuzur Rahman, A. H. M., 1973, *Exports of Manufactures from Developing Countries*, (Centre for Development Planning, Rotterdam University Press).

Morall, J. F., 1972, *Human Capital, Technology & the Role of the U.S. in International Trade* (University of Florida Press, Gainesville).

Schydlowsky, D. M. (forthcoming), 'Argentina', in *Development Strategies in Semi-Industrial Countries* by B. Balassa and Associates.

Stern, R. M., 1975, 'Testing Trade Theories', in *International Trade and Finance*, ed. P. B. Kenen (Cambridge University Press).

Appendix

APPENDIX TABLE 1

SECTORAL CHARACTERISTICS FOR 184 PRODUCT CATEGORIES (in dollars)

SECTOR	PRODUCT CATEGORY	p_i^s	h_i^s	k_i^s	p_i^f	h_i^f	k_i^f	p_i^s/h_i^s	p_i^s/h_i^f
1.	COTTON FABRICS (GREY)	11770.	15906.	27676.	2871.	5819.	8690.	.740	.493
2.	SYNTHETIC FABRICS	11690.	22165.	33855.	3734.	6446.	10180.	.527	.579
3.	WOOLLEN FABRICS	9490.	20229.	29719.	3792.	6248.	10040.	.469	.607
4.	NARROW FABRICS	6820.	15092.	21912.	3778.	5742.	9520.	.452	.658
5.	HOSIERY + KNIT FABRICS	6930.	10406.	17336.	4501.	5269.	9770.	.666	.854
6.	KNIT OUTERWEAR	4410.	12826.	17236.	2609.	5511.	8120.	.344	.473
7.	KNIT UNDERWEAR	4330.	6864.	11194.	2083.	4817.	7000.	.631	.424
8.	COTTON FABRICS (FINISHED)	13170.	23804.	36974.	3349.	6611.	9960.	.553	.507
9.	WOVEN CARPETS + RUGS	11550.	23188.	34738.	4995.	6545.	11540.	.498	.763
10.	NONWOVEN CARPETS + RUGS	10400.	24937.	35337.	9569.	6721.	16290.	.417	1.424
11.	YARN + THREAD, EXCEPT WOOL	11710.	11396.	23106.	3652.	5368.	9020.	1.028	.680
12.	WOOLLEN YARN + THREAD	1620.	1595.	3215.	799.	1221.	2020.	1.016	.654
13.	FELT GOODS	13280.	38588.	51868	6985.	8085.	15070.	.344	.864
14.	LACE + EMBROIDERY	4530.	28545.	33075.	4853.	6787.	11640.	.159	.715
15.	TEXTILE PADDINGS	9460.	24145.	33605.	6336.	6644.	12980.	.392	.954
16.	COMBED FIBERS + PROCESSED TEXTILE WASTE	9420.	14905.	24145.	4080.	5720.	9800.	.620	.713
17.	NONRUBBERIZED COATED FABRICS	12370.	44198.	56568.	7024.	8646.	15670.	.280	.812
18.	CORDAGE + TWINE	9100.	19327.	28427.	4880.	6160.	11040.	.471	.792
19.	TEXTILE GOODS NES	11640.	29568.	41208	7247.	7183	14430.	.394	1.009
20.	MENS AND BOYS OUTER APPAREL	1680.	9450.	11130.	3181.	4869.	8050.	.178	.653
21.	NONKNIT UNDERWEAR	1920.	7320.	9240.	3042.	4648.	7690.	.262	.655
22.	TIES, CORSETS + GLOVES	1990.	15577.	17567.	4324.	5476.	9800.	.128	.790
23.	WOMENS AND CHILDRENS CLOTHING	2070.	12453.	14523.	3383.	5167.	8550.	.166	.655
24.	HATS + CAPS	2050.	11217.	13267.	3405.	5045.	8450.	.183	.675
25.	FUR GOODS	5320.	46677.	51997.	11051	8589.	19640.	.114	1.287

No.	Product							
26.	LEATHER CLOTHING	1860.	7783.	9643.	2739.	5211.	7950.	.239	.526
27.	CURTAINS + DRAPERIES	3220.	12276.	15496.	3605.	5145.	8750.	.262	.701
28.	TEXTILE BAGS + SACKS	5810.	11581.	17391.	3592.	5078.	8670.	.502	.707
29.	CANVAS PRODUCTS	2410.	19684.	22094.	3306.	5884.	9190.	.122	.562
30.	PRESERVED WOOD	11820.	8618.	20438.	5618.	6072.	11690.	1.372	.925
31.	SAWMILL PRODUCTS	10940.	10586.	21526.	4058.	6272.	10330.	1.033	.647
32.	PREFABRICATED WOOD	5990.	22740.	28730.	4596.	7484.	12080.	.263	.614
33.	VENEER + PLYWOOD	11850.	21362.	33212.	4370.	7350.	11720.	.555	.594
34.	WOODEN BOXES + CRATES	5570.	3358.	8928.	4131.	5549.	9680.	1.659	.744
35.	COOPERAGE PRODUCTS	7880.	15868.	23748.	3935.	6805.	10740.	.497	.578
36.	WOOD PRODUCTS NES	9450.	8952.	18402.	4925.	6105.	11030.	1.056	.807
37.	FURNITURE + FIXTURES	4520.	21678.	26198.	4431.	6669.	11100.	.209	.664
38.	WOOD PULP	88000.	47474.	135474.	16028.	11132.	27160.	1.854	1.440
39.	PAPER, EXCEPT FOR CONSTRUCTION	49260.	39829.	89089.	8651.	10369.	19020.	1.237	.834
40.	PAPERBOARD	42830.	35581.	78411.	13657.	9943.	23600.	1.204	1.373
41.	STATIONERY	8460.	20604.	29064.	6941.	7869.	14810.	.411	.882
42.	PAPER BAGS + CONTAINERS	11950.	16255.	28205.	5366.	8004.	13370.	.735	.670
43.	PAPER PRODUCTS NES	16340.	22431.	38771.	13600.	8620.	22220.	.728	1.578
44.	BUILDING PAPER + PAPER PRODUCTS	30400	27341.	57741.	8656.	9114.	17770.	1.112	.950
45.	NEWSPAPERS + PERIODICALS	8490.	34984.	43474.	7946.	8494.	16440.	.243	.935
46.	BOOKS	7820.	38557.	46377.	12964.	8856.	21820.	.203	1.464
47.	MISCELLANEOUS PUBLISHING	8780.	36563.	45343.	5313.	8647.	13960.	.240	.614
48.	ENGINEERING + PRINTING	8870.	33713.	42583.	7047.	9513.	16560.	.263	.741
49.	INORGANIC CHEMICALS	53480.	39282.	92762.	19675.	10556.	30230.	1.361	1.864
50.	ORGANIC CHEMICALS	75450.	48748.	124198.	25581.	11509.	37090.	1.548	2.223
51.	PLASTIC MATERIALS + PRODUCTS	17790.	14789.	32579.	8559.	7911.	16470.	1.203	1.082
52.	SYNTHETIC RUBBER	69420.	51211.	120631.	26251.	11759.	38010.	1.356	2.233
53.	CELLULOSIC MANMADE FIBERS	34300	8002.	42302.	8746.	7434.	16180.	4.287	1.176
54.	SYNTHETIC FIBERS	40820.	28863.	69683.	13757.	9523.	23280.	1.414	1.445
55.	BIOLOGICAL + MEDICINAL PRODUCTS	17670.	42256.	59926.	28068.	10862.	38390.	.418	2.584
56.	SOAP + CLEANSERS	18830.	30622.	49452.	34207.	9693.	43900.	.615	3.529
57.	TOILET PREPARATIONS	8770.	17967.	36737.	39617.	8433.	48050.	.488	4.698
58.	PAINTS	11650.	26604.	38254.	12644.	9296.	21940.	.438	1.360
59.	DYEING + TANNING EXTRACTS	27530.	9239.	36769.	12141.	7559.	19700.	2.980	1.606

APPENDIX TABLE 1 (continued)

SECTOR	PRODUCT CATEGORY	p_i^s	h_i^s	k_i^s	p_i^f	h_i^f	k_i^f	p_i^s/h_i^s	p_i^s/h_i^f
60.	FERTILISERS	39710.	10748.	50458.	11543.	7707.	19250.	3.694	1.498
61.	MISC. AGRICULTURAL CHEMICALS	30560.	24698.	55258.	29967.	9103.	39070.	1.237	3.292
62.	ADHESIVES + GELATIN	18500.	34856.	53356.	14986.	10124.	25110.	.531	1.480
63.	EXPLOSIVES	6760.	26423.	33183.	1887.	9273.	11160.	.256	.204
64.	PRINTING INK	10810.	29033.	39843.	8726.	9534.	18260.	.372	.915
65.	CARBON BLACK	62230.	38391.	101161.	30489.	10521.	41010.	1.598	2.898
66.	MISC. CHEMICAL PREPARATIONS	17820.	26071.	43891.	17251.	9239.	26490.	.684	1.867
67.	PETROLEUM REFINING + PRODUCTS	126110.	65679.	191739.	31310.	11910.	43220.	1.922	2.629
68.	ASBESTOS + ASPHALT PRODUCTS	19810	43088.	62898.	11119.	9651.	20770.	.460	1.152
69.	TIRES + TUBES	23050.	45124.	68174.	11792.	10958.	22750.	.511	1.076
70.	FOOTWEAR	2200.	1557.	3757.	3360.	5611.	8970.	1.413	.599
71.	RECLAIMED RUBBER	21620.	22534.	44154.	4059.	8691.	12750.	.959	.467
72.	MISC. RUBBER PRODUCTS	10280.	20621.	30901.	5413.	8507.	13920.	.499	.636
73.	LEATHER	7470.	23815.	31285.	4840.	7480.	12320.	.314	.647
74.	LEATHER INDUSTRIAL BELTING	5130.	25564.	30694.	6324.	7656.	13980.	.201	.826
75.	LEATHER UPPERS	3250.	8041.	11291.	4144.	5896.	10040.	.404	.703
76.	LEATHER BAGS + PURSES	2370.	3113.	5483.	3509.	5401.	8910.	.761	.650
77.	MISC. LEATHER GOODS	2890.	7623.	10513.	2567.	5863.	8430.	.379	.438
78.	FLAT GLASS	35560.	49700.	85260.	12076.	11054.	23130.	.715	1.092
79.	GLASS CONTAINERS	9980.	7366.	17346.	5710.	6260.	11970.	1.355	.912
80.	CEMENT + CONCRETE	41110.	31110.	72220.	11447.	9193.	20640.	1.321	1.245
81.	BRICK + STRUCTURAL CLAY TILES	14700.	8708.	23408.	4252.	6948.	11200.	1.688	.612
82.	REFRACTORIES	22060.	30907.	52967.	8609.	9171.	17780.	.714	.939
83.	VITREOUS PLUMBING FIXTURES	11810.	24748.	36558.	7498.	8562.	16060.	.477	.876
84.	VITREOUS CHINA FOOD UTENSILS	5360.	1861.	7221.	3390.	6260.	9650.	2.880	.541
85.	EARTHENWARE FOOD UTENSILS	3520.	0.	3520.	764.	5606.	6370.	R	.136
86.	PORCELAIN PRODUCTS	9620.	11122.	20742.	3743.	7197.	10940.	.865	.520
87.	CONCRETE + BRICK PRODUCTS	11980.	20101.	32081.	6702.	8088.	14790.	.596	.829
88.	LIME	46700.	28313.	75013.	8969.	8911.	17880.	1.649	1.006
89.	GYPSUM PRODUCTS	49070.	33163.	82233.	12184.	9396.	21580.	1.480	1.297

90.	CUT STONE PRODUCTS	7100.	7783.	14883.	3072.	6858.	9930.	.448	.912
91.	ABRASIVE PRODUCTS	15580.	29249.	44829.	8467.	9013.	17480.	.939	.533
92.	ASBESTOS PRODUCTS	13320.	23891.	37211.	6199.	8471.	14670.	.732	.558
93.	MINERAL WOOL	21330.	32757.	54087.	11098.	9362.	20460.	1.185	.651
94.	MISC. NONMETALLIC MINERAL PRODUCTS	12330.	22278.	34608.	4827.	8313.	13140.	.581	.553
95.	STEEL + STEEL PRODUCTS	37850.	31089.	68939.	6729.	10631.	17360.	.633	1.217
96.	IRON FOUNDRIES	11460.	23994.	35454.	4569.	9511.	14080.	.480	.478
97.	STEEL FOUNDRIES	11440.	14716.	26156.	4112.	9208.	13320.	.447	.777
98.	WROUGHT COPPER	23400.	30342.	53742.	8544.	10036.	18580.	.851	.771
99.	WROUGHT ALUMINIUM	32930.	30085.	63015.	5647.	10013.	15660.	.564	1.095
100.	NONFERROUS METALS NES	19760.	25371.	45131.	9154.	9546.	18700.	.959	.779
101.	ALUMINIUM CASTINGS + STAMPINGS	13160.	37694.	50854.	4745.	10025.	14770.	.473	.349
102.	BRASS, BRONZE + COPPER CASTINGS	10260.	21309.	31569.	4502.	9138.	13640.	.493	.481
103.	IRON + STEEL FORGINGS	13070.	34100.	47170.	4765.	11145.	15910.	.428	.383
104.	PRIMARY METAL PRODUCTS NES	15840.	18649.	34489.	6554.	9476.	16030.	.692	.849
105.	METAL CONTAINERS	18720.	39734.	58454.	10848.	9902.	20750.	1.095	.471
106.	CUTLERY	10100.	20473.	30573.	13694.	7976.	21670.	1.717	.493
107.	HAND + EDGE TOOLS	8650.	29390.	39040.	7959.	8871.	16830.	.897	.294
108.	HANDSAWS + SAWBLADES	7780.	18343.	26123.	6609.	7761.	14370.	.852	.424
109.	HARDWARE NES	10200.	28076.	38276.	6925.	8735.	15660.	.793	.363
110.	SANITARY + PLUMBING FIXTURES	10560.	25764.	36324.	6391.	8509.	14900.	.751	.410
111.	NONELECTRIC HEATING EQUIPMENT	7070.	24427.	31497.	7057.	8373.	15430.	.843	.289
112.	STRUCTURAL METAL PRODUCTS	6930.	27283.	34213.	5264.	8656.	13920.	.608	.254
113.	PLATEWORK + BOILERS	9010.	34228.	43238.	7293.	9347.	16640.	.780	.263
114.	BOLTS + NUTS	11800.	36358.	48158.	6527.	9563.	16090.	.683	.325
115.	SAFES + VAULTS	6110.	38511.	44621.	13432.	9778.	23210.	1.374	.159
116.	FABRICATED METAL PRODUCTS NES	10120.	26116.	36236.	6257.	8543.	14800.	.732	.388
117.	STEAM ENGINES + TURBINES	13460.	45537.	58997.	7183.	11257.	18440.	.638	.296
118.	INTERNAL COMBUSTION ENGINES	15990.	24173.	40163.	8019.	10411.	18430.	.770	.661
119.	FARM MACHINERY	10230.	20823.	31053.	6930.	8810.	15740.	.787	.491
120.	CONSTRUCTION + DRILLING MACHINERY	10600.	35814.	46414.	6483.	10287.	16770.	.630	.296
121.	CONVEYING + CARRYING EQUIPMENT	6610.	30535.	37145.	7443.	9757.	17200.	.763	.216
122.	INDUSTRIAL TRUCKS + TRACTORS	7110.	26440.	33550.	7309.	9351.	16660.	.782	.269.
123.	MACHINE TOOLS	11620.	41454.	53074.	5639.	10851.	16490.	.520	.280

APPENDIX TABLE 1 (continued)

SECTOR	PRODUCT CATEGORY	p_i^s	h_i^s	k_i^s	p_i^f	h_i^f	k_i^f	p_i^s/h_i^f	p_i^s/h_i^f
124	METAL + WOODWORKING MACHINERY	9320.	23959.	33279.	6747.	9103.	15850.	.389	.741
125	FOOD PRODUCTS MACHINERY	7570.	29204.	36774.	6928.	9622.	16550.	.259	.720
126	TEXTILE + LAUNDRY MACHINERY	9440.	21364.	30804.	7610.	8550.	16160.	.442	.890
127	PAPER MAKING MACHINERY	10960.	31110.	42070.	5966.	9814.	15780.	.352	.608
128	SPECIAL INDUSTRY MACHINES NES	8540.	39041.	39481.	6868.	9802.	16670.	.276	.701
129	AIR COMPRESSORS + PUMPS	8880.	27219.	36099.	7770.	9430.	17200.	.326	.824
130	BALL + ROLLER BEARINGS	15800.	30400.	46200.	4714.	9746.	14460.	.520	.484
131	INDUSTRIAL FURNACES + OVENS	2760.	8020.	10780.	2566.	4004.	6570.	.344	.641
132	GENERAL INDUSTRIAL MACHINERY NES	7910.	24793.	32703.	6738.	9182.	15920.	.319	.734
133	TYPEWRITERS	10250.	25301.	35551.	12402.	9238.	21640.	.405	1.342
134	COMPUTERS	7400.	41578.	48978.	9217.	10863.	20080.	.178	.849
135	CALCULATING + ACCOUNTING MACHINES	7560.	20586.	28146.	8275.	8765.	17040.	.367	.944
136	SCALES + BALANCES	4870.	23451.	28321.	6893.	9047.	15940.	.208	.762
137	OFFICE MACHINERY NES	9210.	26824.	36034.	9625.	9385.	19010.	.343	1.026
138	AUTOMATIC MERCHANDISING MACHINES	7190.	7716.	14906.	6431.	7479.	13910.	.932	.860
139	REFRIGERATION MACHINERY	8320.	20541.	28861.	8307.	8753.	17060.	.405	.949
140	NONELECTRICAL MACHINERY NES	7950.	22605.	30555.	5102.	8968.	14070.	.352	.569
141	ELECTRIC MEASURING INSTRUMENTS	5670.	30040.	35710.	6232.	8838.	15070.	.189	.705
142	TRANSFORMERS, MOTORS + GENERATORS	8500.	28378.	36878.	5660.	8670.	14330.	.300	.653
143	CARBON + GRAPHITE PRODUCTS	24760.	29715.	54475.	10636.	8804.	19440.	.833	1.208
144	HOUSEHOLD COOKING EQUIPMENT	6690.	22527.	29217.	6044.	8086.	14130.	.297	.748
145	HOUSEHOLD REFRIGERATORS + FREEZERS	8870.	33611.	42481.	8603.	9197.	17800.	.264	.935
146	ELECTRICAL HOUSEWARES + FANS	6240.	10702.	16942.	9004.	6906.	15910.	.583	1.304
147	SEWING MACHINES	10810.	38991.	49801.	6884.	9736.	16620.	.277	.707
148	ELECTRIC LAMPS	9380.	13094.	22924.	10608.	7142.	17750.	.751	1.485
149	LIGHTING FIXTURES	6650.	19563.	26213.	7006.	7794.	14800.	.340	.899
150	RADIO + TV EQUIPMENT	5450.	42988.	48438.	4951.	10129.	15080.	.127	.489
151	PHONOGRAPHIC RECORDS	6250.	9939.	16189.	8232.	6828.	15060.	.629	1.206
152	TELEPHONE + TELEGRAPH APPARATUS	9360.	37508.	46868.	6941.	9579.	16520.	.250	.725
153	ELECTRONIC COMPONENTS + ACCESSORIES	7910.	22078.	29988.	3909.	8041.	11950.	.358	.486

No.	Category							
154.	STORAGE BATTERIES	9940.	34723.	44663.	7780.	9310.	17090.	.286	.836
155.	PRIMARY BATTERIES	7750.	14431.	22181.	12803.	7277.	20080.	.537	1.759
156.	XRAY APPARATUS + TUBES	5860.	42854.	48714.	7132.	10118.	17250.	.137	.705
157.	AUTOMOTIVE ELECTRICAL EQUIPMENT	8440.	34409.	42849.	7764.	9276.	17040.	.245	.837
158.	MOTOR VEHICLES + BODIES	13210.	25855.	39065.	13616.	11064.	24680.	.511	1.231
159.	TRAILERS	3720.	6420.	10140.	4832.	7338.	12170.	.579	.659
160.	AIRCRAFT	6820.	41483.	48303.	5339.	12121.	17460.	.164	.440
161.	AIRCRAFT ENGINES + EQUIPMENT	8830.	35132.	43962.	4268.	11482.	15750.	.251	.372
162.	SHIPS + BOATS	5730.	32125.	37855.	1538.	9392.	10930.	.178	.164
163.	LOCOMOTIVES + PARTS	11780.	50318.	62098.	18106.	11204.	29310.	.234	1.616
164.	RAILROAD CARS	9660.	36258.	45918.	1771.	9799.	11570.	.266	.181
165.	MOTORCYCLES, BICYCLES + PARTS	5940.	15325.	21265.	4381.	7709.	12090.	.388	.568
166.	SCIENTIFIC INSTRUMENTS + CONTROL EQUIP.	6040.	35157.	41197.	5394.	9016.	14410.	.172	.598
167.	OPTICAL INSTRUMENTS	6600.	43467.	50067.	5965.	9845.	15810.	.152	.606
168.	MEDICAL APPLIANCES + EQUIPMENT	6470.	25155.	31625.	8762.	8008.	16770.	.257	1.094
169.	OPHTHALMIC GOODS	6020.	15288.	21308.	6438.	7022.	13460.	.394	.917
170.	PHOTOGRAPHIC EQUIPMENT + SUPPLIES	17720.	57378.	75098.	21716.	11234.	32950.	.309	1.933
171.	WATCHES + CLOCKS	3840.	17270.	21110.	6386.	7224.	13610.	.222	.884
172.	JEWELRY + SILVERWARE	4680.	24708.	29388.	6119.	7911.	14030.	.189	.773
173.	LAPIDARY WORK	6370.	29030.	35400.	8507.	8343.	16850.	.219	1.020
174.	MUSICAL INSTRUMENTS + PARTS	5250.	17739.	22989.	4287.	7213.	11500.	.296	.594
175.	GAMES + TOYS	5069.	3585.	8654.	3922.	13408.	17330.	1.414	.293
176.	CHILDRENS VEHICLES	6860.	10903.	17763.	4554.	6526.	11080.	.629	.698
177.	MISC. SPORTING GOODS	5180.	8676.	13856.	5305.	6305.	11510.	.597	.826
178.	WRITING INSTRUMENTS + MATERIALS	6630.	15678.	22308.	6327.	7003.	13330.	.423	.904
179.	COSTUME JEWELRY	3260.	5329.	8589.	4988.	5972.	10960.	.612	.835
180.	BUTTONS	5120.	11302.	16422.	4470.	6570.	11040.	.453	.680
181.	NEEDLES, PINS + FASTENERS	6560.	11756.	18316.	6765.	6615.	13380.	.558	1.023
182.	BROOMS + BRUSHES	5800.	5540.	11340.	5336.	5994.	11330.	1.047	.890
183.	HARD FLOOR COVERINGS	28460.	38547.	67007.	15684.	9296.	24980.	.738	1.687
184.	MISCELLANEOUS MANUFACTURES NES	4920.	8842.	13762.	4484.	66316.	10800.	.556	.710

NOTE ON THE CORRESPONDENCE OF THE PRODUCT CATEGORIES WITH THE US STANDARD INDUSTRIAL CLASSIFICATION AND
THE UN STANDARD INTERNATIONAL TRADE CLASSIFICATION, SEE APPENDIX TABLE 2

FOR AN EXPLANATION OF THE DEFINITIONS AND SYMBOLS USED, SEE EQUATIONS (1) AND (3) IN THE TEXT.

APPENDIX TABLE 2

CORRESPONDENCE OF THE SECTOR CLASSIFICATION SCHEME WITH THE
STANDARD INDUSTRIAL CLASSIFICATION AND THE STANDARD
INTERNATIONAL TRADE CLASSIFICATION

Sector	SIC	SITC
001	2211	652.1
002	2221, 2262	653 less 653.2, 653.3, 653.4, 653.9
003	2231	653.2
004	2241	655.5, 655.9
005	2251, 2252, 2256, 2259	841.4 less 841.43, 0.44
006	2253	841.44
007	2254	841.43
008	2261	652.2
009	2271	657.5
010	2272, 2279	657.6, 657.8
011	2281, 2282, 2284	651 less 651.2, .5, .8, .9
012	2283	651.2
013	2291	655.1
014	2292, 2395, 2396, 2397	654.0
015	2293	655.8
016	2294, 2297	262.6, .7, .8, .9; 263.4, 266.23
017	2295	611.2, 655.4
018	2298	655.6
019	2299	651.5, 651.9, 653.3, 653.4, 653.9
020	2311, 2321, 2327, 2328, 2329	841.11
021	2322, 2341	841 less 841.11, 841.12
022	2323, 2342, 2381, 2389	841.2
023	2331, 2335, 2337, 2339 2361, 2363, 2369	841.12
024	2351, 2352	655.7, 841.5
025	2371	842
026	2386, 3151	841.3
027	2391, 2392	656.6, 656.9, 657.7
028	2393	656.1
029	2394	656.2
030	2411, 2491	242
031	2421, 2426, 2429	243, 631.8
032	2431, 2433	632.4
033	2432	631.1, 631.2; 631.4 less 631.42
034	2441, 1442, 2443	632.1
035	2445	632.2
036	2499	244, 631.42, 632.7, 632.8, 633
037	25	821, 895.1
038	2611	251
039	2621	641 less 641.5, 641.6
040	2631, 2641	641.5

APPENDIX TABLE 2 (continued)

Sector	SIC	SITC
041	2642, 2645, 2649, 2761 2782	642.2, 642.3
042	2643, 2651, 2652, 2653, 2654	642.1
043	2646, 2647, 2655	642.9
044	2661	641.6
045	2711, 2721	892.2
046	2731, 2732	892.1, 892.3
047	2741, 2751, 2752, 2771	892.4, 892.9
048	2753, 3555	718.2
049	2812, 2813, 2816, 2819	513 less 513.27, 514, 515, 533.1, 561.1
050	2815, 2818	321.8, 512, 521, 531, 532.3, 551.2
051	2821, 3079	581, 893
052	2822	231.2
053	2823	266.3
054	2824	266.21, 266.22
055	2831, 2833, 2834	541 less 541.9
056	2841, 2842, 2843	554
057	2844	553
058	2851	533.3
059	2861	241.2, 532 less 532.3, 599.6
060	2871, 2872	561 less 561.1
061	2879	599.2
062	2891	599.5
063	2892	571.1, 571.2
064	2893	533.2
065	2895	513.27
066	2899	551.1, 571.3, 599.7
067	2911, 2992, 2999	331 less 331.01; 332
068	2951, 2952	661.8
069	3011	629.1
070	3021, 3141, 3142	851
071	3031	231.3
072	3069	621, 629 less 629.1, 841.6
073	3111	611 less 611.2
074	3121	612.1
075	3131	612.3
076	3161, 3171, 3172	831
077	3199	612.2, 612.9
078	3211	644.3, 664.4, 664.5
079	3221, 3229, 3231	651.8, 664 less 664.3, 664.4, 664.5; 665
080	3241, 3273	661.2
081	3251, 3253, 3259	662.4
082	3255, 3297	662.3, 663.7
083	3261	812.2

APPENDIX TABLE 2 (continued)

Sector	SIC	SITC
084	3262	666.4
085	3263	666.5
086	3264, 3269	663.9, 666.6, 723.2
087	3271, 3272	663.6
088	3274	666.1
089	3275	273.2
090	3281	661.3
091	3291	663.1, 663.2, 697.9
092	3292, 3293	663.8, 663.2, 697.9
093	3296	663.5
094	3299	663.4
095	3312, 3313, 3315, 3316, 3317, 3566, 3481, 3493	693.2, 693.3, 694.1, 698.3, 698.6, 719.9, 67 less 671.3, 678.1, 678.5, 679
096	3321, 3322, 3494, 3497	678.1, 678.5, 679.1, 719.92
097	3323	679.2
098	3351	682 less 682.1
099	3352	684 less 684.1
100	3356, 3357	681, 683.2, 685.2, 686.2, 687.2, 688, 689 less 689.13, 693.1, 723.1
101	3361, 3461	697.2
102	3362, 3369, 3392	698.9
103	3391	679.3, 698.4
104	3399	671.3
105	3411, 3491, 3496	692.2
106	3421	696
107	3423	695.1, 695.22, 695.23
108	3425	695.21
109	3429	698.1
110	3431, 3432	812.3
111	3433	719.13, 812.1
112	3441, 3442, 3444, 3446, 3449	619, 693.4
113	3443	692.1, 692.3, 711.1, 711.2, 711.7
114	3452	694.2
115	3492	698.2
116	3499	719.66, 729.91
117	3511	711.3, 711.6, 711.8
118	3519, 3714	711.5
119	3522	712, 719.64
120	3531, 3532, 3533, 3544, 3545	695.24, 695.25, 695.26, 718.4, 718.51, 719.91, 719.54
121	3534, 3535, 3536	719.31
122	3537	719.32
123	3541, 3542	715.1

APPENDIX TABLE 2 (continued)

Sector	SIC	STIC
124	3548, 3553	715.22, 715.23, 729.6, 719.52, 719.53
125	3551	718.3, 719.62
126	3552, 3582, 3633	717.1 less 717.14, 725.02
127	3554	718.1
128	3559	715.21, 717.1 less all but 717.14, 717.2, 718.5 less 718.51, 719.19, 719.51, 719.61, 719.8
129	3561, 3564, 3586	719.21, 719.22
130	3562	719.7
131	3567, 3623	719.14, 729.92
132	3569	719.11, 719.23
133	3572	714.1
134	3573	714.3
135	3574	714.2
136	3576	719.63
137	3579	714.91
138	3581	719.65
139	3585	719.12, 719.15
140	3599	719.99
141	3611	729.5, 729.99
142	3612, 3621	722.1
143	3624	729.96
144	3631	697.1
145	3632, 3639	719.4, 725.01
146	3634, 3635	725 less 725.01, 725.02
147	3636	717.3
148	3641	729.2, 729.42
149	3642	729.94, 812.4
150	3651, 3662	724 less 724.91, 729.7, 729.93, 891.1
151	3652	891.2
152	3661	724.91
153	3671, 3672, 3673, 3674, 3679	722.2, 729.3, 729.95, 729.98
154	3691	729.12
155	3692	729.11
156	3693	726
157	3694	729.41
158	3711, 3712, 3713	732 less 732.9
159	3715, 3791, 3799	733.3
160	3721	734 less 734.92
161	3722, 3723, 2739	711.4, 734.92
162	3731, 3732	735
163	3741	731.1, 731.2, 731.3
164	3742	731 less 731.1, 731.2, 731.3
165	3751	732.9, 733.1

APPENDIX TABLE 2 (continued)

Sector	SIC	SITC
166	3811, 3821, 3822	861.8, 861.9 less 861.92, 861.94
167	3831	861.1, 861.3
168	3841, 3842, 3843	541.9, 733.4, 861.7, 899.6
169	3851	861.2
170	3861	861.4, 861.5, 861.6, 862
171	3871	864
172	3911, 3912, 3914	897.1
173	3913	667
174	3931	891 less 891.1, 892
175	3941, 3942	894.2
176	3943	894.1
177	3949	894.4
178	3951, 3952, 3953, 3955	895 less 895.1
179	3961	897.2
180	3963	899.5
181	3964	698.5
182	3991	899.2
183	3996	657.4
184	3999	613, 861.92, 861.94, 894.5, 899 less 899.2, 899.5, 899.6

12 The Exchange Rate Regime and the Integration of the World Economy

William M. Corden
Australian National University, Canberra

INTRODUCTION

The original purpose of this paper was to discuss the implications of the present exchange rate regime and the one that preceded it. What are its implications for economic growth, for the international division of labour, and for co-operation in economic development?

In fact its implications are somewhat indirect. Exchange rates are monetary phenomena and the exchange rate regime is important mainly for its effects on monetary policies, and more generally on aggregate demand policies. The effects on such matters as economic growth depend on how demand policies affect economic growth. The central issue turns out to be the integration or disintegration of the world economy. The exchange rate regime influences the transmission of disturbances and of monetary trends between countries, and the degree to which countries can carry on independent monetary policies. This, in turn, does have wide-ranging effects, notably on economic stability; and, indirectly, on growth.

Section I of this paper will deal with the key characteristics of the present system, which will be compared with the preceding Bretton Woods system, as well as with the two polar theoretical systems of completely fixed rates and free-floating rates. Section II considers the implications for growth, stability, and the division of labour. Finally, Section III discusses at the level of general theory an issue of current importance, namely, to what extent world economic recovery depends on the economic recovery of the major nations, especially the United States, Germany, and Japan. This issue is closely related to the central theme of this paper, which is the degree of integration of the world's economy.

I shall be concerned only with the market economies, excluding the socialist countries. Furthermore, I shall not deal with special problems of developing countries. In general I shall have the OECD countries in mind, although most of the discussion is as applicable to developing market economies as to the developed ones.[1]

I. THE PRESENT SYSTEM

It is well known that the present exchange rate system is a very varied one.[2] A few major countries float their currencies relative to the dollar, with little or no

[1] I am indebted to H. W. Arndt, and to other members of the Economics Seminar, Research School of Pacific Studies, Australian National University, for valuable comments on an earlier draft.
[2] International Monetary Fund, *Annual Report for 1976* (Washington, 1976) pp. 24–7, 70–2.

intervention. Some intervene a great deal but make no kind of exchange-rate commitment. Some have fixed their rates to particular other currencies, or to a basket of currencies, or the SDR (which is a particular basket of currencies).

What is really comes to is that we have an international *laissez-faire* system (endorsed by the 1976 Jamaica Agreement) where few governments of larger economies feel genuinely inhibited about exchange-rate alterations. Any fixed exchange rate mystique has gone. Even the countries that are part of the European snake, and so have tied their currencies to the D-mark, have not made any firm, long-term commitments. Notably France – the government of which usually advocates fixed rates in international counsels – has felt free to join and leave the snake several times. The system is not *laissez-faire* in the Adam Smith sense that governments do not intervene and all action is private action. Rather, there is *laissez-faire* for governments or their monetary authorities, since they are not subject to international inhibitions or controls. By contrast, in a truly fixed rate system they are not free; they are committed to a price, namely the exchange rate. Similarly, if they were committed to a free-floating system they would not be free; they would be committed to a quantity, namely the quantity of foreign exchange reserves, the level of which should not alter if they do not intervene in the foreign exchange market. Only in the system of managed floating – which we have now for key countries – are they committed neither to a price nor to a quantity. In this system the monetary authorities buy and sell foreign claims – mainly dollars – for various reasons. They may aim to stabilise the exchange rate temporarily; they may aim to smooth fluctuations in it; or they may simply be engaging in what they believe to be optimal variations in official lending or borrowing from the United States or its banks.

Alternative Systems

The Bretton Woods system of 'fixed but adjustable par values' was certainly not a truly fixed rate system. Countries often did alter their exchange rates, usually devaluing in relation to the dollar. It differed from the present system in two ways. First, adjustments were larger and more jerky; secondly, there was some attempt to keep rates fixed. The first characteristic has often been discussed, and its disadvantages noted. In particular, it led to destabilising speculation involving profits for speculators at the expense of central banks. But the second characteristic is more relevant to the present discussion. There was some attempt to maintain the par values. The degree of commitment to fixity of rates, though never absolute, was certainly much greater than it is now. If we envisage a continuum with a system with absolute commitment to fixed rates at one end – that is, a system of true monetary integration – and a system at the other end where no virtue at all is seen in maintaining constant the relative prices of any two moneys for even a limited period of time – then the world has moved significantly in the direction of the latter. The 1976 Jamaica Agreement endorsed the *fait accompli* of this move, but it is clear that the idea of moving back in the other direction – whether for the world as a whole or for groups of countries – is still in the air and has certainly not been given up by many interested persons.[3] It is also still an issue whether limited areas of complete monetary integration – i.e. areas within which exchange rates are irrevocably fixed even though they may alter together relative to the outside world – should be established at some stage. I need hardly mention the currently moribund European monetary integration proposal.

In comparing these various systems the central point from which all else follows would seem to be that in a fixed rate system the economies are monetarily integrated while a flexible exchange rate system gives countries monetary independence. Putting it very simply: in a fixed-rate system, when the rest of the world inflates, the country must inflate also. More specifically, the monetary policies of the major economies, especially of the United States, will govern its own policies. In contrast, if the exchange rate is flexible the country can inflate ahead of the rest of the world, reconciling its excess inflation rate with external balance by continuous depreciation of the currency; or it can follow a less inflationary policy than the rest of the world, appreciating its currency appropriately. One can then say that the movement from the Bretton Woods system to the present system has increased the monetary independence of many countries.

The Inflation Transmission Process in the Fixed-rate System

Let me spell out further the transmission process in a fixed-rate system.[4] I shall consider the case of a country such as Germany. Germany, initially, has a rate of price and wage inflation below that of its trading partners, and it is running a current account surplus. The exchange rate need not be irrevocably fixed, but it is fixed for the time being; and while it is, this sort of transmission process is likely to take place. I shall distinguish the price transmission of inflation from monetary transmission.

(*a*) *Price transmission.* Prices of the country's tradeable goods will tend to rise along with world prices, while prices of non-tradeables will rise less. The continuous change in relative prices will bring about production shifts (toward the tradeables) that will lead to an increasing current account surplus, as well as a continuous squeeze on real incomes of non-tradeable-goods producers. All this assumes that monetary and fiscal policies allow this process to go on.

At this stage one can say only that there has been a transmission of foreign inflation to the tradeable-goods sector. If the country wishes to maintain a rate

[3]On the Jamaica Agreement, and the state of international monetary reform, see A. Kafka, *The International Monetary Fund: Reform without Reconstruction*, Essays in International Finance, No. 118 (Princeton, 1976); and E. M. Bernstein, *et al.*, *Reflections on Jamaica*, Essays in International Finance, No. 115 (Princeton, 1976).

[4]There is an extensive literature on the inflation transmission process. See L. B. Krause and W. S. Salant, *Worldwide Inflation* (Brookings Institution, Washington, 1977); and also W. H. Branson, 'Monetarist and Keynesian Models of the Transmission of Inflation', *American Economic Review*, 65 (1975).

of domestic price increase (an average of tradeable and non-tradeable-goods inflation) which is lower than the world rate of inflation, it would have to regulate monetary and fiscal policies in order to ensure that for every rise in the foreign, and hence tradeable-goods, inflation rate, there is also an appropriate decline in the domestically generated, non-tradeable-goods inflation rate. If there is downward rigidity of money wages, or a downward limit to the rate of increase in money wages, full offsetting of the tradeable-goods inflation may not be possible, and a rise in foreign inflation will then, indeed, lead to some rise in the average rate of domestic inflation.

(*b*) *Monetary transmission.* A current account surplus means that the private sector or the public sector or both are continuously accumulating financial assets or reducing liabilities. The argument that in a fixed-rate system foreign inflation must eventually be transmitted through the monetary mechanism rests on the idea that such continuous accumulation cannot go on, or even if it can technically, it will not in practice do so because countries will not find it in their interests to let it go on. They will eventually have to, or want to, inflate their surplus away. Thus, there will eventually be *monetary* transmission of inflation to supplement the price transmission.

In monetary terms, the continuance of the surplus requires sterilisation of monetary inflows. The rise in the foreign assets of the banking system must be offset by an appropriate decline in the domestic assets. But even if this is technically possible, it is a situation of continuous portfolio disequilibrium, having possibly to be maintained by a continuously growing budget surplus. A distinction might be drawn between *automatic* transmission of inflation in so far as sterilisation is efficiently and speedily conducted, there will eventually be policy transmission. A growing surplus may be possible, but it is unlikely to be thought desirable. It will not be compatible with portfolio equilibrium of the public sector.

All this can be avoided with a flexible exchange rate. A rise in foreign prices can be associated with an appropriate appreciation of the currency so that the domestic currency prices of tradeables rise no faster than the domestic prices of non-tradeables. If the central bank does not intervene in the foreign exchange market at all, the balance of payments will stay in equilibrium. The central bank will not acquire any foreign assets, and therefore, it will not be faced with the choice of either decreasing the domestic assets of the banking system (sterilisation) or allowing the money supply to increase (import of inflation).

Transmission Processes in the Flexible-rate System

What I have presented thus far is a very simple argument which has often been propounded; namely, that a flexible exchange rate system, unlike a fixed-rate one, enables a country's monetary authorities to regulate the supply of money according to their choice, or at least leaves them as free to do so as they would be in a closed economy. In contrast, this is not always possible in a fixed-rate system because of the difficulty of sterilisation, which even if technically possible will not usually be thought desirable for any length of time. Now this needs to be qualified. In a flexible rate system *real* disturbances will still be transmitted from country to country, and these may have monetary consequences. It is still possible to import inflation from abroad.

A domestic relative price change may result from changes in foreign conditions. With money wages tending to be rigid downwards, though flexible upwards, to avoid unemployment this relative price change will then have to involve a rise in the general price level. Three highly relevant examples can be given.

(*a*) *Short-term capital inflow*. Foreign developments bring about a short-term disturbance in the capital market. Capital flows into a country, perhaps because of an increase in foreign savings or a reduction in investment opportunities abroad. The currency of the country appreciates as part of the transfer process. Since one is concerned with a portfolio adjustment the whole process will be temporary. Furthermore, short-term capital responds readily to changes in expectations, so that the movement may be reversed very suddenly. With a flexible exchange rate the country will find the prices of its tradeable goods, and possibly the general price-level, fluctuating in response to capital movements. To avoid absolute falls in the prices of its tradeable goods (in order to avoid unemployment in that sector when money wages are rigid downwards), it may need to make a monetary expansion some part of the adjustment. The adjustment will then be brought about by a rise in the prices of non-traded goods rather than a fall in the domestic prices of traded goods.

(*b*) *Improvement in terms of trade*. Suppose that the major world economies experience a boom. There will be a shift in the terms of trade in favour of raw materials producers, because prices of manufactured goods and wages in industrial countries tend to be somewhat less flexible upwards than prices of basic materials. A raw material exporting country will find the prices of both its exports and its imports rising, but export prices will rise relatively more. It can certainly appreciate its currency as the world boom develops and so avoid a rise in its average domestic price-level, and hence any need for monetary expansion. But in that case it would be left with an absolute fall in the domestic prices of importables. In the presence of downward rigidity of money wages this might lead to unemployment in the import-competing sector. So the authorities may prefer to appreciate rather less – just sufficient for the domestic prices of importables to stay constant. With export prices higher it will be necessary for the prices of non-traded goods to rise to maintain balance in the non-traded market as well as external balance. Finally, the average domestic price-level will have risen, a rise which will be associated with a monetary expansion. The original current account surplus would have been eliminated partly by appreciation and partly by monetary expansion. There will have been a transmission of foreign inflation even though the exchange rate instrument was available.

(*c*) *Deterioration in terms of trade*. A similar story applies in the case of a raw material importer, such as the United Kingdom, where the terms of trade deteriorate as a result of a world boom.

At a constant exchange rate, with the money-wage level initially given, and with monetary policy aimed at internal balance, the UK balance of payments may improve or worsen, depending on the price elasticity of demand for imported commodities. The more realistic assumption is that the elasticity is less than unity, so that the balance of payments deteriorates. (This is the assumption one makes when analysing the effects of the oil-price rise, to which this analysis applies completely.) Sterling then depreciates. The sterling prices of imports rise, firstly because their foreign currency prices rose (the terms of trade deteriorated), and secondly because of the depreciation. The prices of exportables will rise, though to a lesser extent, because of the depreciation. With money wage rigidity downwards the prices of non-tradeables will not fall, or at least their fall will be limited by the extent to which profit margins in that sector can be squeezed. On balance, then, the average price level will rise, and monetary policy will have to be sufficiently expansionary to ensure full employment with this higher price level. Hence, price inflation has been imported by the United Kingdom: continuous inflation if the terms of trade continuously deteriorate, and otherwise a once-for-all price rise.

This story could be continued to bring in another familiar consideration. The foreign relative price change may not just bring about a once-and-for-all rise in the average price level, but it may have a continuous effect. We no longer assume that the money wage level stays constant. After a while, the price rise stimulates money wage increases aimed to restore real wage levels. Further monetary expansion is then needed to maintain employment. This will be followed by further depreciation, which further raises prices, wages, and so on. An inflationary process has thus been generated by the terms of trade effects on the world boom. Inflation results from an attempt to maintain a level of real wages which is no longer compatible with the terms of trade. Essentially, this inflationary process is brought about by the *real* effects of the world boom. The workers in Britain are made poorer as a result of the terms of trade deterioration, and in their attempt to shift this loss away from themselves an inflationary process is set in motion.

The general conclusion is that while it is indeed true that a considerable degree of monetary independence can be obtained once the exchange rate constraint is abandoned, domestic monetary policies will still be affected by the outside world through external influences on domestic prices. Unless countries choose to cut themselves off from world trade and capital flows they cannot be fully insulated.

II. THE EXCHANGE RATE REGIME AND ECONOMIC GROWTH

In what ways might an exchange rate regime affect economic growth? One might query whether there is any relationship at all. After all, under the Bretton Woods system which operated from 1945 to 1971 it was possible for the high growth rate of Japan to coexist with the low rate of Britain. Since the period of managed floating began we have had the great boom or 'growth' year of 1973 as well as the slump of 1974–75. One might conclude that growth depends on many things which are, no doubt, the subject of many papers at this Congress; but international monetary arrangements are unlikely to be significant. Yet it has certainly been popular among politicians and journalists to blame the world monetary system (or the current non-system) for the world's economic troubles. The feeling that there is some connection between the international monetary and trading system, on the one hand, and domestic economic prosperity. on the other, lies behind numerous so-called high-level conferences, seminars, and the like.

In the 1960s it was common in Britain to blame the country's problems and low-growth rate on the commitment of successive governments to maintaining the sterling exchange rate, supposedly because of some 'exchange rate fetishism' or because of a desire to prevent the 'collapse' of the international monetary system. In addition, the concern at the time with a shortage of international liquidity reflected a fear of deflation and resultant low growth. At present it is quite common to blame instability of export earnings as well as domestic unemployment on the international monetary system. Concern with the exchange rate regime also figures in discussions about the New International Economic Order.

A simple but agnostic answer to the question of how the exchange rate regime affects growth is the following. Presumably there is some appropriate monetary policy that will help to attain the optimal rate of growth and more generally to maximise the social welfare of a particular country, given the constraints of other policies. Probably it is stability of the rate of inflation rather than the magnitude of the rate of inflation that is relevant. In the short run, policies that lead to more inflation may well raise a country's rate of growth, but it would be at the cost of slowing it down later. The relationship between monetary policy and rate of growth is itself a large subject which I shall not pursue here. I shall assume for the moment that monetary stability and predictability foster growth and instability and that uncertainty handicaps it.

The issue, then, is whether in any particular case the monetary authorities would pursue a more stable (and hence pro-growth) policy when they are free agents – that is, when their country is insulated from the world with a flexible exchange rate – than they would if compelled to import the stability or instability of the rest of the world. If we are concerned with fostering the social welfare of the various national members of the international community, the pursuit of an optimal rate of growth being one ingredient of this, then we would favour a flexible rate system (if we believed that national governments and monetary authorities are the best judges of their own countries' economic welfare and pursue, in some sense, national goals). On the other hand we would favour a fixed rate regime if we felt that countries would be better off being subject to the monetary policies of the major nations, especially the United States, which between them determine the world rate of inflation.

If one wanted to give advice to countries about the choice of exchange rate regime from the point of view of economic growth, one would first have to decide how monetary policies affect economic growth. My own view is that stable policies are more conducive to growth, except in the very short run. This does not necessarily mean stable rates of growth of money supply (M), however it is defined. It is more likely to mean reasonably stable rates of growth of money expenditure (MV), at least relative to growth in labour productivity. This is certainly contrary to a view that was popular in Britain until 1973, namely, that high rates of growth require the maintenance on a continuous basis of high levels of 'pressure of demand'. The difficulty about this latter view is that it does not allow for the endogeneity of wages. Next, one would have to decide whether one expects the monetary policies of the principal world nations – especially the United States – to be more or less favourable to growth than the policies of particular countries if left to themselves. For example, if one advises the political or monetary authorities of a country to commit that country to an exchange rate fixed to the US dollar, one is really saying that one has no faith in that country's authorities and thinks it would be better if their policies were tied to those of the United States.

It is not easy to say whether a firm exchange rate commitment is desirable. Until the mid-sixties the United States pursued policies of stability. Hence a commitment to fixed rates relative to the dollar meant essentially that other countries imported stability. For a country such as Britain, this meant in inhibition to inflation, which at least in the short run could be seen as having anti-growth effects but which in the medium run avoided the sort of inflationary explosion – and inevitable growth-inhibiting, counter-inflationary policies later – that we have seen in 1973–75. But the US policy stance changed, and after a time a country such as Germany could take the view that it could protect its stability only by breaking with the fixed exchange rate system and appreciating its currency. Today one might suggest to a country that for the sake of stability and growth, it should tie its exchange rate to the D-mark. But can one be sure that Germany will always follow stable monetary policies?

The issue of a fixed exchange rate commitment seems rather academic now. It is improbable that a firm, binding commitment to maintain fixed rates will be entered into by many countries. If a country's exchange rate is fixed to that of another currency, or to a basket, it can only be a temporary, uncertain commitment. There is no real external discipline. Rather, economic costs are imposed by sharp changes in exchange rates, and by the sharp changes in policy direction that go with it. If it is better for growth that private planning be based on predictable policies and wage contracts on correct expectations, it is surely desirable to have gradual changes rather than sharp and unpredictable ones. This is indeed the familiar argument against the Bretton Woods system of stable but adjustable par values.

Managed Floating and Growth

So far I have compared a fixed rate system with a flexible-rate one, the main point being that in a fixed-rate system a country loses freedom in its monetary policies, other than in the short term, when some sterilisation of domestic effects may be possible. Another comparison to make is between free floating and managed floating. In the managed floating case, monetary authorities have the freedom to engage in 'accommodating' official borrowing or lending, perhaps to offset fluctuations in short-term private capital movements. In a free-floating system they do not allow themselves this freedom. Which system is more conducive to growth?

One would expect that no simple answer can be given. If private capital movements are erratic, perhaps in response to irrationally changing expectations, official intervention managed by wise non-erratic officials may foster stability, and so perhaps growth. But perhaps the private capital movements are based on correct expectations of wise sceptical corporate treasurers, while governments try to sustain exchange rates at unsustainable levels, thus substituting erratic large changes for predictable small ones. One might expect growth, or at least the efficiency of the economy, to be hindered by this, Whether foreign borrowing or lending by the government fosters or retards the growth of national income (as distinct from national product) depends on how foreign rates of return obtainable on foreign exchange holdings or other investments compare with local social rates of return.[5]

Finally, it should be noted that probably growth is fostered by policies that encourage (though not *over*-encourage) flows of international trade and investment.

The Exchange Rate Regime and the International Division of Labour

What sort of exchange rate regime encourages the free flow of international trade and investment – and hence the international division of labour? There are two considerations. First, let us provisionally assume that restrictions on trade, such as tariffs and quotas, and controls on capital movements, are unaffected by the choice of exchange rate regime. The main point now is that unpredictably fluctuating exchange rates are inconvenient to trade. There is certainly no clear evidence that the widespread floating of exchange rates since March 1973 had adverse effects on trade, but from *a priori* reasoning one might conclude that, other things equal, it is better for international trade and investment flows that there are firmly fixed rates between different moneys. This certainly makes a case for wise intervention in a managed floating system.

But one cannot argue for fixed rates on these grounds: other things are *not*

---

[5] A discussion of the broader welfare issues of the choice of exchange rate regime, the optimality of intervention or maintaining particular rates, and so on, is in J. Williamson, 'Payments Objectives and Economic Welfare', *Staff Papers*, XX, November 1973.

equal. It is also better for international trade and investment flows that the value of domestic money in terms of domestic and foreign goods stays constant, or is predictable. If there is foreign inflation, then to fix the domestic currency to the foreign one means fixing it to foreign money but not to foreign or domestic goods. Trade in moneys may be helped, but conversion of moneys into goods, and vice versa, will not be. A steady and appropriate appreciation of the domestic currency combined with stable domestic monetary policies may fix the value of the local currency in terms of goods, either domestic or foreign. This is likely to be more beneficial for economic efficiency and growth than fixing it in terms of foreign money. There may thus be a case for managed floating – indeed there is bound to be a case for 'wise managing' – but on such grounds there is no strong case for fixing rates. The issue remains whether the exchange rate regime encourages monetary policies to be more stable.

The second consideration is by far the most important. It is also well known, so I can be brief. Fixed rates, or temporary commitments to fixed rates, as in the Bretton Woods system, encourage the use of trade and investment restrictions to deal with balance of payments problems. The fact that the relatively free international trading and investment system was not destroyed by the crisis of 1974–75 must be due to a considerable extent to the fact that in 1974 countries felt free to alter exchange rates. A flexible rate system therefore certainly helps the international division of labour. This is probably the most important single argument in favour of flexible rates. It is true that sometimes countries may control private capital flows in order to avoid changes in exchange rates – in turn, in order to avoid effects on domestic relative prices and sectional real incomes – but it does seem that, on balance, such flows are less likely to be controlled when the two distinct freedoms of floating and of managing the float are available to the authorities.

Co-operation in Economic Development

Part of the title for this session of the Congress is 'co-operation for economic development'. What is the relevance of the exchange rate regime and international monetary arrangements for this? It will be recalled that this paper is not concerned with problems specific to developing countries, and therefore I do not deal with aid, the aid-SDR link, and so on.

A number of points can be made, following simply from the earlier discussion. In a fixed system – or one where there is some commitment, if not irrevocable, to fixed rates – co-operation in monetary and fiscal policies is more necessary than in a flexible-rate regime. Countries are more dependent on each other; the larger economies, especially, can more easily destabilise the smaller ones, and the larger economies themselves are more interdependent. Since co-operation and international conferences are not virtues in themselves (unless monetary union is seen as a road to political union, as it naively was in Europe at one time), this hardly makes a case for fixed rates.

Nevertheless, even in a flexible-rate regime countries remain interdependent, as outlined earlier. The ups and downs of the United States affect the terms of trade of many countries and can have seriously destabilising effects. Even if we prefer the international *laissez-faire* system, where each major country makes its own adjustments to the events of the outside world and to changing domestic trade-offs and preferences, it remains true that national adjustments are best made with maximum information, with maximum warning of external shocks, and indeed with the least such shocks. Beyond that, it need only be pointed out that customs unions and various acts of bilateral or regional co-operation do not require fixed rates. Perhaps it is only for fiscal integration that monetary integration becomes a prerequisite.[6]

III. DOES WORLD RECOVERY DEPEND ON THE UNITED STATES?

It was often said in 1976 and early 1977 that world recovery in output, profits and rates of growth depended on recovery in the United States, Germany, and Japan, most especially the first two. The implication of innumerable newspaper articles, often based on ideas fed from official sources and on discussions at OECD meetings, was that countries such as Britain and France could not restore their economies unless the largest economies led the way. Unemployment in Britain and France was thus blamed on the recession in the United States. An American or German expansion would lead to a favourable multiplier effect in other countries. While I shall be referring to US expansion here, more recently the pressure seems to have been put particularly on Germany to expand.[7]

The preceding discussion in this paper is certainly relevant to this popular approach. It rests on the idea that there is still an important degree of monetary integration between countries. More particularly, it seems to rest on two assumptions. First, output, profits, and growth are demand-determined, at least to a significant extent in the short run. Secondly, exchange rates are fixed. One can perhaps concede the first assumption. But what of the second? Is this approach not based on fixed exchange-rate thinking in a world where exchange

[6]See W. M. Corden, *Monetary Integration*, Essay in International Finance, No. 93 (Princeton, 1972).

[7]See *Newsweek*, 14 March 1977, p. 19. 'The big issue in Europe as spring approaches is ... how long the West Germans can resist the importunities of the U.S. and their European neighbors to heal up the German economy in order to speed up the pace of recovery in the rest of the industrialized world.' The same day the United Press sent the following dispatch from Ottawa. 'The Western world was counting on the U.S. to lead it out of its current economic doldrums, the British Prime Minister, Mr Callaghan, said yesterday. He told a news conference following the first of his two scheduled talks with the Canadian Prime Minister, Mr Trudeau: "We know and understand that the success of the U.S. means the success of all of us." Mr Callaghan said there were 12 million people unemployed in Western industrialised countries and predicted that without some concerted economic action they would face "slow growth, high unemployment and increased balance of payments problems."'

rates are no longer constrained? If the British monetary authorities wish to engage in a monetary expansion without the US having expanded and without creating a balance of payments problem, they are surely free to do so provided they are willing to allow sterling to depreciate. In this way the extra UK demand could be wholly diverted on to UK goods. This is so elementary a proposition from the 'theory of internal and external balance' that one feels that there must be more to the popular argument. Let me explore a number of possible ways of rescuing it.

(1) US Expansion a Sufficient but not Necessary Condition: It is true that in the short run a US expansion would lead to monetary expansion in many other countries, as it has in the past. First, exchange rates are not generally *free*-floating, so that exchange-rate appreciations relative to the dollar would not be rapid enough to avoid some domestic impact in other countries even if this insulation were desired. Secondly, monetary sterilisation, even if it were desired, is not usually rapid or complete enough to avoid some transmission of the US expansion. But this does not rescue the popular argument. A US expansion is a sufficient condition for short-term expansion in other countries, but not a necessary one.

Countries would indeed get their domestic expansions if the US expanded – especially if they wanted it and avoided either rapid appreciation or sterilisation. But they could still have their expansions without the United States expanding. If the US expanded, the money supplies of other countries would increase because the *foreign assets* of their banking systems increased. In the absence of the US expansion the same money supply increases could be brought about by expansion of the *domestic assets* of the banking systems.

(2) Fear of 'Beggar-my-Neighbour' Devaluations: It might be argued that countries are not in practice willing to devalue sufficiently to improve the competitiveness of their traded-goods industries so as to offset the adverse balance of payments effects of a domestic expansion greater than in other countries. Further, even if they did try to devalue to the necessary extent, other countries would not let them, devaluing in relation to the dollar or SDR themselves. They would regard the original devaluating as a 'competitive devaluation'. In other words, there is a rigidity in *real* exchange rates, meaning exchange rates in relation to relative domestic cost-levels. But this is not convincing.

If other countries did react in such an adverse way to an expanding economy's attempt to maintain its balance of payments position, it would be a highly irrational reaction. The fact is that the traded goods industries of other countries benefit from the consequences of the expansion and lose from the consequences of the devaluation. The aim is simply for the two effects to be offset, so that on average the neighbours will not be 'beggared'.

(3) Low Elasticities: Reluctance to engage in unilateral expansion may reflect 'elasticity pessimism'. It is true that foreign trade elasticities tend to be

low in the short run, but they are usually sufficiently high in the long run for devaluations associated with policies of domestic stability ('internal balance') to be effective.[8] A country that expands ahead of its neighbours and wants to avoid a very large devaluation at the same time is thus likely to go into current-account deficit for some time, though this may be eliminated after a while, and perhaps converted into a surplus. If private speculators foresee that the current account will improve in time, then private capital movements may cover the short-term deficit. Otherwise it would be quite proper to use official reserves for the purpose, the central bank, in effect, doing the speculating.

(4) One-Sided View of US Expansion: The following one-sided argument might also be made. If the US expands, the demand for UK exports will expand. Given initial unemployment and excess capacity in the UK, employment in the UK will then increase without much pressure on wages and prices. The UK balance of payments will improve, which will make possible an appreciation of sterling (or lesser depreciation than would have happened for other reasons). This appreciation will actually raise real wages, and so moderate any pressures for money wage increases. This process can then be compared favourably with the effects of a unilateral UK expansion. In this case also, in the first instance, UK employment would increase. But the extra demand for imports and some diversion of potential exports to the home market would worsen the balance of payments. As pointed out earlier, it would be necessary to devalue, which would raise prices and lower real wages, and the favourable effect of the devaluation on the balance of payments and employment would be negated. If this were followed by further devaluation, a wage–price–devaluation spiral would have been initiated.

The argument seems persuasive, and it is certainly familiar. The fallacy is that it considers the effects of the US expansion only on the demand for UK exports and ignores the effect on import prices. It assumes that the UK terms of trade improve. But it must be remembered that the rise in UK import prices that normally results from a world expansion will lower real wages directly and, in so far as it worsens the balance of payments and thus gives rise to devaluation, also indirectly. When the effects of higher export demand and higher import prices are combined, it is by no means clear which way real wages would move in the first instance and hence whether pressure on money wages to increase would be weakened or strengthened. As a first approximation one should, presumably, look at the net effects on the terms of trade.

(5) Terms of Trade Effects of US Expansion Let us now consider the effects of a US and world expansion on exporters of basic commodities. Such an

---

[8]A good case study in support of this view is in J. R. Artus, 'The 1967 Devaluation of Sterling', *Staff Papers*, XXII, November 1975. The crucial caveat is 'associated with policies of domestic stability'. It must be stressed that for elasticities to be relevant there has to be a real relative price change.

expansion would improve their terms of trade, since the prices of basic commodities relative to manufactures usually rise in a boom.

From the broad income point of view, it is obvious that commodity exporters should welcome such expansion. But the main point to be made here is that monetary expansion in these countries would probably be less inflationary, and hence easier, in this situation. Their Phillips curves will move in a favourable direction.

In the absence of the improvement in their terms of trade, and with exchange rate flexibility, a domestic monetary expansion would lead to depreciation and, in the first instance, a reduction in real wages. In time money wages would rise, so partially or wholly restoring the original real wage levels and reversing the original increases in employment. But if at the same time the terms of trade improved owing to the US expansion, the depreciation might be avoided (on balance there might even be an appreciation), the domestic currency prices of imports might not need to rise, and it might be possible to avoid an initial fall in real wages, and so an eventual reversal of the increase in employment owing to a compensating money wage increase.

But the matter is different *for importers* of basic commodities. In a world of flexible exchange rates it seems strange for the British Chancellor of the Exchequer, and presumably the governments of quite a few other commodity-importing countries, to welcome or urge a US expansion. These countries are competitive with the US – not complementary. When the US, Germany, and Japan expand, the terms of trade turn *against* Britain and France. Surely their full employment policies will become more difficult, at least if there is some tendency towards real wage rigidity downwards.

UK real wages are likely to fall when the UK terms of trade deteriorate. The rise in import prices will provoke money wage increases designed to compensate, followed by devaluation, followed by further wage increases and so on. In so far as real wages finally recover to the pre-expansion situation, there will be increased unemployment. A deterioration in the terms of trade will shift the short-term Phillips curve in an unfavourable direction and may also raise the 'natural' rate of unemployment.

To summarise, one could probably argue that a world expansion would benefit those countries which would gain improved terms of trade as a result. But even in these cases a sudden expansion would give rise to domestic adjustment problems, and the benefits may be more potential – depending on wise concurrent domestic policies – than actual. As for other countries, such as the UK, one can argue that they are free to expand domestic monetary demand now, if they really believed that this would help their domestic problems and provided they were willing to alter exchange rates appropriately and accept the consequences of this. One suggests that their reluctance to expand monetary demand reflects a correct assessment that the benefits for employment would only be short-term, and the costs in increased domestic price inflation would not be worth it.

13 The Developing Countries' Gain from Export Prices Indexation: a Crude Model

J. Bénard
University of Paris, France

INTRODUCTION

It is possible, with the help of a very aggregated model, to study some of the economic aspects of price indexation of primary products exports from developing countries with respect to prices of their imports from industrialised countries.[1] This model is crude in the sense that it is extremely aggregated and ignores such important phenomena as oligopolistic international trade and international monetary flows. The model deals with an international trade that is restricted to two goods and two sets of countries: (i) the manufactured good produced exclusively by the set of all industrialised countries belonging to the market economy, and (ii) the non-oil primary product supplied exclusively by the set of all non-oil producing developing countries but competing, on the industrialised countries' market, with a substitute which is produced by industrialised economies and is therefore considered a manufactured good.

On the basis of a simple, static, macroeconomic model that confronts aggregate supply and demand functions for primary exports, a cost function of the manufactured good, and an equilibrium equation of this simplified international trade, we aim to determine the following:

(*a*) the equilibrium conditions of this trade, first without and then with indexation;
(*b*) the gain for developing countries from indexation and its sensibility to variations of demand or supply;
(*c*) the evolution of this gain through time and its behaviour when the buffer stock balance is wholly equilibrated over a period of several years.

The parameters of the model have been statistically estimated for the period 1955–74, and the results have been applied to our problem of the gain from indexation. We have dealt exclusively with a 'direct indexation procedure'; that is, with a barter term of trade freezing. Although this model may be useful for studying the most simple indirect indexation procedure, which freezes the 'income terms of trade', we do not deal here with that type of indexation.

[1] We thought of this model when we were participating in a very short-lived UNCTAD advisory working group chaired by Professor Houthakker, which met in Geneva during the spring of 1975 for studying the ways and consequences of such indexation.

I. THE MODEL STRUCTURE AND ITS STATIC EQUILIBRIUM

Structure of the Model. Let us name the following:

X_{21} = Exports of primary products from developing countries to
          industrialised countries
Y = GNP of industrialised countries
Q = Developing countries' production capacity for primary products
w = Domestic cost factors in industrialised countries (wage rates,
      monopolistic and competitive profits, taxation, etc.)
P_1 = Manufactured good price
P_2 = Developing countries' primary good price
      (both expressed in some common standard currency)

Structurally, the model will consist of the four following equations:
(1) *Exports (from 2 to 1) demand function*:

$$X_{21} = k_1 Y^\alpha p_2^\epsilon p_1^\lambda \tag{1}$$

with: α and $\lambda > 0$ and $\epsilon < 0$
λ is the crossed price elasticity of demand for product 2 with respect to its substitute price in country 1. For instance: the demand elasticity of oil with respect to nuclear energy price; or cotton demand elasticity with respect to synthetic fibres price. k_1 is a scale positive coefficient.

(2) *Exports (from 2 to 1) supply function*:

$$X_{21}^\vee = k_2 Q^\beta p_2^\eta \tag{2}$$

with β, η and $k_2 > 0$
(3) *Cost function of manufactured goods*:

$$p_1 = k_3 w^\omega p_2^\sigma \tag{3}$$

with $\omega > 0$, $0 \leqslant \sigma < 1$ and $k_3 > 0$
(4) *International trade equilibrium for good 2*:

$$sX_{21} = X_{21}^\vee \tag{4}$$

with $s \equiv 1 + s_2$ where s_2 is the buffer stock coefficient, such as

$$\underline{s_2} \leqslant s_2 \leqslant \overline{s_2} \quad \text{and} \quad \underline{s_2} < 0, \overline{s_2} > 0$$

which respectively design the floor and ceiling limits of the accumulation (or exhaustion) of stocks of good 2.
Stocks accumulation means $s_2 > 0$ and $s > 1$ and stocks depletion means $s_2 < 0$ and $s < 1$.

Equilibrium Conditions: If the industrialised countries' GNP (Y), the primary products capacity of production (Q) and the domestic cost factors in industrialised countries are exogenous, the model allows us to calculate the *equilibrium terms of trade*, as these are, in this case, endogenous. Letting down:

$$\gamma \equiv \frac{\eta - \epsilon - \lambda\sigma}{1 - \sigma} \tag{5}$$

and

$$K \equiv \frac{k_1 k_3 \lambda - \gamma}{k_2} > 0 \tag{6}$$

we will have:

$$\frac{p_2}{p_1} = \left(K s Y^\alpha Q^{-\beta} w^{\omega(\lambda - \gamma)} \right) \frac{1}{\gamma} \tag{7}$$

Export prices *indexation* of developing countries' primary products with respect to the price of their imported manufactured goods amounts, in our model, to keeping constant the terms of trade P_2/P, that is, to freezing:

$$\frac{P_2}{P_1} = A = \text{constant.}$$

From that moment, equation (7) can be satisfied only if one of its right-hand side variables becomes endogenous. The stocking parameter may adapt to its required level through the formula

$$s = \frac{A^\gamma Y^{-\alpha} Q^\beta w^{\omega(\gamma - \lambda)}}{K} \tag{7'}$$

But as soon as s has reached one of its limits, it becomes exogenous and we must find another candidate. According to the economic relations between the two groups of countries, we will assume that industrialised countries' variables behave autonomously whereas those of developing countries will adapt. Therefore, Q will become endogenous here and we will get:

$$Q = \left(A^{-\gamma} s Y^\alpha w^{\omega(\lambda - \gamma)} \right) \frac{1}{\beta} \tag{8}$$

As γ will be probably positive, Q will vary in the same direction as Y and s, but in the opposite direction as A. Its relation with w will depend on the fact whether γ is greater or lesser than γ.

II. THE GAIN FROM INDEXATION

Definition and Formalisation

This gain is one which the developing countries are supposed to receive thanks to the indexation of their foreign trade with industrialised countries. We define it, in real terms, as the import surplus originating in industrialised countries, which developing countries receive thanks to indexation. That is,

$$G \equiv X_{12} - X'_{12} \tag{9}$$

where:

X_{12} = imports from industrialised countries when there are indexation of developing countries' export prices and a buffer stocks policy;

X'_{12} = the same imports but there is no such indexation nor a buffer stocks policy.

If, for the sake of simplification we assume that exchanges between the two groups of countries are strictly equilibrated in both cases (but taking buffer stocks into account when indexation exists), we will get:

$$p'_1 X'_{12} = p'_2 X'_{21} \Rightarrow X'_{12} = \frac{p'_2 X'_{21}}{p'_1} \tag{10}$$

$$p_1 X_{12} = p_2(1 + s_2)X_{21} \Rightarrow X_{12} = \frac{p_2 s X_{21}}{p_1} \tag{11}$$

As in this model both industrialised countries' GNP (Y) and their domestic cost factors (w) are considered exogenous, we will assume that the indexation procedure modifies all the other price and quantity variables except for these. As for s, it exists only with indexation and must respect the limits,

$$\underline{s_2} \leqslant s_2 \leqslant \overline{s_2}$$

Combined with the structural equations (1) to (4), these new equilibrium relations will give us:

$$G = \left(s(Aw^{\omega})^{\theta} - (KY^{\alpha}Q'^{-\beta}w^{\omega\lambda}) \frac{\theta}{\gamma} \right) k_1 k_3^{\lambda+\theta-1} Y^{\alpha} w^{\omega(\lambda-1)} \tag{12}$$

where: A is the indexation parameter

$$\theta \equiv \frac{1 + \epsilon + (\lambda - 1)\sigma}{1 - \sigma} \; ; \; K = \frac{k_1 k_3^{\lambda-\gamma}}{k_2}$$

and Q' is the developing countries' production capacity for primary products which they export towards industrialised countries when there is no indexation. This formula allows us to specify the conditions which determine the existence of an actual indexation gain (i.e. G > O) and the effects upon it of the various variables: s, Y, w, and Q'.

Existence of a Positive Gain from Indexation

Equation (12) shows that G has the same sign as its right-hand-side parenthesis. For a positive gain from indexation it is then necessary that this parenthesis be positive. As can be seen from our mathematical appendix, it is necessary that

$$w < \left(\frac{s^{\gamma/\theta} A^{\gamma} Q'^{\beta}}{K Y^{a}} \right) \frac{1}{\omega(\lambda - \gamma)} \tag{13}$$

for θ/γ and $\lambda - \gamma$ both positive.

So, it is only if the domestic cost factors in the industrialised countries are inferior to a given level expressed by the above inequation (13) that indexation becomes profitable. Further, it induces a loss.

Factors Affecting the Gain from Indexation
Calculating the partial derivatives of function (12) with respect to its explanatory variables s, Y, Q', and w, allows us to see how the gain from indexation varies when one of these variables changes while the others stay constant (1). Let us remind ourselves that s represents the buffer stock policy, Y and Q' the economic growth of the two groups of countries, and w the inflationary factors in developed economies. Algebra corroborates economic reasoning as it shows that G always increases with the buffer stock rate s, but we know that the latter cannot exceed a given ceiling s̄. On the other hand there are strong probabilities for G increasing when the primary products production capacity Q' is increased independently (it is sufficient for that achievement that θ be positive, which is most probable). Thirdly, the gain from indexation increases with either industrialised countries GNP (Y) or their domestic cost factors (w) only if the latter do not exceed certain limits, the one for the action of GNP being superior to that for the action of cost factors.

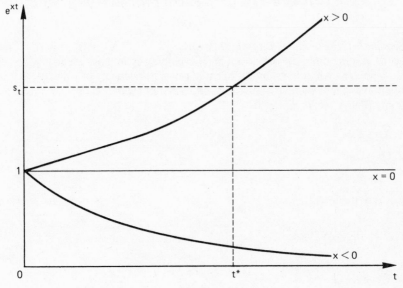

Fig. 13.1

Let us write down M_1, M_2, and M_3 for the respective ceilings which the domestic cost factors in the industrialised countries must not exceed in order to let the gain from indexation be positive or vary in the same direction respectively as Y or w. With the econometric values calculated, we then can discover that $M_3 < M_2 < M_1$. This order, from the more to the less compelling constraint upon w, means that the increase of developed countries' domestic costs (w) is the first to provoke adverse effects upon the gain from indexation as the increase of these countries' GNP (Y) is still favourable. When w passes on M_3, it induces a first decrease of G. But along with the increase of w, the one of Y induces later on (in M_2) an additional decrease of G. And finally it is only when w is over M_1 that the gain from indexation becomes a loss.

the sign of \ As w is:	$< \quad M_3 \quad <$	$M_2 \quad <$	$M_1 \quad <$
G	> 0		< 0
$\dfrac{\partial G}{\partial Y}$	> 0		< 0
$\dfrac{\partial G}{\partial w}$	> 0	< 0	

III. EVOLUTION OF THE GAIN FROM INDEXATION THROUGH TIME

Economic Growth and Gain from Indexation

Let us assume that both developed and developing economies are facing economic growth at constant exponential rates, respectively of y and q', as inflation expands in industrialised countries at a constant exponential rate r. So at any time, t, we have:

$$Y_t = Y_0 e^{yt}$$
$$Q'_t = Q_0 e^{q't} \tag{14}$$
$$w_t = w_0 e^{rt}$$

Let us write down:

$$X \equiv [\alpha y - \beta q' + \omega(\lambda - \gamma)r] \frac{\theta}{\gamma} \tag{15}$$

$$V \equiv \alpha y + \omega \frac{\epsilon + \lambda}{1 - \sigma} r$$

and some other auxiliary variables or parameters such as Z_0, K etc (1). From these expressions and from equations (12) and (14), we arrive at:

$$G_t = z_0(s_t - e^{xt})e^{vt} \tag{16}$$

As $z_0 e^{vt}$ is necessarily positive, G_t has the same sign as its parenthesis in (16). So, the gain from trade is positive at a time t, if and only if:

$$e^{xt} < s_t \tag{17}$$

Let us distinguish among three cases at time t:

Positive buffer stock policy ($s_t > 1$)
No buffer stock policy ($s_t = 1$)
Negative buffer stock policy ($s_t < 1$)

The third occurs when there is excess demand for primary products.

Positive Buffer Stock Policy ($s_t > 1$)
This case can be illustrated by the three curves above, as x is positive, nul, or negative.

In the first hypothesis ($x > 0$) the gain from indexation begins by being positive, decreases, is nul for $t^* = L_n s_t/x$ then becomes negative.

With the second and third hypothesis ($x \leqslant 0$) the gain from indexation is always positive.

No buffer stock policy ($s_t = 1$)
If there is no buffer stock policy, $s_2 \geqslant 0$ and $s = 1$. Then equation (16) writes:

$$G_t = (1 - e^{xt})z_0 e^{vt} \tag{18}$$

and G_t will be positive only if $e^{xt} < 1$, which obviously implies that $x < 0$.

Negative buffer stock policy ($s_t < 1$)
The three hypotheses of the first case lead here to opposite conclusions as Fig. 13.2 shows it. Here for $x \geqslant 0$, condition (17) can never be satisfied. It can be for $x < 0$ but only when $t > t^{**}$ with $t^{**} = L_n s_t/x > 0$.

The following table gathers all those cases and exhibits where condition (17) is satisfied and those where it is not.

	$s_t < 1$	$s_t = 1$	$s_t > 1$
$x < 0$	(17) satisfied only for $t > t^*$	(17) always satisfied	(17) always satisfied
$x = 0$	(17) never satisfied	(17) never satisfied	(17) never satisfied
$x > 0$	(17) never satisfied	(17) never satisfied	(17) satisfied only for $t > t^{**}$

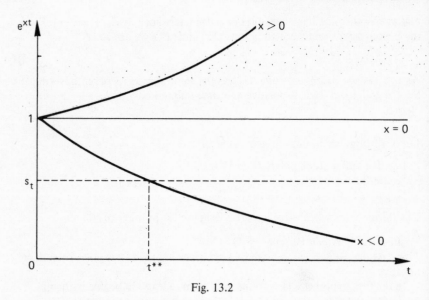

Fig. 13.2

One can notice that most often parameter x must be negative to ensure that the gain from indexation is positive. We will face this condition again when dealing with a buffer stock policy equilibrated over several periods. The economic significance of x (or of its opposite $-$ x) arises from the fact that it sums up the very conditions for the gain from indexation to be positive. So we might name it the 'gain from indexation existence parameter'. What formula (15) shows is that x is a linear combination of both developed and developing countries' GNPs and of domestic cost factors in developed economies, weighted by their respective elasticities in export equations and affected by a combination of exports price elasticities (θ/γ).

Effects of an Equilibrated Buffer Stocks Policy upon the Gain from Indexation
Buffer stocks policy practically appears to be necessarily linked with indexation. It amounts to the stocking agency buying primary products when supply exceeds demand in order to ease the market and support the prices. Then it sells the primary products when the demand exceeds supply and price goes up. So the agency works self-financing. The stocking index s is therefore superior to one (and $s_2 > 0$) during the first phase and inferior (and $s_2 < 0$) during the second; but the overall balance is equilibrated only if for the two periods considered together stocks have been entirely used up.

More generally, for a set of periods $t = 0 \ldots T$ and in the wordings of our model if we call $R_{(t)}$ the stocking (or destocking) made in t, so that $R_{(t)} = s_2(b)X_{2b}(b)$ we must have upon this set of periods:

$$\int_{t=0}^{T} R(t)dt = 0$$

What is the consequence of this rule upon the overall gain from indexation over these periods?

Starting from equation (16) *this overall gain* will be written:

$$G \equiv \int_{t=0}^{T} G(t)dt = z_0 \int_{t=0}^{T} (e^{vt} - e^{(v+x)t})dt + \int_{t=0}^{T} s_2(t)e^{vt}dt$$

In this formula, the last integral represents the cumulated effect of (sometimes positive, sometimes negative) stocking. If the latter is to globally disappear over the whole set of periods $(0 \dots T)$, the corresponding integral must disappear too, so that we are left with:

$$G = z_0 \int_{t=0}^{T} (e^{vt} - e^{(v+x)t})dt \tag{19}$$

This implies that the stocking coefficient $s_2(t)$ has to follow a time schedule consistant with this condition. For a given horizon T, several time schedules usually will check it.

As z_0 is necessarily positive, G will be positive if and only if:

$$\int_{t=0}^{T} e^{vt}dt > \int_{t=0}^{T} e^{(v+x)t}dt$$

which implies, wherever be the sign of v, that $x < 0$.

The condition: $x < 0$, still appears here as a crucial requirement for an indexation policy of developing countries exports being favourable to these countries as well as in the short as in the medium term.

We need now to check whether world trade statistics during the last two decades will allow us to estimate the parameters of our model and to calculate figures for x.

IV. A TENTATIVE ECONOMETRIC ESTIMATE

The parameters of the three behavioural functions of our model (1), (2) and (3) have been estimated over the periods 1955–74 (20 observations) and 1955–72 (18 observations), as for the second estimate it keeps off the important price and wage rises and the beginning of recession during the years 1973 and 1974.

Gathering and Analysing Statistical Data
The two sets of countries which are considered are the market-economy

developed countries and the developing countries other than oil exporters.

The 'market-economy developed countries' are represented by the OECD countries: Western Europe, North America, and Japan, according to the list appearing in the volume *Statistics of National Accounts of OECD Countries* for 1957–66.[2] Compared with the wider list of the 1974 volume, the following countries have been omitted: Finland, Yugoslavia, Australia, and New Zealand.

The 'developing countries other than oil exporters' are determined from lists and statistics of the UN *Handbook of International Trade and Development Statistics* 1972 and 1976.[3]

Variables have been defined as the following:

X_{21} = 1963 constant prices and exchange rates exports of non-oil primary products by developing countries other than oil exporters, towards market-economy developed countries.
Account unit: 1963 10^6 US $.
Sources: *HITDS* (UN, 1972 and 1976).

Y = 1963 constant prices and exchange rate GNP (at market prices) of market economy developed countries.
Account unit: 1963 10^6 US $.
Sources: *SNA* (OECD) 1960–61 (1964); 1957–66 (1968); 1961–72 (1974), 1974, Vol. I (1976).

Q' = 1960 constant prices and exchange rates GNP (at market prices) of non-European and non-oil-exporting developing countries.
Account unit: 1960 10^6 US $.
Sources: *National Accounts of Less Developed Countries* (OECD Development Center), Vol. 1950–66 (July 1968); Vol. 1959–68 (June 1970); Vol. no. 9 (Dec 1975).

Failing better, GNP has been taken as an indicator of the primary products production capacities of developing countries. OECD estimates in 1960 $ have been kept. The only conversion rate which was available for these countries was linking the $68 and the $63 estimates. Its value was 1.05 (therefore very weak). Between $63 and $60 estimates this rate would have been still weaker and it seemed useless to make such an uncertain and small correction which, being homothetic for all the years concerned, would have induced no changes into the econometric regressions.

p_1 = Unit value index for the exports of manufactured goods by the market developed economies (MDE) to all countries (1963 = 100).
Sources: *HITDS* (UN, 1972 and 1976).

p_2 = Unit value index for the exports of non-oil primary products by

[2]From now on, designated *SNA* (OECD, and date).
[3]From now on, designated *HITDS* (UN, and date).

developing countries towards the market developed economies
(1963 = 100).
Sources: *HITDS* (UN, 1976).
w = Domestic cost factors index in market developed economies
(1963 = 100). This index has been defined as the ratio of the average
index of hourly earnings in manufacturing industries of the main
OECD industrial countries (g) on the one hand, and of an average
index of labour productivity in the same industries of the same
countries (π) on the other.

Countries which were investigated for these statistics are Canada, the United
States, Japan, France, the Federal Republic of Germany, Italy, and the United
Kingdom.

Sources for g: OECD, *Main Economic Indicators* (various issues)
Sources for π: OECD, ibid.
UN, *Yearbook of National Accounts* (1957–73)
ILO, *Yearbook of Labour Statistics* (1960–73).

Numerical Results
Since our model is overidentified we used both the classical econometric
estimations through ordinary least squares regressions (OLS) and a method
with limited information, that of two stages least squares regressions (2SLS).[4]
We applied both methods to the period with the troubled last years (1955–74)
and to the period without them (1955–72).

Estimates of the model equations over the period 1955–74

OLS method

$$\text{Log } X_{21} = -0.1962 + 0.6711 \text{ Log } Y - 0.5164 \text{ Log } p_2 + 0.6005 \text{ Log } p_1$$
$$(0.6012) \ (0.0632) \qquad (0.0892) \qquad (0.1482)$$
$$R^2 = 0.9871 \qquad\qquad DW = 1.3847 \ (1.00 - 1.68)$$
$$(1.1)$$

$$\text{Log } X_{21}^{\vee} = 0.1050 + 0.8495 \text{ Log } Q - 0.2397 \text{ Log } p_2$$
$$(0.3060) \ (0.0281)$$
$$R^2 = 0.9835 \qquad\qquad DW = 1.4588 \ (1.10 - 1.54)$$
$$(1.2)$$

$$\text{Log } p_1 = -2.2630 + 1.2732 \text{ Log } w + 0.2164 \text{ Log } p_2$$
$$(0.1073) \ (0.0602) \qquad (0.3291)$$
$$R^2 = 0.9708 \qquad\qquad DW = 0.9233 \ (1.10 - 1.54)$$
$$(1.3)$$

[4]I wish to express my thanks to my colleague Professor G. Rottier for having been
so helpful in the choice of estimation methods and the criticism of their results; and
also to Mme I. Peaucelle, who collected some of the statistical data and made the com-
putations with the help of Mr Sastre.

As can be seen, the correlation coefficients are very good everywhere but the Durbin and Watson test indicates that residuals autocorrelation, if it can be rejected in the case of equation (1.2) cannot be so in equation (1.1) and even appears to be positive in equation (1.3), which for that reason cannot be used. In equations (1.1) and (1.2) the coefficients of every variable are statistically significant, but this is not the case for the constants, which are never significally different from zero. Regressions made without any structural constants lead to values of elasticity coefficients very close to those obtained here.

Finally, it will be noticed that the coefficient of p_2 in equation (1.2) is negative even though it represents a price elasticity of export supply for primary products and must have therefore been positive. This probably means that for export prices of such products, the demand effect is stronger.

2SLS method

$$\text{Log } X_{21} = -0.5094 + 0.6895 \text{ Log Y} - 0.4003 \text{ Log } p_2 + 0.4946 \text{ Log } p_1 \quad (2.1)$$
$$(0.8082) \ (0.0848) \qquad\quad (0.1422) \qquad\qquad (0.2215)$$

$$\text{Log } X_{21}^{\smallsmile} = 0.1038 + 0.8213 \text{ Log Q} - 0.1654 \text{ Log } p_2 \quad (2.2)$$
$$(0.3134) \ (0.0299) \qquad\quad (0.0452)$$

$$\text{Log } p_1 = -2.5301 + 1.4726 \text{ Log w} + 0.0769 \text{ Log } p_2 \quad (2.3)$$
$$(0.3559) \ (0.1391) \qquad\qquad (0.0864)$$

Here the Durbin and Watson test loses its significance, and so does the correlation coefficient R^2, as the number of observations (20) is too low for allowing its asymptotic properties to be meaningful. Thus we are left with the standard deviations of the various coefficients. Again we find that the constant terms have high standard deviations, except in equation (2.3), and so could be neglected. The same situation occurs for Log p_2 coefficient in equation (2.3). But in the other cases the situation is satisfactory. Compared with the OLS results, the 2SLS exhibit an increase for α, ε, η and ω, a quasi stability for β and a decrease for λ and σ. Again η (the price elasticity of primary countries' exports in equation 2.2) is negative.

Estimates for the Period 1955–72
OLS method

$$\text{Log } X_{21} = 0.6755 + 0.5502 \text{ Log Y} - 0.4231 \text{ Log } p_2 + 0.9738 \text{ Log } p_1$$
$$(0.4662) \ (0.0557) \qquad\quad (0.0698) \qquad\qquad (0.1431)$$
$$R^2 = 0.9930 \qquad\qquad\qquad\qquad \text{DW} = 1.7430 \ (0.93 - 1.69)$$
$$(3.1)$$

$$\text{Log } X_{21}^{\smallsmile} = -0.5201 + 0.85904 \text{ Log Q} - 0.1316 \text{ Log } p_2$$
$$(0.5977) \ (0.0298) \qquad\quad (0.0952)$$
$$R^2 = 0.9825 \qquad\qquad\qquad\qquad \text{DW} = 1.0985 \ (1.05 - 1.53)$$
$$(3.2)$$

$$\text{Log } p_1 = -0.57841 + 1.1885 \text{ Log } w - 0.0594 \text{ Log } p_2$$
$$(0.4598) \quad (0.0794) \qquad (0.0776)$$
$$R^2 = 0.9388 \qquad\qquad DW = 1.8798 \ (1.05 - 1.53)$$
$$(3.3)$$

The estimate for equation (3.1) is better than in (1.1) since all its parameters are more significant (better students' tests) and since the DW coefficient is greater than the superior limit beyond which residuals autocorrelation vanishes. Meanwhile, the estimate for equation (3.2) is rather worse than in (1.2) since a positive residuals autocorrelation almost appears there. And if residuals autocorrelation vanishes in equation (3.3), then the estimate of σ (coefficient of P^2) is not at all significant.

We find again that all the constants are not significantly different from zero and again that the elasticity η in equation (3.2) is negative instead of being positive as the economic reasoning would imply.

2SLS method

$$\text{Log } X_{21} = -0.3502 + 0.4748 \text{ Log } Y - 0.4699 \text{ Log } p_2 + 1.1779 \text{ Log } p_1 \quad (4.1)$$
$$(0.5881) \ (0.0675) \qquad (0.0979) \qquad\qquad (0.1780)$$

$$\text{Log } X_{21}^{\sim} = -1.4454 + 0.8611 \text{ Log } Q + 0.0599 \text{ Log } p_2 \quad\quad (4.2)$$
$$(0.7296)(0.0307) \qquad (0.1261)$$

$$\text{Log } p_1 = -0.4260 + 1.2116 \text{ Log } w - 0.1150 \text{ Log } p_2 \quad\quad (4.3)$$
$$(0.4744) \ (0.0737) \qquad (0.0919)$$

Again the constant term is not significant in any equation and so could be nullified.

The coefficients of every variable in any equation are reliable, apart from those of Log p_2 both in eq. (4.2) and in eq. (4.3). The sign of η becomes positive, as economic reasoning implies, but at the price of a statistically non-significant value, as we have just said.

Compared with those of OLS method applied to the same period, these results exhibit substantial increases for λ (eq. 4.1) and η (eq. 4.2), again a quasi-stability for β (eq. 4.2) and ω (eq. 4.3), but a decrease for α, ε (eq. 4.1) and σ (eq. 4.3).

Nevertheless we must remember that, in the case of an overidentified model, such as ours, the 2SLS method gives intrinsically better results than the OLS method can do. So, for both periods, we will pay more attention to the 2SLS results.

Existence of the gain from indexation
We have seen that a positive gain from indexation, as well as at every moment t as over a set of periods over which the buffer stock policy would be equilibrated as a whole, does exist if and only if the coefficient x is negative.

Remind that x is expressed by equation (15) i.e.:

$$x = [\alpha y - \beta q' + \omega(\lambda - \gamma)r] \frac{\theta}{\gamma}$$

From the previous econometric estimations we calculated four values for x, two for each observation period by both types of regressions. The growth rates used (y, q' and r) were those observed in each period. The results appear in the following table.

Calculation of x

Equations	Parameters	Period 1955–74		Period 1955–72	
		OLS	2SLS	OLS	2SLS
1	α	0.6711	0.6895	0.5502	0.4748
	ϵ	−0.5164	−0.4003	−0.4231	−0.4699
	λ	0.6005	0.4946	0.9738	1.1779
2	β	0.8495	0.8213	0.85904	0.8611
	η	−0.2397	−0.1654	−0.1316	0.0599
3	ω	1.2732	1.4726	1.1885	1.2116
	σ	0.2164	0.0769	−0.0594	−0.1150
Growth rates	y	0.0405	0.0405	0.0416	0.0416
	q'	0.0489	0.0489	0.0464	0.0464
	r	0.0219	0.0219	0.0145	0.0145
Gain from indexation coefficient (%)	x	−0.77 <0	−0.91 <0	−0.96 <0	−0.77 <0

We have also tried less orthodox calculations, either using the best estimates of various equations in any period (with the OLS method), or taking an average of elasticities estimations (with the 2SLS method) and nullifying σ in any case and η in the second one. All these calculations gave us negative x. So, in all our estimates, *x is always negative.*

Applied to both periods, 1955–74 and 1955–72, our model therefore seems to conclude in favour of the profitability of export prices indexation upon their manufactured goods import prices, for non-oil exporting developing countries. This has been checked by a simulation calculus for these periods. Without any buffer stock policy ($s_t = 1$), and with two values of parameter A,[5] this simulation exhibits variable but constantly positive gains from indexation.

Nevertheless this conclusion has to be seriously qualified.

[5] $A = \dfrac{p_2(1955)}{p_1(1955)} = 1.380$ and $A = \dfrac{p_2(1955-64)}{p_1(1955-64)} = 1.117$

We will notice first that the values obtained for x are not far from zero. Their negativity therefore is trustworthy only if it is based upon very good econometric estimates. But we have noticed that, unfortunately, some of the available statistics used and some of the resulting regressions are not very good. The values obtained both for η (which logically must have been positive) and for σ are far from being satisfactory. The strong aggregation of the model, particularly for products, is probably partly responsible for these defects. It would be therefore fitting to disaggregate it into some wide groups of products of which export supply and demand functions perhaps would give better econometric estimates for their parameters and, if so, would lead to stronger results.

However, we felt that, as it is, the present model allows us to analyse more closely some of the factors which determine the possible gain from indexation. So it will contribute to clarify a debate where *a priori*s and taboos are frequent. We think that four conclusions do rise from it, for the moment:

(1) Indexation, as such, is not necessarily a gain. To achieve a permanent advantage from indexation, it is necessary that growth rates, both of developed and developing countries, and the inflation rate of developed countries combine with supply and demand elasticities for primary product exports in such a way that they result in a negative value of parameter x. Now this negativity is unstable since the components of x are very much affected by trade cycle fluctuations.

(2) The synthetic quasi-necessary condition for having a positive gain i.e. x < 0, points out that the existence of the gain does not depend on buffer stock policy, even if this policy is practically unescapable (but of course the amount of the gain does depend on it).

(3) The buffer stock policy comes into the play for enlarging the export possibilities, but both the limits put on it by financing considerations and the overall equilibrium condition (19) compel it to follow one of the various paths consistent with these conditions.

(4) Equilibrium with indexation implies that, with the decreed fixity of international prices ratio, another variable will adapt itself. When the stocking coefficient has reached one of its limits, the adaptation will probably be made through the production capacity of exportable primary products in developing countries or the latter's GNP (cf. equation 8).

So, paradoxically, indexation, which aims at enabling the developing economies to escape world market random fluctuations, compels their production to adapt to these fluctuations.

(5) Last, but not least, as the model is most aggregated, it does not exhibit the harmful consequences of price indexation upon development efficiency. Price indexation, by its very nature, is a price structure freezing, and as such it opposes an efficient allocation of resources, both in international trade and in the internal growth of developing countries. But if no other means can actually be established for financing development in poor countries on a large scale, we may ask whether an imperfect method is worse than no method at all.

Mathematical Appendix

I. SIGN OF AND FACTORS AFFECTING G

From equation (12) i.e.:

$$G = \left(s(Aw^\omega)^\theta - (KY^\alpha Q'^{-\beta} w^{\omega\lambda}) \frac{\theta}{\gamma} \right) k_1 k_3^{\lambda+\theta-1} Y^\alpha w^{\omega(\lambda-1)}$$

we derive the following conditions (for γ and $\theta > 0$ and $\gamma < \Omega\lambda$)

(1) $G > 0$ iff: $w < \left(s^{\gamma/\theta} \dfrac{A^\gamma Q'^\beta}{KY^\alpha} \right) \dfrac{1}{\omega(\lambda - \gamma)} \equiv M_1$

(2) $\dfrac{\partial G}{\partial Y} > 0$ iff: $w < \left[\left(\dfrac{\gamma(1-\sigma)}{\eta + 1 - \sigma} s \right)^{\gamma/\theta} \dfrac{A^\gamma Q'^\beta}{KY^\alpha} \right] \dfrac{1}{\omega(\lambda - \gamma)} \equiv M_2$

(3) $\dfrac{\partial G}{\partial w} > 0$ iff: $w < \left[\left(\dfrac{\gamma(\epsilon + \lambda)}{\epsilon + \lambda + \eta(\lambda - 1)} s \right)^{\gamma/\theta} \dfrac{A^\gamma Q'^\beta}{KY^\alpha} \right] \dfrac{1}{\omega(\lambda - \gamma)} \equiv M_3$

(4) $\dfrac{\partial G}{\partial Q'} > 0$ iff: $\dfrac{\theta}{\gamma} > 0$ which has been assumed here.

so $\dfrac{\partial G}{\partial Q'}$ is always positive.

The ordering of M_1, M_2 and M_3 will follow this of the corresponding multipliers of s in the three previous inequalities.

(1) $M_2 < M_1$ iff: $\dfrac{\gamma(1-\sigma)}{\eta + 1 - \sigma} < 1$

that is: $\sigma(1 - \lambda) < \epsilon + 1$, which is econometrically checked.

(2) $M_3 < M_2$ iff: $\dfrac{\gamma(\epsilon + \lambda)}{\epsilon + \lambda + \eta(\lambda - 1)} < \dfrac{\gamma(1-\sigma)}{\eta + 1 - \sigma}$

that is: $\eta(\epsilon + \lambda) < \eta(1 - \sigma)(\lambda - 1)$.

Here we face two alternatives:

(2.1) $n > 0$ (as it must theoretically be)

then $M_3 < M_2$ implies $\epsilon + 1 < \sigma(1 - \lambda)$ which is contradictory with the condition for $M_2 < M_1$. So, in that case, we will have $M_2 < M_3$.

But then, we must rank M_3 and M_1. And we see, for instance, that $M_3 < M_1$ *iff*:

$$\frac{-\gamma(\epsilon + \lambda)}{\epsilon + \lambda + \eta(\lambda - 1)} < 1$$

that is: $\gamma < 1 + \eta \dfrac{\lambda - 1}{\epsilon + \lambda}$

(2.2) $\eta < 0$ (as it is econometrically checked)

then, dividing both members of the second inequality of section 2 by η, yields

$$\sigma(1 - \lambda) < \epsilon + 1$$

which we have already got for $M_2 < M_1$ and is econometrically verified.

(3) So we may conclude that, for the period statistically observed, we have the ordering:

$$M_3 < M_2 < M_1$$

II. EVOLUTION OF G_t THROUGH TIME

With growth equations (14) introduced into relation (12) we get:

$$G_t = \left[s_t(k_3^\gamma A^\gamma w_0^{\omega\gamma} e^{\omega\gamma r t})^{\theta/\gamma} - \left(\frac{k_1 k_3^\lambda}{k_2} Y_0^\alpha Q_0^{-\beta} w_0^{\omega\lambda} e^{(\alpha y - \beta q' + \omega\lambda r)t} \right)^{\theta/\gamma} \right]$$
$$\times k_1 k_3^{\lambda-1} Y_0^\alpha w_0^{\omega(\lambda-1)} e^{[\alpha y + \omega(\lambda-1)r]t}$$

But from (8) we get also:

$$A^\gamma = KY_0^\alpha Q_0^{-\beta} w_0^{\omega(\lambda-\gamma)}$$

Notice that in this equation $s_0 = 1$ as in the base period, that is, before indexation there is no buffer stock policy linked to indexation. So, putting

$$Y_0^\alpha Q_0^{-\beta} w_0^{\omega\lambda}$$

into common factor of our brackets, noticing that

$$k_3^\gamma K = \frac{k_1 k_3^\lambda}{k^2}$$

which will also be put into common factor, and letting down:

$$Z_0 \equiv \frac{k_1^2 k_3^{2\lambda-1}}{k^2} Y_0^{2\alpha} Q_0^{-\beta} w_0^{\omega(2\lambda-1)}$$

we write:

$$G_t = (s_t - e^{[\alpha y - \beta q' + \omega(\lambda-\gamma)r](\theta/\gamma)t}) Z_0 e^{[\alpha y + \omega(\lambda+\theta-1)r]t}$$

And with:

$$x \equiv [\alpha y - \beta q' + \omega(\lambda - \gamma)r] \frac{\theta}{\gamma}$$

$$o \equiv \alpha y + \omega(\lambda + \theta - 1)r = \alpha y + \omega \frac{\epsilon + \lambda}{1 - \sigma} r$$

the expression for G_t simplifies into:

$$G_t = (s_t - e^{xt})Z_0 e^{rt}$$

As $Z_0 e^{rt} > 0$, $G_t > 0$ iff:

$$e^{xt} < s_t \qquad \text{Q.E.D.}$$

Index

Entries in the index in bold type under the names of participants in the Conference indicate their Papers or Discussions of their Papers.

192   *Index*